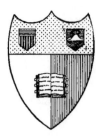

Cornell University

Ithaca, New York

COLLEGE OF ARCHITECTURE

LIBRARY

Date Due

JUL 22 1959		
NOV 1 1974		
NOV 1 2 1981		
DEC 1 7 1982		
JUN 22 1989		
	(bd)	23 233

SAN LUIS REY DE FRANCIA

(St. Louis, King of France)

New Series. Local History

SAN LUIS REY MISSION

BY

Fr. ZEPHYRIN ENGELHARDT, O.F.M.

Author of "Missions and Missionaries," "Franciscans in California,"
"Franciscans in Arizona," "Holy Man of Santa Clara,"
"San Diego Mission," Etc.

"Colligite quae superaverunt fragmenta,
ne pereant." Joan, vi, 12

Cum Approbatione Ecclesiastica

SAN FRANCISCO, CAL.
THE JAMES H. BARRY COMPANY
1921

The publication of this volume has been rendered possible
through the interest taken in the history of Mission
San Luis Rey by the Rev. Fr. Dominic Gal-
lardo, O. F. M., pastor in charge, aided by
substantial donations from Mr. Jerome
O'Neil of Santa Margarita Ranch
and Mr. Cave J. Couts of
Vista, California.

Ar. C

F . *c* ..

S - *r* | *c*

CONTENTS

vi   Contents

Page

CHAPTER XI.

CHAPTER XII.

CHAPTER XIII.

CHAPTER XIV.

viii   Contents

CHAPTER XV.

CHAPTER XVI

CHAPTER XVII.

APPENDIX

ILLUSTRATIONS

X   Illustrations

FIRST MILITARY DISTRICT
II
SAN LUIS REY MISSION
(1798 - 1865)

THE OLD
FRANCISCAN
MISSIONS
IN
CALIFORNIA.

CHAPTER I.

T HE need of a mission between San Diego and San Juan
Capistrano was recognized at an early date. Between
these two points lay many Indian rancherías; and, as the
reader will have learned from the narrative on Mission San
Diego, the overburdened Fathers of this Mission were frequently called to the outlying rancherías in order to minister
to the sick. Moreover, the distance between San Diego and
San Juan Capistrano could not be covered in a day, a fact
which made traveling very unsafe. Finally, on July 23,
1795, Governor Diego Borica issued an order directing
Ensign Juan Pablo Grijalva to examine the territory for a
suitable site. Fr. Presidente Lasuén appointed Fr. Juan
Mariner of Mission San Diego to accompany the exploring
party and to report the discoveries. On August 17, 1795,
Ensign Grijalva, Fr. Mariner, and six soldiers set out from
San Diego. Fr. Mariner kept a diary in which from day
to day he noted the movements of the expedition. A translation of it is herewith given entire. It reads as follows:

Report on the survey which we made in company with Don Pablo
Grijalva, Corporal Juan Vicente Felix, etc., commenced on the seven-
teenth of August and concluded on the twenty-sixth of the same month.

1. We went by way of Rancho San Luis, and, going through the
Cañada de Alisos on the left, we passed two rancherías which had a
fairly large pagan population. We camped for the night in a valley
of considerable size having two large rancherías.

2. Next morning we found two large rancherías, and in the afternoon we passed by two others. Then we reached another valley which
is called Esechá. Here is where the large water ditch ran, but which
at present is entirely dry. The valley has much good land which is
very humid, and it contains five good-sized rancherías. A league and

a half beyond, there is a very large ranchería in which I counted one hundred and nine men, and back of this, there are three other rancherías. The large one is called Samptay Luscat. The valley abounds in live oak, sycamore, alder, willow, and pine trees.

3. In the morning we continued on our way through a thicket of various kinds of oak trees. The sierra is covered with pines. Between the sierra and Pamó, we passed two large rancherías which have a goodly population of pagans. Then we arrived in a valley which we named San Joseph. It may be more than three and a half or four leagues long and a league and a half wide. It is occupied by ten large rancherías all surrounded by oaks, sycamores, alders, willows, and pines that extend down to the ravine below. Here we came to a long ditch, the water of which comes from the sierra and passes by the ranchería of Jajopin on the right. We discovered also three springs flowing from below the ranchería of Tauhí. There is much good land.

We continued the examination, and, in the valley which the Indians pointed out to us, we discovered an extensive and deep marsh, in the upper portion of which were three large springs bubbling up high, as though they were boiling. The water is very good, and it could easily be conducted to irrigate the soil, which is very good. This valley is on the other side of Pamó, toward the northeast and distant about a league and a half. It is such a good place that all say, and I also, that it is suitable not only for a mission, but for both presidio and mission. Señor Felipe said that, when the road is opened, one could make the distance from the presidio (of San Diego) in one day. The Indians call this valley Jatir Jo.

In the afternoon we set out and proceeded along the arroyo, which leaves this valley very much narrowed and which, until leaving the Cañada de San Juan Capistrano el Viejo, is everywhere densely covered with large trees such as oaks, sycamores, pines, alders, and willows. The heights all around are overgrown with pines. There is a very large population of savages.

On the second day of our journey, at about ten in the morning, we entered the territory where the language of San Juan Capistrano is spoken. By the time we reached this place, we had passed twenty-six rancherías, which generally were large and in which the *Mau* language of San Diego is used.

In the afternoon before sunset we passed a ranchería which is called Palé. It has a great deal of running water which can easily be taken out. It has also very much good soil. What I saw in company with Don Pablo was enough for sowing sixty fanégas of beans. When I saw this and noticed that we were already approaching the cañada, I told Don Pablo to give orders that the other side be examined. As the thick growth of underbrush impeded our progress, he sent Señor Felipe and Claudio ahead; and these reported that there was very good land for sowing fifty fanégas of wheat and fifteen fanégas of corn, and that there was a level plot on which to place the mission. It is true that it still lies in the cañada between San Dieguito and the sierra of Pamó. There is an unlimited amount of good timber, plenty stones, firewood, and good pasture land. It has also five rancherías that speak the language of San Juan Capistrano. According to the estimate of all, it is about two leagues and a half distant from the cañada and about six leagues from the *camino reál.* A league farther down, the water of the arroyo ceases to run; but there are springs as far as San Juan Capistrano el Viejo, where we arrived the next day at about ten in the morning or a little earlier. We surveyed the entire cañada and found deep springs or wells from which the water could not flow or easily be taken out. Timber is lacking, as also firewood and stone. The soil, too, is unsuitable because it contains too much sand. Only a few spots near the hills are good. We went to examine the laguna and found that the little water it had comes from four sources, only one being from the rain. We applied crowbar and pickaxe; but we could not make the water flow, because these wells are very deep and the land lies high. This water doubtless comes from above and passes on underground.

We surveyed Santa Margarita and found the laguna more than a yard and a half deep. There are six or eight springs; but they are so deep that the water does not flow, except the water in the three close to the sierra, which is very little at that. There is a dearth of firewood and stone, and the place lies far distant from the road.

We examined Las Flores; but we did not discover more running water than that from the road, and from the dry arroyo above, and it has only a small spring. The rancherías, including Santa Margarita and Las Flores, that speak the language of San Juan Capistrano, number fourteen. So in all we passed forty and we were close by said places.

In my opinion and in the opinion of the others, the place nearest San Juan Capistrano el Viejo is the ranchería of Palé, which has all facilities and is in the center of said language as though in a round jar; but the great forest impedes access to it. In the valley the Indians say that, if a mission were established, they would become Christians. They said the same with much pleasure in the ranchería of Palé. This, Rev. Fr. Presidente, is the truth before God and upon my conscience.[1]

According to Bancroft,[2] Grijalva's report contained the names of the following rancherías not given by Fr. Mariner:

---

[1] Fr. Mariner, *Diario,* August 26, 1795. *Sta. Barb. Arch.,* Bancroft, vol. i, p. 553.

[2] *History of California,* vol. i, p. 563.

"Mescuanal, Tonapa, Ganal, Mocoquil, and Cuami, in the valley called Esechá; moreover, Tagui, Gante, Algualcapa, Capatay, Tacupin, Quguas, Calagua, Matagua, and Atá, in another valley three leagues distant; furthermore, Curila, Topame, Luque, Cupame, Páume, and Palé, three leagues from the former valley and speaking the language of San Juan Capistrano; then, Palin, Pamame, Pamua, and Asichiqmes, lower down; Chacápe and Pamamelli, in the Santa Margarita Valley; and finally Chumelle and Quesinille, in the region of Las Flores."

Writing to Governor Borica, on January 12, 1796, Fr. Presidente Lasuén recommended as a suitable site for the contemplated Mission of San Luís Rey the place called Palé, fourteen leagues from San Diego, eighteen leagues from San Juan Capistrano, and six leagues from the camino reál.[3] After he had seen the locality, however, Fr. Lasuén wrote to Borica: "The site of Sonquich, equivocally called Palé, is not suitable, because it is ten leagues from the camino reál."[4]

A new exploration of the territory between San Diego and San Juan Capistrano was ordered by the governor. Accompanied by Fr. Presidente Lasuén and Fr. Santiago, the latter stationed at San Juan Capistrano, Corporal Pedro Lizalde, with seven soldiers and five Indians, set out from Mission San Juan Capistrano. "The party separated to return north and south at Old Capistrano, which they doubtless selected at the time, October 6, as the best mission site, for we hear no more of the Palé of former expeditions." Thus, rather enigmatically, Bancroft puts it.[5] The fact is that, after the country round had been explored anew, Fr. Lasuén decided on the valley which Fr. Juan Crespi, when passing there with the Portolá expedition in July, 1769,[6]

3 Sta. Barb. Arch., ad annum.
4 September 28, 1797. "Lo vi, y no sirve absolutamente." Archb. Arch., no. 113.
5 Bancroft, vol. i, pp. 562-563.
6 See Missions and Missionaries, vol. ii, p. 28.

SAN LUIS REY MISSION DISTRICT

had already noted as a favorable locality for a mission and which on that occasion he had christened San Juan Capistrano. Since the founding of Mission San Juan Capistrano, in 1776, this place had been known as San Juan Capistrano *el Viejo* or *Old* Capistrano, to distinguish it from the Mission of the same name. From this region the Fathers of San Diego had already obtained many good neophytes.

When Governor Borica received the report of the Fr. Presidente, he issued orders under date of February 27, 1798, to the comandante of the San Diego presidio, instructing him to furnish a guard "and to require from the soldiers personal labor in erecting the necessary buildings, without murmuring at site or work, and with implicit obedience to Fr. Lasuén,"[7] who named the feast of St. Anthony of Padua, June 13, 1798, as the day on which the new Mission should be formally established. Viceroy Branciforte himself had chosen the patron saint, St. Louis, King of France.[8] What happened then Fr. Lasuén reported to the governor as follows:

Blessed be Jesus!

Señor Governor:—At last I have the happy satisfaction of communicating to Your Honor that on this date, the feast of St. Anthony of Padua, on this site called by the natives *Tacayme* and by the first discoverers San Juan Capistrano, halfway between the missions of San Juan Capistrano and San Diego, assisted by the Captain of the Cavalry Don Antonio Grájera, by the Reverend Fathers and Apostolic Preachers Juan Norberto de Santiago, missionary of Mission San Juan Capistrano, and Antonio Peyri, destined for this Mission, by the soldiers destined for its protection, by many neophytes from San Juan Capistrano, and by a great multitude of gentiles of both sexes and all ages who manifested ineffable satisfaction and pleasure, I blessed the water, the place, and the great cross which we raised and venerated. We then chanted the Litany of All Saints. Afterwards I sang the High Mass, during which I preached the sermon and exhorted all to co-operate in the great work. We concluded the function by singing the *Te Deum Laudamus.*

After an interval of about an hour and a half, some pagans, who

---

7 Bancroft, i, p. 563.

8 See *Missions and Missionaries*, vol. ii, pp. 494, 496.—See Appendix A.

had assisted, spontaneously brought twenty-five male and twenty-nine female children and asked me to baptize them. On this same morning and in the afternoon, therefore, in the little *enramada* which had been constructed yesterday and which today had served for the holy Mass, I solemnly baptized all fifty-four.

Seven young men and twelve young girls also wanted to be baptized. But I told them that it was necessary first to be instructed, wherefore the nineteen remained to receive instruction. Thanks be to God!

Thus possession was taken of this site and it was dedicated in honor of San Luis Rey de Francia. In this manner, the Mission of this sacred title was begun in conformity with the orders of His Excellency the Marqués de Branciforte, Viceroy of New Spain, and with those of Your Honor. God preserve Your Honor in His grace many years.—San Luis Rey, June 13, 1798.—Fr. Fermín Francisco de Lasuén.[9]

An eye-witness of this happy event, the Rev. Domingo Rivas, supplies some interesting details, which throw much light on the situation. He writes:

I shall relate what I myself have seen at the founding of this Mission. In the year 1798, since I happened to be at the presidio of San Diego at the time when they were about to establish the Mission of San Luis Rey, the comandante of said presidio, who was the late Don Antonio Grájera, induced me to accompany him in order to witness the founding. I gladly accepted the invitation out of mere curiosity to see what I had many times desired to witness. We reached the site of the proposed establishment in the afternoon of June 12. We found three religious there; they had been there two days, working for the following day, which was the feast of San Antonio de Padua, in order to make the beginning of the new Mission. I could not help being touched, when I beheld a venerable old man seated on a bundle of blankets. It was the Rev. Fr. Presidente of the Missions, Fr. Fermín Francisco de Lasuén, a man already more than seventy years of age. With him were the Fathers Juan de Santiago and Antonio Peyri. He was giving directions for completing, that very evening, the church and the dwelling for the religious. The shortness of the time which it took to construct the two rooms indicates of what nature the structures were and of what material they must have been built. Neither apartment exceeded ten yards in length and five in width, and their walls were nothing more than poles and branches of trees, so that they are perfectly described

---

[9] Fr. Lasuén to Borica, *Archb. Arch.*, no. 143.

TWO VOLUNTEER FRIARS ABOUT TO LEAVE FOR THE MISSIONS

by saying that they were *sicut tugurium in cucumerario,* like a lodge in a garden of cucumbers.[10]

On the following day, in the morning, High Mass was celebrated by the Rev. Fr. Presidente, and the two associate missionaries did the singing. I assisted them at this because I had some knowledge of ecclesiastical chant. There was a pathetic sermon in keeping with the object and the circumstances, the preacher being the celebrant himself. When holy Mass was concluded, the *Te Deum* was sung in thanksgiving. Here the function of the morning ended. In the afternoon there was another function which, though different from that in the morning, was very edifying. From me it drew tears of joy as I beheld the same venerable old man, re-vested with alb, stole, and cope, and assisted by the two companions, commencing to gather the fruit of their labors by administering the holy sacrament of Baptism to thirty and more little ones, the oldest of whom was only five years of age. With this function closed the first day of the new Mission.

The Fr. Presidente remained there about three or four days more, selecting together with Fr. Antonio Peyri the places where grain might be planted, where the church could be erected, and where the dwelling of the Fathers and the other necessary quarters of the Mission should be built. In the meantime, Fr. José Faura arrived, who was the religious assigned as companion to the Rev. Fr. Antonio Peyri. When the Fr. Presidente and Fr. Santiago had departed, these two remained alone to perfect the work confided to them.

The hardships these two religious must have endured, I leave to the consideration of the reader. He will easily comprehend them if he bears in mind that those two Fathers were appointed to establish a settlement without any other aid than some pickaxes, a dozen plowshares, half a dozen crowbars, some blankets, a quantity of flannel, and two dozen bolts of cloth with which to clothe the naked Indians. This is all that could be sent to the Fathers by the Fr. Procurator of the College of Mexico out of the $1000 which he received from the royal treasury [11] for founding a new Mission.[12]

---

[10] Isaiah, i, 8.

[11] From the Pious Fund, rather. In addition the following church goods were sent for the new Mission: 1 baul, 5 ornamentos abiados, 3 corporales, 3 cingulos, 3 manteles, 3 roquetes, 3 albas, 3 amitos, 3 purificadores, 3 manotejos, 5 palias, 3 manguillos, 2 guardapolvos, 1 almaisol, 5 frontales, 1 ritual, 1 misal, 3 platillos, 2 alfombras, 3 pares de vinageras, 2 Santos Cristos, 2 calices, 1 crismera, 2 aras, 1 copon, 1 pila bautismal, 1 fierro de hacer hostias, 1 campana de 5 arrobas, 1 concha, 1 campanita, 13 monedas, 2 arillos, 1 Santo Titular. —(*Inventario de 1808.*)

[12] Rivas, *Parecer en Repulsa, etc., Las Misiones de la Alta California,* Mexico, 1914, pp. 185-187.

Work on the new Mission proceeded at a brisk rate. Mindful of the governor's warning, the soldiers rolled up their sleeves and helped to prepare the material for the necessary structures. By July 12, Fr. Lasuén could report that already six thousand adobes had been made.[13] From San Diego, the Fr. Presidente wrote under date of July 27 to Governor Borica, who manifested great interest in missionary progress, that he had left Mission San Luis Rey on July 18, 1798, six weeks after the founding. "I left there," he wrote, "thirty-six, baptized single Indians, nineteen married couples, and eight catechumens. More than eight thousand adobes had been made, 175 beams have been brought to the Mission, and the foundations have been completed for five rooms which measure thirty-two varas (about ninety feet). What is necessary now are doors, windows, tables, chairs, empty barrels, etc." [14]

Governor Borica communicated the happy news to the viceroy under date of August 1, 1798, and reported that, besides the seventy-seven Indians already baptized, there were under instruction the three principal chiefs of neighboring rancherías with their wives and twenty-nine additional persons.[15]

On August 29, 1798, Fr. Lasuén wrote to Borica from San Buenaventura that at San Luis Rey already as many as 147 Indians had been baptized, and that the marriages of twenty-eight Indian couples had been blessed by the two missionaries. Three rooms were completed and occupied. The foundations of two other rooms had been laid. The Fathers were doing well, indeed.[16]

Unfortunately, the Mission Registers of San Luis Rey are lost. The title pages always contained the dates of the founding and the names of the missionaries. Much historical information could have been secured from these precious volumes, information which can not be obtained

13 *Archbishop's Archives*, no. 144.   14 Ibidem, no. 147.
15 *California Archives, Provincial Records*, vi, p. 406.
16 *Archb. Arch.*, no. 153.

En 27 de Octubre de 1813, el R.P. Ex Lr. de Filosofia Fr. Vicente
Fran.co de Sarria, Comis.o Prefecto de las Misiones que son del cargo
del Colegio de Propaganda Fide de San Fernando de Mexico, visitó este
Libro de Patentes y lo halló en el debido metodo y orden. Y p.a que conste
lo firmó conmigo el infra escrito Secret.o de la Vijita =

Fr. Vicente Fran.co de Sarria
Comis.o Prefo.

Fr. Fran.co Suñer
Secret.o

En 8 de Agosto de 1816 el R.P. Ex-Lector de Filosofia Fr. Vicente
Fran.co de Sarria Comisario Prefecto de las Misiones, que en el cargo
el Colegio de Propaganda Fide de S.n Fernando de Mexico, visitó este
Libro de Patentes, y lo halló cabal. Y para que conste lo firmó conmigo
el infra escrito Secret.o de la visita.

Fr. Vicente Fran.co de Sarria
Comis.o Prefto.

Fr. Joaquin Pasqual Nuez
Secret.o

En 21 de Julio de 1818. el R.P. ex L.r de Filosofia
Fr. Vicente Fran.co de Sarria, Comis.o Prefecto de las
Misiones que están al cargo del Colegio de Propag.da Fide
de S.n Fernando de Mexico, visitó este Libro, de Patentes, y lo halló cabal. La Pastoral de N.ro R.mo de
Yndias del 28 de Agosto de 1816, se está actualm.te
copiando. Y para que conste lo firmó conmigo el Infra-
escrito Secretario de la Visita.

Fr. Vicente Fran.co de Sarria
Comis.o Prefto.

Fr. Jayme Escude
Secret.o

AUTOS-DE-VISITA OF FR. V. F. DE SARRIA ON FLYLEAF
OF MISSION REGISTERS

from any other source. We shall have more to say on this subject later on. From the *Informes Generales* or *Annual Reports,* however, we learn that by the close of the year, that is, by December 31, 1798, only six months after the founding of the Mission, Fathers Antonio Peyri and José Faura had baptized 210 Indians of all ages, had blessed thirty-four marriages, and had buried five deceased; 214 Indians, 106 male and 108 female, had made their home with the Fathers at the Mission. Truly, the beginning was auspicious and in this regard surpassed the record of any of the twenty-one missions. The live stock, at the end of the first six months, consisted of 162 head of cattle, 600 sheep, 28 horses, and 10 pack mules. It was customary for the older missions to make contributions in behalf of a new establishment. According to Bancroft,[17] Santa Barbara, San Gabriel, San Juan Capistrano, and San Diego together contributed for San Luis Rey 64 horses, 28 yoke of oxen, 310 head of cattle, and 508 sheep.

At the close of 1798 the two missionaries reported to Fr. Lasuén that the rooms for the Fathers, the soldiers' quarters, and the dwelling for the corporal of the guard, were finished and roofed with thatch and earth, and that likewise all the adobes had been made. The walls of another building, as also the building for the girls, had gone up, but owing to the rains, it had not been possible to roof these structures. They were completed the next year, 1799. Five other apartments were added, of which one served as a house for the boys, one as a weaving room, one as a store room for the wool, and the other two as *truegas.* The walls of all these structures were of adobes, and they measured an adobe and a half in thickness.[18] The roof was covered with tules.[19]

As Fr. Palóu would say, Satan must have grown jealous

---

[17] *History of California,* vol. i, p. 564, note.

[18] An adobe measured usually 18 inches in length, 12 inches in width, and 4 inches in thickness. Hence the walls were about 27 inches thick.

[19] *Cal. Arch., Prov. Rec., Missions,* vi, pp. 43, 88.

from the start when he beheld the marvelously successful beginning, which presaged the wonderful progress of the Mission made during the next thirty-two years under the energetic and patient administration of its founder, Fr. Antonio Peyri. Some one must have complained to Governor Borica that the missionaries of San Luis Rey neglected to hold the usual election of Indian officials. This foolish regulation, introduced by Governor Neve, but the source of untold damage to the missions, was observed, however, by the Fathers on the first occasion, January 1, 1799, only six months after the admission of the first convert. The elections were held, and in the evening of the same day Fathers Peyri and Giribet reported to the Governor that the accusation was false, and that the Indian neophytes had elected Telmo and Felix as alcaldes and Mateo and Alejo as regidores for the ensuing year.[20]

For a while during the year 1798, Fr. José Panella stayed at San Luis Rey. This was during the absence of Fr. Antonio Peyri, whom ill health compelled to use the hot baths [21] near Mission San Juan Capistrano. Bancroft claims that Fr. Panella rendered himself unpopular on account of his strictness, and that Fr. Lasuén had to call him away.[22] The whole story appears muddled. The truth probably is that Fr. Peyri returned from the baths in better health, and that Fr. Panella accordingly returned to San Diego. Some disgruntled Indians may then have boasted that the missionary had been transferred at their instigation.

---

[20] See *Missions and Missionaries*, vol. ii, pp. 336-346, 540-543; vol. iii, pp. 397, 455, 487.

[21] They are twelve miles to the east and are very beneficial for those afflicted with rheumatism, as the writer himself experienced.

[22] Bancroft, vol. i, p. 564.

CHAPTER II.

FROM the very beginning, as we have seen, the Fathers in charge of the new Mission displayed a lively building activity. This was owing to the fact that the Indians applied in ever-increasing numbers for admission into the Christian fold. Dwellings had to be provided, work shops erected, implements and live stock cared for; but the energetic Fr. Peyri and his assistant were equal to the occasion.

At the end of 1800, the Fathers reported to the Fr. Presidente that a capacious guardhouse for the soldiers, a storeroom for the corporal, and a dwelling for each of the six guards of the Mission had been built. All these structures consisted of adobe walls that were one adobe and a half in thickness. The flat roof was formed of poles covered with earth. The walls for the two rooms of the Mission buildings proper had been raised, but they could not be roofed on account of rains. In the same year the number of baptized neophytes had reached 371, the marriages blessed to date numbered seventy-eight, while fifty-six Indians had died. The Mission population comprised 337 neophytes.

Live stock also had increased considerably, the Mission owning 450 head of cattle, 1,600 sheep, 146 horses, and 14 mules. Notwithstanding that experiments had to be made and the climate and soil had to be tested, the harvest during the same year (1800) yielded 1,000 fanégas or 1,600 bushels of wheat, 60 fanégas of barley and 20 fanégas of corn.

Improvements continued in subsequent years, as we learn from the annual reports of the two resident missionaries.

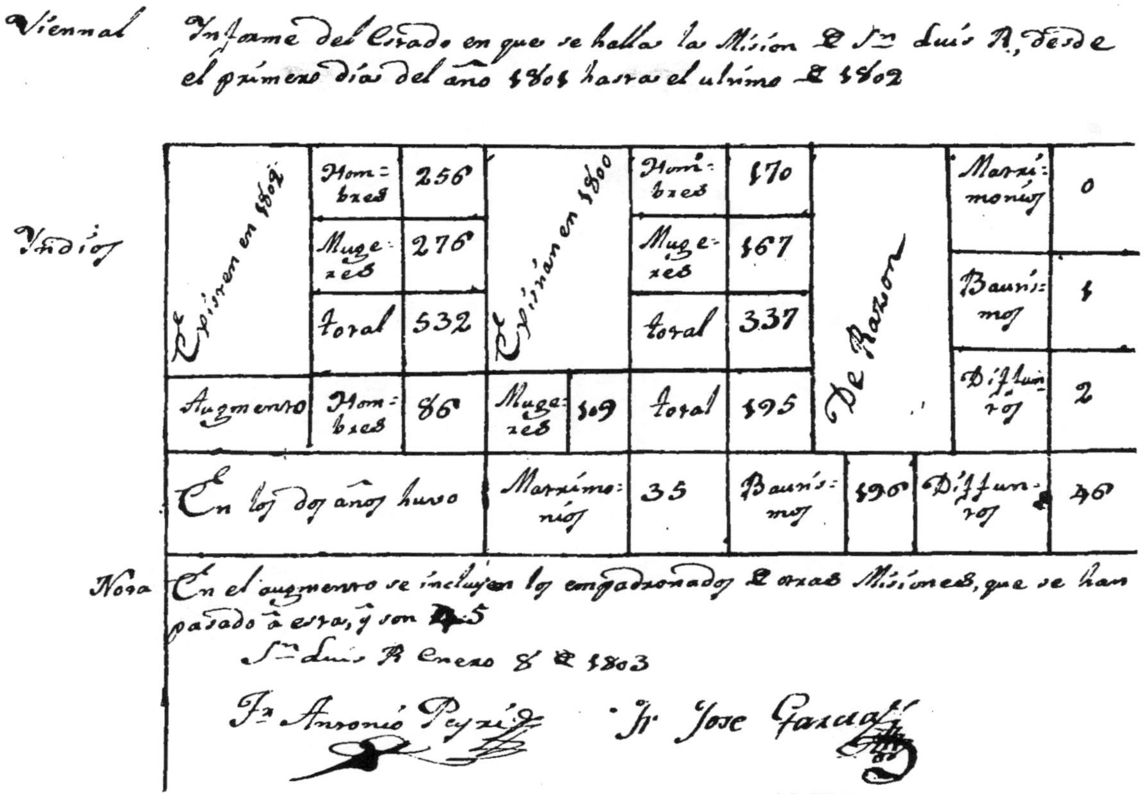

Viennal — Informe del Estado en que se halla la Misión de Sn Luis R. desde el primero día del año 1801 hasta el último de 1802

Indios

Existieron en 1802	Hombres	256	Existían en 1800	Hombres	170	De Razon	Matrimonios	0
	Mugeres	276		Mugeres	167		Bautismos	1
	Total	532		Total	337		Difuntos	2
Augmento	Hombres	86	Mugeres 109	Total	195			
En los dos años huvo			Matrimonios	35	Bautismos	190	Difuntos	46

Nota — En el augmento se incluyen los empadronados de otras Misiones, que se han pasado a esta, y son [illegible]5

Sn Luis R. Enero 8 de 1803

Fr. Antonio Peyri — Fr. Jose Garcia

STATE OF THE MISSION IN 1802. FACSIMILE

The year 1801 saw a marked change in the roofing of the buildings. The Fathers write that a large granary was built, that two rooms were added to the others, and that the two rooms, left uncompleted in the previous year, were now roofed. One-half of all the Mission buildings were *roofed with tiles made on the spot*. The remainder would be tiled in the coming year, please God, the missionaries conclude their report.

On December 31, 1802, the Fathers reported more explicitly, supplying the dimensions of the structures so far erected. During that year, four rooms were built of adobe and roofed with tiles. They were to serve as granaries or to be used for any purpose demanded. The dimensions were eleven varas or Spanish yards in length, five varas in width, and five varas in height. Additions were made to the old church structure, but this proving still too small, another church edifice was built of adobe and roofed with tiles. Its dimensions were fifty varas or about 138 feet long, seven varas or about nineteen feet wide, and six varas or about seventeen feet high. This, the Fathers calculated, would suffice to accommodate 1,000 Indians. All the tule roofs disappeared from the Mission and tile roofs replaced them. The year 1802 had, therefore, been an especially active one.

Reports for the year 1803 are missing. The next year, 1804, saw four granaries go up, each twenty varas long, six varas wide, and seven varas high. With this addition the one wing of the Mission, which had remained unfinished, was continued until it connected with another wing, and thus at last was completed the *patio* or inner court, a description of which will be given later. For tanning hides two capacious tanks of brick were constructed. Finally, a boiler of the same material was built for making soap; its capacity was 750 pounds.

At the close of this same year, 1804, a little more than five years after the founding of this missionary center, 308 male and 328 female Indians had settled under the shadow of the Cross. According to the annual reports, there had been 744 baptisms and 189 burials. A number of neophytes from San Diego and San Juan Capistrano had come to live here by permission of their respective missionaries, probably because they originally hailed from this region. This accounts for the difference of numbers in the annual reports and in the padron or Mission roll.

For the year 1805 we have no reports. Those for the next year, however, relate that a capacious apartment was erected for the girls and unmarried women. It had a *patio* or court-yard of its own, which measured twenty-six varas or about seventy-two feet in length and sixteen varas or about forty-five feet in width. This *patio* communicated with the grand inner court of the Mission. At the same time, in the rancho where the cattle were kept, a corral was constructed of adobe posts and covered with tiles. It was 110 varas or more than 300 feet square. Near it was erected an adobe house with tiled roof, probably for the cowherds.

At the end of this year, 1806, the baptismal entries already exceeded the one thousand mark, the actual number being 1,158. Death had called away 333 neophytes, while 256 marriages had received the priestly blessing. At the close of 1807 the resident Indian population comprised 1,025 souls.

During 1808 two rows of buildings in the *patio* were raised to the height of the main building, and two corrals, previously begun, were completed. An adobe wall was erected around two springs near the Mission. This report was signed by Fathers Antonio Peyri and Domingo Carranza, whereas the previous ones, 1801-1807, had been signed by Fathers Peyri and José García.[1]

---

[1] These notes on the building activities of all missions, more or less, were taken, in the summer of 1904, from the *California Archives, State Papers, Missions,* destroyed since, at that time in the U. S. Land Office, on Commercial Street, San Francisco. We drew from this source, because the Annual Reports for the years preceding 1810 have not as yet been discovered. Those at Santa Barbara of the period mentioned are incomplete, except the reports on agriculture, stock raising, and spiritual affairs, which begin with the year 1783, for some missions much earlier.

In the Inventory of 1808, Fr. Peyri himself notes that the church was enriched during 1808 with a crucifix for the pulpit, a silver censer with boat, a statue of San Luis Rey two varas and a quarter in height, and an oil painting one vara high, which represented Christ being baptized by St. John.

According to the Annual Report of December 31, 1810, which is signed by Fr. Estevan Tápis, then Presidente of all the missions, and by Fr. Peyri, a granary was built at the Rancho de Pala. This is the first time that mention is made of Pala. At the Mission itself, the vineyard was enclosed on two sides by an adobe wall. In the church, which is mentioned in this connection for the first time, a silk chasuble for first-class feasts and four albs were procured.

During this same year, 1810, an extraordinary number of converts were received—432! seventy-four marriages were blessed, and thirty-four deceased neophytes received Christian burial. The Indian population at the Mission in that year rose from 1,121 to 1,571, of whom 778 were males and 739 females. Only a missionary similarly situated will be able to comprehend what it meant to feed and clothe, to keep occupied, to instruct in spiritual doctrine and in mechanical arts, and to amuse and satisfy such a vast family of fickle Indians.

We should be pleased to describe this phase of missionary activity at San Luis Rey, but here, as elsewhere, the Fathers observed absolute silence on this subject. The hardships they endured and the successes and failures they met with were left to the Recording Angel. Let the reader consult toward the end of the narrative the tables on agriculture and stock raising as carried on by this chief of missionary establishments; from them he can draw his own conclusions. The farmer will readily understand and marvel at the struggles the missionaries had to undergo with climate and soil; the stock raiser will appreciate what the figures tell regarding his department; the teacher or principal of a school blessed with a few hundred unruly boys will know how to sympathize with the missionaries who day and night had between

BAPTISMAL FONT AT SAN LUIS REY

two and three thousand insatiable Indians about them; and, above all, the missionary will grasp what heroism was needed to maintain such a mission as San Luis Rey. Yes, even the police authorities will wonder how the Fathers ever contrived to keep peace among their jealous and childish wards. Had all white people, the settlers, soldiers, and officials, assisted the missionaries in promoting the spiritual and temporal welfare of the neophytes,—had they but refrained from putting obstacles in the way of the overburdened Fathers,—the patriarchal family of Mission Indians would have been an ideal congregation of happy and care-free creatures. Unfortunately, the guards, recruited largely from the scum of Mexican society, were given to naught but to idleness and self-gratification; wherefore, the unselfish missionaries were bound to come in conflict with the military on the subject of Indian rights, for which the soldiers had no regard whatever. Trouble of this kind began early at San Luis Rey. A few instances which have been recorded will enlighten the reader. On April 8, 1810, Fr. Peyri found it necessary to complain to Comandante Francisco M. Ruiz of San Diego that the troops were occupying the Las Flores and Santa Margarita rancherías, where the Mission grazed its sheep. These pastures were needed, Fr. Peyri said, and he would not believe that the soldiers acted upon orders from the Governor.[2]

Two days later, probably because he had not received a satisfactory answer from Ruiz, Fr. Peyri wrote to Governor Arrillaga. He showed that the Mission needed the land, since there had been a drought and the cattle were suffering in the sierra from lack of sufficient pasture.[3]

Again, on May 10, 1810, Fathers Peyri and Carranza jointly complained to Governor Arrillaga that the land around Las Flores was overrun by the horses of the presidio soldiers.[4]

Such and other troubles caused by the soldiers, more than the hardships experienced in serving the neophytes, con-

---

[2] *Archb. Arch.*, no. 356.   [3] Ibidem, no. 358.   [4] Ibidem, no. 365.

tributed to the nervous breakdown of many a peace-loving
friar, here as elsewhere. During the same year, 1810, Fr.
Domingo Carranza, owing to habitual ill health, petitioned
Fr. Presidente Lasuén for the permit to retire to the Mother
College. He had served on the mission two years longer
than the required ten. He was, therefore, entitled to return
to Mexico. Having received the permission of his superior,
Fr. Carranza asked Governor Arrillaga for the necessary
passport, which was accorded him on October 28, 1810.[5]

In 1811, the Fathers at San Luis Rey made plans for a
more worthy church edifice. It was at this time that the
foundations for the present structure were laid. No other
work in the way of building was undertaken during this year.
Fr. Peyri and Fr. Geronimo Boscana signed the report on
December 31, 1811.

During the year 1812 the adobe walls of the new church
rose to the height of the cornice, and the wall around the
vineyard, mentioned in the previous year, was completed.
The vineyard was thus made secure against animals.

On December 31, 1813, the Fathers wrote that a wing had
been added to the main row of buildings. Along the front
of the latter a corridor had been erected, the remains of
which could still be seen some years ago. In the patio
the arches of the corridor had reached one-half the proposed
height, and more material had been collected to continue the
work on the new church.

On October 6, 1812, the Spanish Minister of Foreign Relations in Mexico, Don Ciriaco Gonzalez Carvajál, addressed
to all civil and ecclesiastical authorities in the Spanish
dominions a list of thirty-six questions regarding the natives
of their respective districts. The missionaries in California
received this *Interrogatorio* in 1814.[6] Fathers Peyri and
Suñer replied to the questions as follows:

"This Mission is composed of pure native Indians of this
district, without any mixture, and is guarded by five soldiers

5 *Archb. Arch.*, no. 370.
6 *Missions and Missionaries*, vol. iii, pp. 10-11.

under a corporal, who have their families and belong to the presidio of San Diego.

"The language of these Indians is called *Tamancus*. However, many of the neophytes, especially the men, speak and understand the Spanish idiom, though not perfectly.

"These Indians have a natural love for their children, but they entertain love for their wives only if the women please them or because of the children. The latter they let live as they please, without any education, or any application to agriculture or mechanical arts. The neophytes, however, no longer live in that way, because the vigilance and zeal of the Fathers will not permit it, and these missionaries spare no means for promoting civilization.

"Although the gentiles as well as the neophytes may not manifest any particular fondness for the Europeans or Americans, they being children in this respect, yet we have never, since the founding of the Mission, known them to manifest any formal hatred toward either Europeans or Americans.

"In these Indians is observed an inclination to read and to write on paper. But it is because they are moved by the novelty or the curiosity of it more than by its utility, wherefore they quickly grow tired of it. In their pagan state they have no idea whatever of characters or writings, and therefore they do not use characters nor the bark of trees or plants for writing.

"It seems to us that the easiest and simplest way of getting them to devote themselves to speaking and understanding the Castilian tongue is emulation fostered by means of premiums, especially as regards the children. We have had no difficulty in getting them to speak and understand Spanish. For this reason the majority of the neophytes speak either one or the other language, especially the men. Of those born in the Mission, all speak Castilian.

"Mildness, submissiveness, and humility, the effects of their pusillanimity and timidity, are the virtues we consider the most dominant in the Indians here. If they sometimes show themselves charitable and generous, it is not because they are such by nature, but always for some purpose of self-interest, that is, because they have something to expect or to fear. If they show themselves compassionate, it is for the relatives; but they regard with indifference the ills, hardships and miseries of those who are not relatives.

"These Indians have many ridiculous superstitions; for instance, the fisherman who catches a fish and the hunter who kills the rabbit he caught, etc., may not eat of what he has caught, because then the fisherman would not catch and the hunter would not kill any more. In order to win at their games of chance, they will fast one, two, or three days, and in the night preceding the game they will take a drink of what they call *Mani* (which is composed of the root of the *taluacke machucado* mixed with water, which liquid makes them drunk and sometimes turns the stomach), with the understanding that if they lose in spite of this nonsense, they say that it was because the other fasted and drank more. The husband may not touch the wife until the child can walk; if he does, he will have no other child. When the women give birth, the men abstain from meat and all fat for some days, in order that the infants may not die. Thus they cherish very many superstitions, which we have no other method of counteracting than *clama ne cesses*— shout lest you seem indifferent; by this means not a few neophytes by and by are disillusioned.

"In this Mission we use the short catechism, containing in the Indian language and in Castilian what is absolutely necessary for a Christian to know; at the same time, we teach the acts of Faith, Hope, Charity, and Contrition. The Indians are taught in both languages the Pater Noster,[7] Ave Maria, the Credo, the Salve, the Ten Commandments of God, the Precepts of the Church, the Sacraments, and the General Confession or Confiteor.

"Among these Indians we have observed no other idolatry

[7] See Appendix B.

than that with certain birds which they call *Azuts,* a kind
of very large hawk. At the right time, when the birds are
still small, they take them from their nest (as they say,
there are never more than two), and he who captured them
presents them to the chief of the rancheria, who raises them
with much care and attention until they are grown up.
When they have attained a good size, the Indians arrange
for a grand feast with the following ceremonies: In the
night before the feast, they place the *Azuts* or hawks in the
center of a great ring formed by themselves. Then, while
they dance and sing in a most dismal manner, and the old
men and women blow toward every direction, at the same
time making a thousand strange faces and grimaces, they
kill the birds very slowly. As soon as the birds are dead,
they extinguish the fire and all break out into wailing, shout-
ing, and howling like crazy people, and like maniacs strike
blows in a manner that creates horror and confusion. After
a long time, during which this raving lasts, they again start
the fire. Now they skin the birds and throw the flesh into
the fire. Meanwhile, they sing again, but in a more gentle
manner. The feathers are preserved with much care and
veneration until the next day, when they make of them a
skirt, which they put on a boy during the days that the
feast lasts. He dances with it in the center of a large
circle of Indians, who likewise walk to and fro, keeping time
with the boy, who is dancing in the center of the ring. In
this way they dance at intervals. In like manner, other boys
selected for that purpose exchange places with the first boy.
After the feast, the capitano of the rancheria keeps the skirt
with considerable veneration or a species of idolatry. We
have made every effort to ascertain the purpose of these
ceremonies; but we have never learned anything else than
that thus the ancestors have done.

"Their matrimonial contracts they celebrate in this simple
way: The candidate sends a representative (who is always
either the father or a brother) to the parents of the girl
desired, and asks her for wife. If they concede her to him,

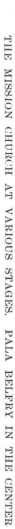

THE MISSION CHURCH AT VARIOUS STAGES. PALA BELFRY IN THE CENTER

the young man sends some seeds, beads, or other trifles to the girl. If she accepts them, the two by that very act are considered married. Among the neophytes, the candidate presents himself to one of the missionaries. The priest conducts the proceedings entirely until he joins the two in wedlock according to the Roman Ritual. But neither among the Christians nor among the pagans does the groom present anything to the father of the bride.

"The method observed by these Indians when they are ill is as follows: In the case of external maladies, such as wounds, they firmly tie the part above the wound in order to prevent the evil from extending farther up. In addition, one of the following remedies is most commonly applied: a plaster of tule leaves (which they call *Pibut*) cooked and crushed; at other times, a poultice made of crushed wild onions (which they call *Queheyaguis*); sometimes an herb, which grows on the seashore, is burnt and the ashes are applied to the wound. We do not know this herb, but they call it *Chaeca*. If the wound is a burn, they follow the same treatment regarding the ligature; but in addition they make a powder of the prickly pear, *Nabot;* at other times, they use the powdered excrements of the jack-rabbit or rabbit, called *Tosajat Posá.* Others use leaves of the sage, called *Casil.* If the malady is from the bite of a poisonous creature, they use a stone similar to chalk, called *Xaclul.* This they soak in the mouth, and as soon as the stone is moistened they apply the spittle to the wound. In the same way they proceed in the case of wounds from poisonous arrows.

"If the illness proceeds from a swelling, never forgetting the ligature, they anoint the swelling with the ointment or oil of the seed of the red pepper (chilcote), called *Ennuix,* until it breaks open. If the illness is internal, they firmly tie up the part that aches most, which we have observed to be the chest of the body. They use also pulverized roots, which, mixed with water, the patient is made to drink. These roots are of the mangrove, called by them *Hichis;* of the

elder, called *Cuta;* of the wild rose of Castile, called *Husla;*
of the reed-grass, called *Hiquix;* and of the ivy, called
Hial. The drinks made of all these, they say, are all purga-
tive; the root of the mangrove also provokes vomiting.

"They do not make use of blood-letting, but they engage
for their infirmities certain quacks, who suck the patient
on the spot where he feels the most pain, and soon from
their mouth they extract blood, and sometimes pebbles, tiny
sticks, bones, hairs, etc. (previously and deceitfully put into
the mouth), and then make the patient believe that this was
the infirmity. Presently they blow a few times to the four
winds, and the sick man is very much satisfied, although he
is more sick than before. They make him observe such a
rigorous diet that ordinarily they will give no food unless
he asks for it.

"With the sick they make use also of superstitious dances,
songs, and blowing, while a wizard makes thousands of
grimaces at the patient, so that in case he does not get well
after the first remedies and avails himself of a quack, this
fellow will not cease until he has killed the patient and
thus made him a martyr to the demon.

"In fine, with regard to the superstitious practices in their
infirmities, idolatries, and witchcraft, they are so reticent,
deceitful, and reserved that, although I have been among
them from the beginning of the Mission, I can only manifest
my ignorance regarding their practices. For they will not
reveal more about these than they can help. Among the
neophytes we are rooting out these ideas, though they, too,
are always Indians.

"About ten leagues from this Mission is a hot spring; but
for lack of information we do not know its qualities. The
Indians make use of it by bathing in it when they are
afflicted with skin diseases, and it seems to do them good.

"During the sixteen years since the founding of this Mission there was little difference between the number of births
and of deaths.

"The Indians distinguish the seasons of the year by calculating the trees as the foliage appears and falls; also by observing the seeds and herbs. The months they calculate according to the moon, and the hours according to the sun. They have never used a calendar. However, the new Christians regulate themselves by the clock of the Mission; and for timing their rest, meals, and work, we sound the bell.

"As to the number of meals in a day, the pagans have no rule; but after the manner of the beasts in the mountains, they eat when it suits them and when they have something to eat. Their food consists at times of deer, rabbits, squirrels, rats, which the men kill, and of acorns and other seeds, which the women gather. It is to be observed, however, that among those who live near the seashore fishes form the more abundant food. To the neophytes three meals are given daily.

"These Indians use no other kind of extraordinary beverage than that made of the *taluache,* and called *Mani.* This beverage does them so much damage that, if they drink much of it and fail to vomit, they die in their drunken stupor, foaming at the mouth.

"We cannot say that they adore the sun or the moon; but we have noticed that when they discover the new moon they will raise a shout and manifest their joy. It has not been possible to discover any other reason for doing this than that their ancestors did so. We have observed also that when there is an eclipse of the sun or moon, they shout or howl at the top of their voices and make noise by clapping their hands, while others strike the earth with a stick or some other object. When asked for the reason, they have always answered us that they were sure some animal was trying to eat the sun or moon, and that they did these strange things in order to frighten the animal away, since they believed that, if the animal ate it, they all would perish. The pagans continue such and similar customs, but we endeavor to wean the neophytes from them little by little.

"Regarding the origin of these Indians, we know nothing; nor is there any tradition regarding it among the Indians.

"At their burials the pagans observe the following ceremonies: As soon as one has died, they throw the corpse on a great pyre; then they come together, that is, the relatives and friends, and stir up the fire as much as they can; meanwhile they howl and weep until the corpse is consumed. On the pile on which they burn the body they throw seeds, beads, and whatever trifles they have. The neophytes likewise throw similar things into the grave, when the Fathers are not looking. They manifest their grief by cutting their hair more or less short, according to the degree of kinship. This is observed especially by the women.

"As to their fidelity to pledges and promises, if they keep their word, it is owing to their timidity; but by nature they are so false that they will break their promises whenever they can. In fact, they are so inclined to lying that, unless it is in their interest, they will tell the truth only out of forgetfulness or fear.

"If at any time they readily make a present of anything, it is on account of kinship or for some especial self-interest; for instance, in order to gain some one's friendship; but when they have no relatives, they seldom offer a gift. This is due to their distrust of one another. If nevertheless they make a present of any beads or other objects, it is with the understanding that it must be returned. Those near the sea usually exchange fish for beads with those of the sierra, so much for so much.

"The most dominant vices of the Indians of both sexes are stealing, lying, and impurity.

"The pagan Indians have no cemeteries, for they conduct their funerals as before stated. The neophytes have a common cemetery and the ceremonies observed are those of the Roman Ritual.

"These Indians are very irascible and entertain hatred a long time for the purpose of revenging themselves. To judge from their acts, they are so cruel that we would experience their cruelties every day were it not for their timidity and cowardice. In their pagan state they have no particular

THE MISSION COMMUNITY IN 1813

chastisement; but for the least trifle they would rise to fight and would readily kill one another. Those of the Mission have generally given up such barbarities; and, as a rule, they are content with complaining to the missionaries.

"We have not heard that in these regions any human sacrifices have been made. If the Indians offered anything at all to their idols, it would consist of acorns and other seeds, which may be inferred from their fondness for their dances and feasts at the time of the harvests.

"In poverty and wretchedness all these Indians are equal, with this difference: that in every ranchería there is one whom they call Capitan *Not*. He governs them in all their battles and feasts and other communal affairs, with the understanding that for every feast all bring him seeds, beads, hides of deer, etc., which he is to distribute to the guests invited from other rancherías.

"The Indians here have no personal servants; but all Christians in common serve the Mission and all in common participate in their service.

"These Indians, it seems, never heard music; for at their dances they use only the chants of their own idiom, which are more sad than cheerful and which to a great extent proceed from a strained throat. The neophytes are much pleased with our music, especially with the pathetic and melodious. They easily learn to play on any musical instrument.

"As has already been said, these Indians had no idea of letters for writing. We return to this subject in order to state that, though they possess reason, they live in the mountains like creatures without reason, and that consequently they never had any men among them distinguished for wisdom or for letters. All have at all times been like so many brutes.

"Although they have some idea of a rational soul, which they call *Chamson,* and which, they believe, will, after death, go down to *Tolmar,* where all are united to live forever in much joy; yet they have no idea of either reward or punishment, nor of final Judgment, Purgatory, and Hell. At present, however, they have an idea of all this, because they heard it from the neophytes and these from the missionaries.

"The gentiles generally go stark naked; but when it is cold they wear a kind of cloak made of the skins of rabbits. The women always use, besides the cloak, a kind of fringed apron. The dress of the male neophytes consists of a blanket, shirt, and pants. That of the women is the same, except that instead of pants they wear a petticoat, which is of wool taken from the sheep of the Mission, and woven there by the neophytes under the care and direction of the missionaries.—San Luis Rey, December 12, 1814.—Fr. Antonio Peyri, Fr. Francisco Suñer." [8]

---

[8] *Sta. Barb. Arch.*, ad annum.

CHAPTER III.

AT the close of 1814, Father Peyri and Suñer report that work on the new church was progressing, that, in fact, it was nearly finished; in addition, other little building was done, which they remark, it was not worth while to describe.

At last the new church was completed, and on October 4, 1815, the feast of St. Francis, it was dedicated. Other work also had been done in that year, but it was of little importance. Thus FF. Peyri and Suñer report on December 31, 1815.

No further mention is made regarding building activity in the several reports sent in till the year 1818. On December 31 of that year, Fathers Peyri and Jayme Escudé inform Fr. Presidente Payeras that at Pala the chapel of San Antonio had been lengthened and that at the same place two large granaries had been built, besides one large apartment for the boys and young men, another for the girls and single women, and other little work of this kind, all of adobe and roofed with tiles.

Some of the work, it seems, had been slovenly done by the hired workmen; for, under date of November 3, 1817, Fr. Peyri writes to Governor Solá, saying with regard to the carpenter and the smith: "We are much afflicted on account of the church; it is absolutely necessary to repair the roof, because the rains have come through and formed a laguna. With the assistance of master Salvador repairs are under way; but the good masons do not know how to place the tiles, and so a whole mountain of difficulties presents itself. Although the smiths might have learned something, they know nothing at present." [1]

Writing to Governor Solá on March 23, 1820, Fr. Jayme Escudé says that there was a great scarcity of water, because not even half of the needed amount of rain had fallen; that in consequence many sheep had died, as also some of the cattle, which was hard to endure, as the Mission now numbered 2,600 souls. At San Antonio de Pala a large number of gentiles applied for Baptism. Some had been baptized this year and many more could be admitted, if there were enough wool to weave into cloth, many sheep having perished. In the past year more than 300 adults had been baptized, besides a large number of children. San Antonio de Pala is surely in as good order and perfection as this Mission itself could be. [2]

On December 31, 1823, Fr. Peyri alone signs the report, saying that in the church and sacristy there was much more than in the past year; that at the Rancho de las Flores there have been constructed in the form of a patio houses and granaries; and that all the buildings were roofed with tiles in that place, which is also called San Pedro.

Fr. Escudé anxiously desired to leave the country, and for that reason he had received from the Fr. Presidente the permit, which was due him for long service. Accordingly, he applied to Governor Solá for the necessary passport. The reply he received was as follows: "I have received your note of August 16. In reply I have to say that I have presented to the Supreme Government the extreme need of priests; for of the majority of those living in the territory some are infirm and others on account of old age are worn out, while the younger ones cannot attend so many missions." [3]   It appears, however, that Fr. Escudé obtained the

---

[1] *Archb. Arch.*, no. 730.

[2] *Archb. Arch.*, no. 1,018, 1,073.

[3] *Cal. Arch., St. Pap., Sacram.*, xviii, 52; *Archb. Arch.*, no. 1,073.

permit later, for he left the territory in the same or early in the next year, 1823. Governor Solá's letter was dated September 19, 1822.

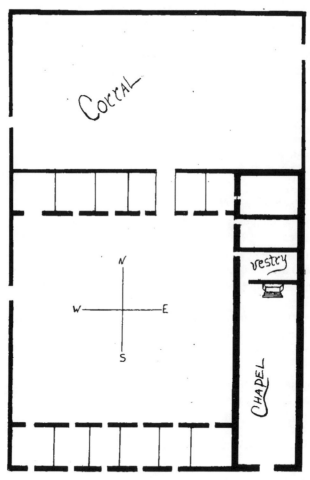

GROUND PLAN OF SAN ANTONIO DE PALA

After this no more building activity is reported. It seems that after the Mexican Independence had been established the Fathers confined themselves to preserving what had so

far been effected and to decorating the interior of the
church. On December 31, 1829, Fr. Peyri, who was alone
now, reported that everything was nicely adorned for divine
worship. On the church edifice a graceful dome was built;
this supported a smaller cupola sustained by eight columns.
This little cupola or lantern was formed of 144 panes of
glass, through which light descended into the sanctuary and
nave below. The vestment case in the sacristy also was
finished this year.

From actual measurements taken on November 5, 1904,
in company with Rev. Fr. Jeremiah O'Keefe, O. F. M., the
superior of the Mexican community, the writer secured the
following details: The ancient mission buildings covered an
area of six and sixty-one hundredths acres. The patio measured 250 feet from corridor to corridor. The Mission had
a frontage of 600 feet, east to west. Along the entire
length, excluding church and cemetery, ran a corridor. The
building ran back 450 feet. The treshing floor was of tile
flagging, and it lay beyond the rear walls of the Mission, on
a slight elevation, somewhat to the west. The church and
main building faced nearly south, about twenty degrees to
the east. Fr. O'Keefe was of the opinion that the reason
why the missionaries, as a rule, did not build squarely facing
cardinal points was that all sides of the mission might have
the benefit of the sun at some time during the day.

The measurement of the church edifice resulted in the following figures: the walls, 6½ feet thick; from the inner
front portal to the transept, 110½ feet; thence to rear wall,
54 feet; the entire inner length of the church, therefore,
164½ feet. Inside width of church, 27 feet. The pillars
of the transept, 25 feet apart; the sanctuary, 29 feet deep;
inside height of the church, 30 feet; outside length of the
church, 177 feet; outside width of the church, 40 feet.

In the following year, 1830, the main altar was gilded, as
also the side altars in the transept. These make a most
agreeable appearance, for they are constructed after modern
patterns.

Once more, at the end of December, 1832, in the report signed this time by Fr. Oliva, who succeeded Fr. Peyri, note is made of additions to church and sacristy. A crucifix of very fine sculpture was obtained, he says, and also a new missal, a new silver ciborium, the cup of which is gold plated.

On October 1, 1822, the imperial commissioner from Mexico requested the Fr. Prefecto to have all the missions reply to a number of questions regarding the state of the establishments. Accordingly, under date of October 5, Fr. Payeras sent a copy of the questions to each mission, with the request that the Fathers comply. The answers follow according to the questions of the formula.

Geographical Situation. The Mission of San Luis Rey, situated in 32½ degrees north latitude, lies south of the territorial capital, Monterey, at a distance of 164 leagues. It has to the east, distant eight leagues, the sierra with some pagan Indians. Of the rest of the Indians which the Mission has in that region, about 1,300 souls are converted to Christianity. They are privileged to have at the foot of the sierra a chapel (by permit of the government), and to arrange it like a mission, the title of which is San Antonio (de Pala). The Christians there are well instructed in the Catholic Religion. They are disposed to obey without repugnance what the government may find expedient to command. To the west lies the Pacific Ocean at a distance of a league and a half. To the north is Mission San Juan Capistrano at a distance of twelve leagues; and to the south is Mission San Diego, fourteen leagues distant. In the same direction toward the southwest, at a distance of thirteen leagues, is the presidio of San Diego.

Cavalry Troops. From the nearest presidio the Mission has a corporal and a squad of five soldiers, which the commander of the presidio increases or decreases according to circumstances.

Inhabitants. The Mission has as American citizens the troops mentioned above, with their families, and the ser-

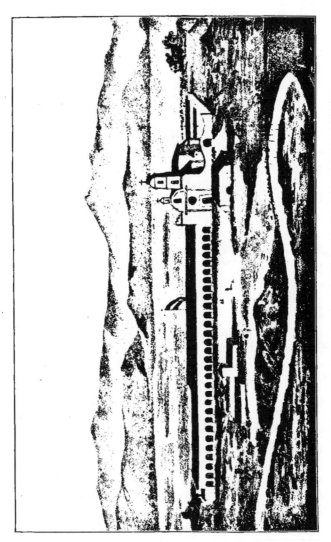

MISSION SAN LUIS REY, ACCORDING TO AN OLD DRAWING

vants, at present three, also with their families. The neophytes at the Mission number 2,663.

Live Stock. There are 500 horses, 150 mules, 12,000 head of cattle, and 20,500 sheep, which four classes of live stock are necessary in this country.

Lands of the Mission. The land belonging to the Mission may be calculated as extending eleven leagues from north to south and fifteen leagues from east to west, for it has a cattle ranch at that distance to the north. The land is to a great extent sterile, and much of it entirely so. For that reason the live stock needs it all; indeed, in years when there is little rain, the stock dies for want of pasture. For cultivation the soil is fairly good and produces, according to good or bad season, from twenty to twenty-five fanégas for one fanéga sown, provided no mishap of any kind occurs. Every year wheat is sown, likewise corn and beans are planted, always in proportion to the needs of the community of neophytes. Generally from two to three hundred fanégas of wheat are sown, according to the circumstances of the year. In proportion, corn and beans and other seeds are planted which, with the meat, will suffice to maintain the community from year to year. The meat is obtained by slaughtering, which takes place every Saturday. To obtain additional provisions the neophytes in the proper season gather wild seeds and berries, or go fishing at the seashore and in the streams. In the twenty-four years since the founding of the Mission, apparently no corner suitable for growing anything has been overlooked in the endeavor to plant grain. Water has been sought as far as eight leagues for the purpose of irrigating; but such spots are few, and for the main crops we have to depend on the rains, which in some seasons were scarce enough. It must be observed also that the fields are very much damaged by locusts, squirrels, crows, blackbirds, and other plagues, which can be driven off only by means of many dogs and scarecrows.

Gold and Silver Mines. No mines have so far been discovered within the territory of this Mission, although for some time the miner Don Pedro Posadas stayed here as guest. Nor have pearl fisheries been discovered. However, there seems to be an abundance of fishes and sardines, which industrious men are seeking to secure for their own benefit.

Fisheries. This Mission, although not more than a league and a half distant from the seashore, cannot be seen from there, because it is situated in a cañada and is hidden behind a ridge. Nevertheless, the native citizens have various places where they fish, going out into the ocean even when the tide is running high. To date, however, no national nor foreign ship has ventured to this point; whence it must be inferred that disembarking would not be easy and would not pay, as there is nothing to be gained from such an attempt.

As to the pagans, some, living in the sierra eight leagues away, have become acquainted with the Christians, but no incursions whatever are to be feared. On the contrary, owing to this acquaintance, they are joining the fold of our holy Religion. I hope that, with the prudent and wise measures which we expect from the Imperial Government, all will be admitted in a short time. In the sierra to the northeast are some savages who have communication with others as far as the Rio Colorado. From this result at times boastings and rumors of meetings and incursions of the savages; but I do not know what number of soldiers would be needed to prevent such meetings and incursions. This is all I have to say on this particular subject.—San Luis Rey, November 22, 1822.—Fr. Antonio Peyri, Missionary.[4]

An interesting summary on the last page of the Padron gives this clear information on the standing of the Indian population of Mission San Luis Rey:

Año 1823 en el fin del año:

Matrimonios	Viudos	Viudas	Solteros	Solteras	Niños	Niñas
De la Mision......308	96	79	354	300	323	272
De S. A. Pala....137	46	58				
Huérfanos 120	00	00				
De Cupa ó Del Valle 37	02	01				

[4] *Sta. Barb. Arch.*, ad annum.

Año de 1824:

Matrimonios	Viudos	Viudas	Solteros	Solteras	Niños	Niñas
De la Mision......300	98	81	387	325	324	272
De S. A. Pala....127	49	61				
Huérfanos ....112 }	5	1				
Del Valle .... 43 }						

In September, 1821, the Fr. Comisario Prefecto, Mariano Payeras, made an official visit to Mission San Diego, and thence, on September 10. he set out with Fr. Sanchez, one of its missionaries, to find suitable sites for new establishments. On September 17 he formally founded the mission station Santa Isabél, and then, after satisfying his missionary zeal by instructing and baptizing, he arrived at a place which he named Guadalupe. Here he raised a cross to mark the site of a prospective mission, about two and a half leagues from Santa Isabél. This happened on September 19.[5]

Then Fr. José Sanchez writes in his *Diario:* "On September 20, at about 4 p. m., we set out for the west on the most wretched road downward through the cañada. The region abounded in poplars and willows, and on the hills were live oaks. We arrived at a ranchería which the Indians and Fr. Prefecto called *Caqui.* This is a very good locality, as water, pastures and live oaks abound, and in the lowlands are alders and willows. In the sierra above are pines and *Palo Colorado* (Redwood) in abundance. After traveling ten leagues, we came to some patches of land cultivated by pagans and Christians. We took a little lunch and then, going through to the lower cañada, we reached San Antonio de Pala, which belongs to San Luis Rey, at about 4:30 p. m., having on this stretch marched two leagues.

"September 21, Feast of St. Matthew. After holy Mass we visited the chapel (as prescribed), and then passed the day in works pertaining to the ministry. From here four of the six soldiers returned to the presidio of San Diego.

"September 22, Saturday. The Fr. Prefecto sang the High Mass in honor of Mary Most Pure. The surrounding

---

[5] See *Mission San Diego.*

territory was examined for the purpose of determining whether at some time a mission could be established here, when the limits between San Luis Rey and Pala would be drawn. It was found that nothing was lacking here for a mission, save that a missionary must be assigned. The place is a little secluded, but it is able to maintain the large number of Indians it already has, and these might be increased. The arroyo which it has is the same that runs to San Luis Rey, and it is lined with willows, poplars, and alders.

"September 23, Sunday. After the holy Mass and sermon by Fr. Prefecto, we listened to some neophytes from San Gabriel and San Juan Capistrano regarding the changing of the Mission. Having satisfied these and having baptized five children of neophytes, we had a pleasant rest of about two hours, watching the pagans and Christians enjoying themselves at dancing after their own fashion. In the afternoon at about 4 o'clock, we started out and traveled toward the north and then toward the east, and soon found ourselves in a cañada which runs northward and then again eastward. In that part where the cañada begins to descend more gently on the other side, was discovered a stone which without doubt had served and still serves these unhappy Indians as an occasion of sin. One look sufficed, owing to its many huge figures and the adjoining thicket, to make it clear what it might signify. The Rev. Fr. Prefecto commanded Fr. Peyri to have it destroyed. From here we turned toward the north through a beautiful cañada until we reached Temécula, at about 5:30 p. m., distant about three leagues from Pala. What we saw on the road this afternoon, as far as the said stone, was poor soil; but there is a little water, and live oaks and alders abound. The rest of the way is well covered with live oak until one emerges on the plain of Temécula.

"September 24. At daybreak we left the lower cañada for the west. The soil is very much saturated with alkali. The water ditch is apparently useless for irrigating because the land lies higher. On the right hand there are some small springs. After wandering toward the north for about a league, we encountered a spring which is not very large and which is called by our people *San Isídro*. Continuing in the same direction, we discovered another called *Santa Gertrudis*. Proceeding in the same direction we stopped at *Jaguara,* so called by the natives, but by our people *San Jacinto*. This is the rancho for the cattle of San Luis Rey, distant from Temécula about eleven or twelve leagues. On the whole stretch there are no trees. The soil is very good; but on reaching *San Jacinto,* its lands, though used for pasture, proved to be of little value on account of the alkali. From this little elevation where the *enramada* is situated, north to south, there are springs. The arroyo which runs from here east to south is covered with álamos for about two leagues. In front of the *enramada,* toward the northeast, is a spring of tepid water. Not far away is fine timber. In fact it is a very extensive locality; but according to observations, it lacks sufficient water. In my opinion, it can serve only for a rancho.

"September 25. The day broke with a little rain and found the Fr. Prefecto ill. He did not find relief until late in the afternoon. We saw only one Indian.

"September 26. At about 4 a. m. the Fr. Prefecto found himself relieved. We left *San Jacinto* and crossed the cañada going toward the west. On the road we found no trees. The soil is mixed with a saline, but it produces grass. After about two leagues and a half, we came upon a laguna of moderate size, which turns toward the south. They say it runs dry in years when there is little rain. From here we went toward the north over a hilly and exceedingly barren country, covered with much brushwood. We ascended and then again descended the sierra with much trouble, passing through a cañada with many *islai* berry bushes. I tasted them and found them pleasant. After a little while we forced our way to the west, returning, on coming out, to proceed northward, and in a short time arrived at San

Bernardino. So we called the place as our people do, while the natives call it *Guachinga*. It belongs to San Gabriel and is distant from the former stop about nine leagues. This cañada has, besides the islai and live oak, plenty of water, and much good soil. There is much *poleo*." [6] Here we leave the two Fathers and resume our narrative.

With the year 1812, worse troubles than those hitherto experienced came upon this Mission as upon the others, in consequence of the revolt in Mexico against Spain, inaugurated by Hidalgo on Sunday, September 16, 1810. Henceforth neither goods for the missions nor salaries for the soldiers in California were supplied by the Mexican Government. In consequence, the whole military department of the territory expected the mission Indians to support the soldiers and their families, and to furnish the equipments, not counting the occasional forced contributions in cash. Most of the historical evidence concerning this matter has been lost or destroyed. Yet there are sufficient documents left to show how the mission Indians in charge of the Franciscans were fleeced in order to support the indolent soldiers, who might have earned a living, and to relieve the *paisanos* and other settlers from contributing. The officials and settlers, indeed, always made the demands on the missionaries so as to escape the odium of oppressing the Indian converts; but that was only a trick to hide the injustice of the transactions; for the missionaries, having made the vow of poverty, could possess nothing and, indeed, never claimed as much as a foot of land or a bushel of grain for themselves. They were merely the legal guardians of their convert Indians and, without compensation, they managed the property accumulated by the thrift of the Indians for the benefit of the whole community.

Here are a few specimen demands made on the Indian community at San Luis Rey. On June 15, 1821, Lieutenant José Maria Estudillo of San Diego demanded from the

---

6 *Sta. Barb. Arch.*, ad annum.

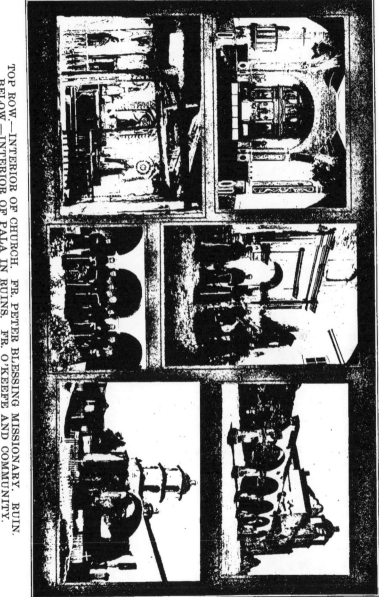

TOP ROW.—INTERIOR OF CHURCH. FR. PETER BLESSING MISSIONARY. RUIN. BELOW.—INTERIOR OF PALA IN RUINS. FR. O'KEEFE AND COMMUNITY. CORNER IN THE CEMETERY.

Mission 652 fanégas of corn and 200 fanégas of beans.[7]
In reply to this demand, Fr. Peyri wrote on June 18: "In
less than a month you have already received $70 worth of
corn and beans. Nevertheless, we shall not only comply,
but we also promise that, though there were at the Mission
no other grain on hand than that which is demanded, we
would cheerfully give the last kernel, in order that the
troops may not suffer and the patriotism we have always
had may become evident.[8] Four days later, however, under
date of June 22, Fathers Peyri and Escudé wrote that Estudillo's request was felt very much, since San Luis Rey was
the most populous Mission, numbering at the time more
than two thousand Indian converts. They thought that the
amount to be contributed should be left to the Fathers to determine, who would decide in accordance with the means on
hand. At all events, they suggested, the presidio ought to furnish the pack mules for transporting the supplies demanded,
as was done elsewhere.[9] It must be borne in mind that for
supplies of this kind the missions received nothing more
than an order on the Mexican treasury, which the missionaries knew very well would never be paid. This state of
affairs continued to the end of the mission period—that is
to say, until the year 1846, when the United States flag
began to wave in California.

At other times, the governor wanted laborers to work on
the fortifications or for other purposes. Of course, the
Indian converts were expected to perform the work. San
Luis Rey, not being in the immediate vicinity of a presidio,
was not troubled on that score. Instead, however, money
had to be contributed. In like manner, money was frequently wanted for other purposes. In that case, the governor would simply ask the Superior of the missions to
furnish the cash. It was then left to the Fr. Presidente or
Comisario to designate the amount each mission had to

---

[7] *Archb. Arch.*, no. 1,223. A fanéga is equal to one hundredweight.
[8] *Archb. Arch.*, no. 1,226.   [9] Ibidem, no. 1,227.

supply according to the poor or prosperous condition it was in at the time.

On December 16, 1820, for instance, Governor Solá requested Fr. Mariano Payeras to furnish $3,000 for governmental purposes. In reply, Fr. Payeras informed the governor that he could not obtain more than $2,000.[10] Of this amount, San Luis Rey was asked to contribute $150.[11] Even the poorest establishment, Mission Soledad, was taxed $100. In a circular dated January 25, 1821, Fr. Payeras asked for clothing for the soldiers and assigned to each mission the amount it had to contribute.

On August 24, 1821, Fr. Payeras asked the Fathers of the San Diego district, in which San Luis Rey was included, to supply ten pack mules and their outfit. In the following year, 1822, on April 17, Fr. Payeras requested the missions to furnish the traveling expenses for Governor Solá, who went to Mexico as representative of California. Mission San Luis Rey offered $100, to be paid the governor in Mexico from the funds which the procurator owed to the Mission. Writing to Collector José M. Herrera on August 14, 1827, Governor Echeandia acknowledges that the missionaries of San Luis Rey had loaned the paymaster $1,000, which was paid most probably under stress and was never returned.[12]

Fr. Peyri had hailed Mexican independence with enthusiasm, and had even adopted the custom of the new rulers of signing communications with *Dios y Libertad*. He readily contributed, therefore, whatever was demanded, as may be seen from the following permit granted to him: "Santa Barbara, December 27, 1829. Inasmuch as there is a manifest decrease in the beasts of burden which serve to transport the hides from Mission San Luis Rey to the port of San Diego, and in consideration of the continued services which the said Mission offers to the national treasury, and

---

[10] *Archb. Arch.*, nos. 1,107, 1,109,   [11] *Sta. Barb. Arch.*, ad annum.
[12] *Archb. Arch.*, nos. 1,191, 1,214, 1,247, 1,369, 2,537.

in view of the petition of the Rev. Fr. Antonio Peyri, missionary of said mission, addressed to me on the 17th instant, that it be permitted to embark 1,500 cattle hides, the majority of which are at the Rancho of Las Flores, on the English frigate *Thomas Nowlan* at the anchorage of San Juan Capistrano, I for this one time grant that said ship may pass on to receive the said hides at said road-stead.—Echeandia." [13]   This concession may have been intended to soothe Fr. Peyri, who had meanwhile grown so disgusted as to demand a passport to leave the territory.

In order to comply with a decree of the territorial legislature coached by Echeandia on October 7, 1827, regarding the extent of the mission property and land, Fr. Peyri drew up the following report:

"The missionary of Mission San Luis Rey, complying with what was ordered by the governor in the proclamation circulated under date of October 8, gives the following information:

"This Mission is situated in a cañada which runs from east to west, named Quechinga by the natives, at a distance of two leagues from the seashore and six leagues from the sierra. It has as neighbors to the south the port and the Mission of San Diego at a distance of about thirteen leagues and a half; to the north Mission San Juan Capistrano at a distance of about twelve leagues and a half. In the east, the Sierra Madre of California is situated at various distances from the seashore, two, three, four, five, six, and seven leagues, the intervening country consisting of cañadas and hills.

"As in the case of the valley in which the Mission is situated, there is no running water nor any spring by means of which a harvest could be secured; therefore, the order to found the Mission caused some difficulties in 1798. It was feared that for want of running water no security could be had of maintaining with the crops a community

---

[13] *Cal. Arch., Prov. St. Pap., Indexes*, xv, pp. 575-576.   •

of native gentiles, who might be attracted to the bosom of our Religion. However, confiding in Divine Providence, we established the Mission in a short time on a mesa situated near a marsh, the water of which by hauling earth we succeeded little by little in forcing up so that it could be reached. By means of two dams the water was then collected so that it sufficed for the assembled Indians and for irrigating a garden. This is the only water on which we can depend; for, although there is an arroyo which runs down from the Sierra Madre, it has abundant water only in the rainy season, from the month of October or November to May or June of the next year, when it is again lost in the sand, so that, the arroyo being then dry, we can not count on it for any seed time.

"To the east at a distance of three leagues the Mission has a locality named San Juan for the cattle; and in the same direction, at a distance of sixteen leagues, there is another district reserved for the sheep, which is famed for its warm springs. There pasture also the flocks of Mission San Diego.

"At a distance of seven leagues, toward the northeast, at the entry of the Sierra Madre, the Mission has a station called San Antonio de Pala, with a church, dwellings, and granaries and with a few fields where wheat, corn, beans, garbanzos, and other leguminous plants are grown. There are also a vineyard and an orchard of various fruits and of olives, for which there is sufficient irrigation, the water being from the stream which runs to the vicinity of this Mission.

"To the north, at a distance of one league and a half, the Mission has a place with a house and garden, and near the beginnings of the sierra a vineyard. This site, lying in a cañada, is called Santa Margarita. The land is cultivated and wheat, corn, beans, and barley are raised. The fields are irrigated by means of the water from the sierra, which, though not plentiful, assures some crops.

"In the same direction, to the north, at a distance of

three leagues, the Mission has the Rancho of San Pedro, known as Las Flores. The place has a house, granaries, and a chapel, which buildings form a square or large patio. Holy Mass is offerd up in the chapel.. In the patio, by means of water taken out of a pool near the sea, corn is raised. In the plain, wheat and barley are raised in season. About one league from the rancho are the pastures for the cattle. The locality is called Las Pulgas.

LEFT—EAR MARK.   RIGHT—CATTLE BRAND

"In the direction of the northeast, in the sierra, at a distance of twelve leagues, the Mission has the Rancho of San Jacinto with a house of adobes for the mayordomos. Here pasture the cattle.

"Between the said ranchos, sites, and stations, there are no mountains whatever; but the valleys and mesas are covered with thickets and underbrush, which are good only for firewood. In the clearings and foothills, cattle and sheep have their pastures.

"Two leagues east of the station of San Antonio de Pala, and nine leagues from the Mission, in the sierra, there is a forest of pines and firs (pinabete) and larches (alerce), where the timber was cut for the buildings of the Mission and of the other stations.

"The cattle brand in use and which has been employed from the beginning of the Mission by higher order, is the figure five, '5'; besides, both ears of the animals are cut. In the figure, too, the same iron will be used, but the marking of the ears will be changed. Only one ear will be cut as before, whilst the other will be pared off as in the accompanying illustration, in obedience to the order issued in the months of March, April, and May.

"The Mission Indians at present own 22,610 head of cattle, 27,412 sheep, 1,120 goats, 280 pigs, 1,501 horses of all kinds, and 235 mules. All these animals are distributed over the ranchos, sites, and stations described. The reason for having them so scattered is the lack of water and pastures, which are difficulties encountered all along this coast region. Necessity compels searching for both in the cañadas which the Sierra Madre offers for the planting of grain as well as for pastures for the live stock, so that we may be able to maintain in community the native converts, as also the gentiles who come to have themselves instructed, preparatory to becoming Christians; and also to supply the troops of the garrison of San Diego with corn, beans, wheat, manteca, soap, blankets, mantles, and shoes.—Mission San Luis Rey, December 22, 1827.—Fr. Antonio Peyri." [14]

---

[14] *Cal. Arch., St. Pap., Missions,* v, pp. 204-208.

CHAPTER IV.

SEVERAL travelers visited San Luis Rey at this period.
Their description of what they saw is interesting and
valuable enough to be reproduced; for the missionaries transmitted nothing of this kind to posterity, save what was
related in the preceding chapter in reply to the questions of
the *Interrogatorio.*

Auguste Duhaut-Cilly, in command of the French vessel
Le Heros, visited the Mission on June 12 and 13, 1827.
He noted his observations as follows: "At last we turned
inland, and after a jaunt of an hour and a half we found
before us, on an elevated piece of land, the superb structure
of Mission San Luis Rey, the glittering whiteness of which
was flashed back to us by the first rays of the day. At the
distance in which we were and in the still uncertain light
of dawn, this edifice, very beautifully modeled and supported
by its numerous pillars, had the aspect of a palace. The
green valley in which the building is situated extends farther
than the eye can see to the north, where the fine landscape
terminates on the summit of high mountains. Here and
there this smiling solitude was enlivened by fat cattle that
looked like white and red spots. Instinctively I stopped my
horse to contemplate alone for a few minutes the beauty of
this spectacle. My friends, the Californians, whom the
observation of nature detained very little, had meanwhile
descended the hill; but I rejoined them a quarter of an
hour later at the Mission.

"The padre was in church and we waited for him in the
corridor. Very soon he came out and received us with that

affability and urbanity that so highly adorned him. He immediately had chocolate served us and then gave orders that beds be made ready for us so that we might rest till dinner time. At noon we all enjoyed the agreeable and jovial conversation of that excellent personage.

"The whole Mission was astir making preparations for the double feast. In the first place, on the following day, June 13, the feast of St. Anthony was to be celebrated. This holiday was rather of a religious character; but, in order to attract more people for the celebration, the Father in charge of the Mission was wont to prepare a free-for-all and to announce the diversions, shows, and games that the Californians enjoyed. Indeed, few inhabitants of this district failed to heed such an agreeable invitation. The vast structure of San Luis had scarcely room for the multitude of men and women that assembled there.

"The second reason for celebrating was the fact that this day happened to be the patronal feast of the missionary himself, as also the twenty-ninth anniversary of the founding of the Mission. The Father related to me how he arrived at 4 o'clock in the afternoon, on June 13, 1798, on this then still uninhabited plain, accompanied by the comandante of San Diego, a troop of soldiers, and workmen. 'Our first care was,' he said, 'to erect some kind of a cabin after the fashion of the savages of this region, since it was to serve as a shelter until the Mission should be built; but on the following morning, before excavating for the foundation, we raised in the open air an altar. Here under the canopy of the sky was offered up for the first time in this valley the holy Sacrifice to the Eternal, which thereafter culminated in such great blessings.'

"The buildings were planned on a grand scale after the ideas of the Father. He himself and alone could have superintended the construction, but he secured the co-operation of a very skilful man who had previously aided in the construction work at Mission Santa Barbara. In fact, although the buildings at Santa Barbara are much more sumptuous, the hand of the same artist will be recognized here.

"The building is shaped in the form of a vast quadrangle measuring five hundred feet on every side. The principal façade is a long peristyle sustained by thirty-two square pillars which support rounded arches. The whole edifice is, indeed, composed of only one story, but its elevation, nicely proportioned, gives it a graceful and noble appearance. It is covered with a flat, tiled roof, around which reached, as much within as without the square, a terrace with an elegant balustrade which makes the structure appear even higher than it is. Within is seen a spacious patio or court-yard, neat and leveled, around which pillars and arches similar to those of the peristyle support a long cloister, by which access is afforded to all parts of the Mission.

"On the right hand of the outside front rises the church with its campanile girded by a double range of columns and railed platforms. The front elevation of this edifice is plain and without columns, but the interior is richly and tastefully ornamented. An earthern waterpipe with faucet supplies the sacristy with water. The rooms in the main front are occupied by the Father and the strangers who visit the Mission. Those fronting on the courtyard are destined for the boys and youths, who, as long as they are not married, live apart from the other Indians. There are also the store rooms for the food supplies, for the tools and implements, and for the looms on which the wool is woven for making the clothes of the Indians, and finally the in-firmary with a special chapel. The infirm could enter the church through the inside corridor without stepping from under cover; thus gracious and superabundant solicitude looked above all to their convenience. Attractive and elegant is the cupola that surmounts that little temple, and Fr. Antonio delighted in letting his good taste shine forth in ornamenting it.

"Besides the immense building thus described by me, are two other very much smaller buildings. One is destined for the mayordomos, and the other for the mission guard, which consists of a sergeant and eleven soldiers. This last structure has a flat roof.

"The vast gardens and orchards with numerous fruit trees, and well cultivated, supply abundant vegetables and fruits of all kinds. The sight of the wide and convenient stairway that leads to the orchard to the southeast put me in mind of the citrus fruit conservatory of Versailles, not because the material was as precious and the architecture as splendid, but because there was some similarity in the disposition, number, and dimension of the steps. At the foot of the stairway are seen two beautiful lavatories in stucco. One of them is a pond in which the Indians bathe every morning; the other serves for washing the linens every Saturday. A part of the waste water runs off into the garden in which numerous conduits preserve continual humidity and freshness. The second orchard, being on higher ground, can be irrigated only by artificial means. A vertical scoopwheel, moved at intervals by two men, lifts the water in time of need. These orchards grow most exquisite olives and produce the best grapewine in all California. I took a sample of this wine with me and I have it still. I kept it seven years. It has the taste of the Paxaret and the color of the Porto purgato.[1]

"Two hundred yards north of the Mission, begins the ranchería or village of the neophyte Indians. This consists of huts thatched with straw, mostly conical in shape, scattered or grouped on a large plot, without order or symmetry. Each of these huts is occupied by one family, and altogether the village is composed of more than two thousand souls. From the beginning, some houses were built of stone and arranged regularly, and this fashion is still observed in several missions. But soon such habitations proved unsuitable for the health of the Indians, who are accustomed to

---

[1] Portai meco de questo vino, ed ancora ne tengo. Da sette anni lo conservo, ed ha il gusto del Paxaret ed il colore del Porto purgato.— p. 45.

DESTROYED GARDEN BELOW THE MISSION. TRACES OF THE STAIRWAY AT THE EXTREME LEFT.

their flimsy hovels; wherefore, some missionaries discarded the houses of stone and let the neophytes put up huts after their own fashion.

"The appurtenances of the Mission do not consist merely of the different buildings that compose it. Within a circumference of ten leagues, Fr. Antonio has established four ranchos, each having an Indian village, a house for the mayordomo, and a pretty chapel. Every Sunday these mayordomos or overseers come to the Mission to give an account to the Father regarding the work of the week and the state of the rancho. Fr. Antonio understands how to arouse emulation among them, by which means he achieves great results for the general prosperity of the Mission. Chiefly on the lands near these ranchos are pastured the great herds and flocks of live stock of San Luis Rey. The number of cattle owned by the Mission amount perhaps to a little less than thirty thousand head, and the sheep number more than twenty thousand.

"At the close of the day, June 12, volleys fired from the loopholes at the barracks, and bonfires started on the plaza, announced the feast of the morrow. The celebration began with a High Mass, chant and music being rendered by the neophyte singers and musicians. There were as many as at Santa Barbara, but they were a great deal less skilful. However, it must be noted that the greater part of the instruments used by them were manufactured at the Mission and that they were of very inferior quality.

"After holy Mass came the bullfight, which lasted a part of the day. Such a game has little in it that is noteworthy. It took place in an inner courtyard. Every horseman proceeded to tease the bull, which, with the head low, rushed now for one and then for another; but such is the dexterity and agility of the men and of the horses that they are scarcely ever touched, although the horn of the bull appeared at every instant to graze along their body.

"From the outset I was stationed with some persons on the doorstep of the Father's room, from which position my eye could sweep over the entire arena; but as soon as I and my companions had taken this position, we were at the mercy of the Indian girls, who for fear of meeting with an accident had been staying about there. They numbered more than two hundred, ranging between the ages of twelve and seventeen years. They were uniformly dressed in red skirt of serge and white waist. Their black hâir was cut half length and flapped about their shoulders. They came in a crowd, asking for rings and pieces of coin. We gratified them by throwing among them at first a few *reales*, which caused them to cast themselves headlong over one another, making very laughable somersaults. Very soon they grew bolder and plied us with much familiarity. Finally they threw themselves upon us and tried to rummage our pockets. The outbursts of their laughter and the uproar of their screams drowned even the bellowing of the bull. It reminded me of the critical situation which I once was in on the island of Java. Being there without weapons of defense, I was assaulted by a troop of monkeys. I grant and acknowledge that those malicious Indian girls of San Luis Rey did not bite; but they scratched and jostled and firmly resolved not to leave in our pockets more money than the monkeys possessed. Now we became aware that it was time to beat a retreat, and we intended to do so in good shape. For that reason we made use of a ruse. Grasping as much as we had left of our small change, we hurled it at as great a distance as we could. No sooner was that done than the entire set darted off to gather the spoils, and we took advantage of that brief truce and decamped. We ascended to the rooms of the Father, and, barricading the door, remained in safety.

"Out here they are not accustomed, as in Spain, to kill the bull. After the Indians had teased, worn out and tormented the beast abundantly for half an hour, they threw open a gate that allowed access to the prairie. No sooner did the animal catch sight of the open gate than he struck for it in a headlong rush, and when out in the open country dashed off at high speed. But lo and behold! as swift as arrows sent from a bow, all the horsemen set out to pursue the bull. The swiftest rider, having overtaken the beast, seized its tail, at the same time applying the spurs to his horse, while the bull toppled over and rolled in the dust. It was intended to play this mean trick on the animal, and it was carried out elegantly. With that the Indian let the bull go to his accustomed pasture, a conquered beast. That is what they call *colear el toro*—to tail the bull.

"Toward evening the horsemen changed their horses for others, and on the esplanade of the Mission arranged a game which they call *la carrera del gallo*—cock chase. It is less perilous and more amusing than the bullfight. A rooster is buried up to his neck. Two hundred paces away stand ready the horsemen that are to take part in the game. With one hand on the saddlebow, they dart forth swiftly as though hurled from a catapult, stooping low, so that in passing they may be able to snatch up the fowl by the neck. At their rate of speed it often happens that the same rider, before securing the coveted object, must run again and again many times. Nor is that the end of the game. If one has picked up the bird, all the other riders rush forward to take it from him. He leads them; they overtake him and a melee of horses and riders follows. They get sprinkled with feathers and blood; the rooster is torn into pieces; and the horsemen, tumbling over one another, become the butt of the laughter of their companions as well as of the fair spectators of the game.

"The races were closed with the horseback game of the *Quattro Canti*—Four Corners. The participants were armed with a good willow switch, with which they struck unmercifully whenever they came near one another. That the game be played well, it was necessary that the switch be used until it was worn to a stub, which was never done till some good hard lash had been dealt on the head or face. The California girls took such great delight in these various games that the noble ladies of the thirteenth and fourteenth centuries might not have experienced as great a pleasure at the splendid tournament in which their cavaliers broke lances in their honor.

"While the *gente de razon* (all non-Indians were so called) amused themselves in this manner, the Indians on their side took to their favorite games. The one that seemed to amuse them most consisted in this: a ring three inches in diameter, made of willows, was sent whirling through the air. During its flight, two slender sticks four feet long were thrown toward it from the opposite direction. The object was to have the sticks run through the ring. If one of the two sticks or if both ran through the ring, or if the ring came to rest on both or on only one stick, the two players scored a number of points. When the two had had their inning, two opponents took their turn, and thus they alternated till the game was finished.

"Other Indians, after the manner of the Bretons (Bassi Brettoni), ranged themselves in two grand opposing parties. Every one was armed with a curved stick and endeavored to drive a wooden ball to a goal, while those of the opposite party tried to send it back to the other goal. It appeared that this game pleased equally men and women.

"It happened also that the married women challenged the single young women to a game. The girls lost the game, which brought tears to their eyes. Weeping they came to Fr. Antonio (Peyri) and complained that the women had abused their strength in that when the girls were on the point of sending the ball their arm was unjustly held back. With a seriousness befitting the judgment of Solomon, Fr. Antonio investigated the case closely. While the information was given and he was listening to the one and to the other side, the good missionary had his eyes half-closed and sat gravely in the corridor. With the forefinger of his right hand resting on his eyebrow and the middle finger, thumb, and hand passing under his nose, forming a sort of square, he appeared to meditate profoundly. Finally, after the Indians had stated their case, he raised his head somewhat and decided the momentous quarrel; but within his cowl he smiled to himself. Later he said to me softly: 'Poor girls! Something must be done for them. In this and similar ways I secured the confidence and respect of these Indians.'

"In fact, his Mission was, among all the missions of California, the one in which those poor Indians received the best treatment.[2] Not only were they well fed and well clad, but on their feast days they were given some money. Every Saturday soap was distributed to the women. On such an occasion all the women passed in review before the missionary Father, and while two men fished from two enormous baskets for each woman the piece of soap to be given to her, Fr. Antonio addressed his words to her. He knew them all. One he kindly commended, another he reproved gently. One he offered a good-natured courtesy, another a paternal admonition. All went away satisfied and charmed.

"After nightfall I went with Fr. Antonio to see the Indian dance. It was a sight as captivating as it was strange. The light of the burning torches made the firmament appear rather dark. Twelve men, with no other clothing on their body than a breechcloth (*taparabo*) and a shirt, the head adorned with a high tuft of feathers, danced in admirable harmony. The pantomime continually represented some scene. They executed it chiefly by beating the earth in time with the music and by making with eyes and arms the gestures indicative of love, hatred, or terror. They held their heads straight, the body inclined forward, and their knees a little bent. The perspiration that covered their whole person was reflected as from a brown mirror by the light of the torches. When the perspiration incommoded them, they scraped it off with a wooden ferule which they held in their hand.

"The orchestra, arranged theater-like in a half-circle, was

---

[2] As the French navigator had not seen nearly all the other establishments, his declaration is rather bold. At all the missions the neophytes were similarly treated like children. Life at all the missions was similar to that described by Cilly for San Luis Rey. For that reason we adopted his charming description, since the Fathers neglected to go into such detail. San Luis Rey was typical of them all.

made up of women, boys, and old men. Back of them stood one or two rows of spectators, who enjoyed the exhibition. The harmony of the songs, which regulated the time measure, were of a mournful and weird strain. It appeared to move the nerves more than the soul, something like the variable sounds of the Aeolian harp in time of a tempest. From time to time the actors rested and the chanting ceased. During such an interval, all present would simultaneously and very noisily expectorate up into the air. This, I was assured, was done to chase away the evil spirits; for, although they are all Christians, they still observe many old superstitious customs, and the Fathers, out of prudence, pretend not to notice them.

"After the ceremonies and the procession of the consecration on the following morning, the games began again and continued in the same way as on the previous day; but this time a gloom fell on the bull chase in consequence of an accident. One of the Indian girls, while disporting herself with others on the porch of the Mission, fell over the balustrade to the pavement of the courtyard and fractured her skull.

"Having completed my business with Fr. Antonio, I, with only two or three persons, returned to San Diego, where I arrived on the evening of June 15." [3]

Another traveler, a trapper, indeed, James Ohio Pattie, claimed to have visited San Luis Rey. After his return to Ohio, he or some one else wrote from memory what he had experienced in California. "February 28, 1829," he writes, "I set forth to the next mission at which I had already been. It was called San Luis (Rey). I reached it in the evening. I found an old priest, who seemed glad to see me. I gave him the General's (Echeandia's) letter. After he had read it, he said, with regard to that part of it which spoke of payment, that I had better take certificates from the priests of each mission, as I advanced up the coast, stating that I

---

[3] Duhaut-Cilly, vol. ii, pp. 40-55.

had vaccinated their inhabitants; and that when I arrived at the upper mission, where one of the dignitaries of the Church resided, I should receive my recompense for the whole. Seeing nothing at all singular in this advice, I concluded to adopt it. In the morning I entered on the performance of my duty. My subjects were Indians, the Mission being entirely composed of them, with the exception of the priests, who are the rulers. The number of natives in this Mission was 3,904.[4] I took the old priest's certificate, as had been recommended by him, when I had completed my task. This is said to be the largest, most flourishing, and every way the most important Mission on the coast. For its consumption fifty beeves are killed weekly. The hides and tallow are sold to ships for goods, and other articles for use of the Indians, who are better dressed in general than the Spaniards (Mexicans). All the income of the Mission is placed in the hands of the priests, who give out clothing and food according as it is required. They are also the guardians of the female part of the Mission, shutting up under lock and key, one hour after supper, all those whose husbands are absent, and all young women and girls above nine years of age. During the day they are entrusted to the care of the matrons. Notwithstanding this, all the precautions taken by the vigilant Fathers of the Church are found insufficient. I saw women in irons for misconduct, and men in the stocks. The former are expected to remain a widow six months after the death of a husband, after which period they may marry again. The priests appoint officers to superintend the natives, while they are at work, from among themselves. They are called alcaldes, and are very rigid in exacting the performance of the allotted tasks, applying the rod to those who fall short of the portion of labor assigned them. They are taught in different trades; some of them being blacksmiths, others carpenters and shoemakers. Those trained to the knowledge of

---

4 Pattie is wrong. The Indians numbered 2,860, about 500 of whom lived at Pala.

music, both vocal and instrumental, are intended for the service of the church. The women and girls sew, knit, and spin wool upon a large wheel, which is woven into blankets by the men. The alcaldes, after finishing the business of the day, give an account of it to the priest, and then kiss his hand, before they withdraw to their wigwams to pass the night. This Mission is composed of parts of five different tribes, who speak different languages."

Pattie's account must not be taken seriously in every particular. Much smacks of *paisano* talk. There is more and worse. Pattie recites what he could not have seen, but must have heard from the Mission enemies. It is false, of course; but we reproduce it here all the same, in order to show the wickedness of the *paisano* chiefs, who thus endeavored to justify their robbery of the Mission property: "The greater part of these Indians," Pattie continues, "were brought from their native mountains against their own inclinations, and by compulsion; and then baptized, which act was as little voluntary on their part as the former had been. After these preliminaries, they had been put to work as converted Indians." [5]

Alfred Robinson, who visited the Mission in the same year, 1829, has this to say on the establishment: "It was yet early in the afternoon when we rode up to the establishment, at the entrance of which many Indians had congregated to behold us, and as we dismounted some stood ready to take off our spurs, whilst others unsaddled the horses. The Rev. Father was at prayers, and some time elapsed ere he came, giving us a most cordial reception. Chocolate and refreshments were at once ordered for us, and rooms where we might arrange our dress, which had become somewhat soiled by the dust.

"This Mission was founded in the year 1798 by its pres-

---

[5] Pattie, *Personal Narrative*, pp. 275-277.—There is outside his book no evidence that Pattie ever visited Mission San Luis Rey, or that he vaccinated there. See the narrative *Mission San Diego* for Smythe's opinion of Pattie and his assertions.

ent minister, Father Antonio Peyri, who had for many years been a reformer and director among the Indians. At this time (1829) its population was about three thousand Indians, who are all employed in various occupations. Some were engaged in agriculture, while others attended to the management of over sixty thousand [6] head of cattle. Many were carpenters, masons, coopers, saddlers, shoemakers, weavers, etc., while the females were employed in spinning and preparing wool for the looms, which produced a sufficiency of blankets for the yearly consumption. Thus every one had his particular vocation, and each department its official superintendent or alcalde; these were subject to the supervision of one or more Spanish mayordomos, who were appointed by the missionary Father, and consequently under his immediate direction.

"The building occupies a large square, of at least eighty or ninety yards each side, forming an extensive area, in the center of which a fountain constantly supplies the establishment with pure water.

"The front is protected by a long corridor, supported by thirty-two arches, ornamented with latticed railings, which, together with the fine appearance of the church on the right, presents an attractive view to the traveler. The interior is divided into apartments for the missionary and mayordomos, storerooms, workshops, hospitals, rooms for unmarried males and females, while near at hand is a range of buildings tenanted by the families of the superintendents. There is also a guardhouse, where were stationed some ten or a dozen soldiers, and in the rear spacious granaries stored with an abundance of wheat, corn, beans, peas, etc.; also large enclosures for wagons, carts, and the implements of agriculture. In the interior of the square might be seen the various

---

[6] A gross exaggeration. The exact number was 25,500. Robinson did not, like Duhaut-Cilly, take the trouble to secure the correct figures from Fr. Peyri, but here and in some other statements merely repeated the absurd stories of the mission enemies. Robinson is more readable than exact.

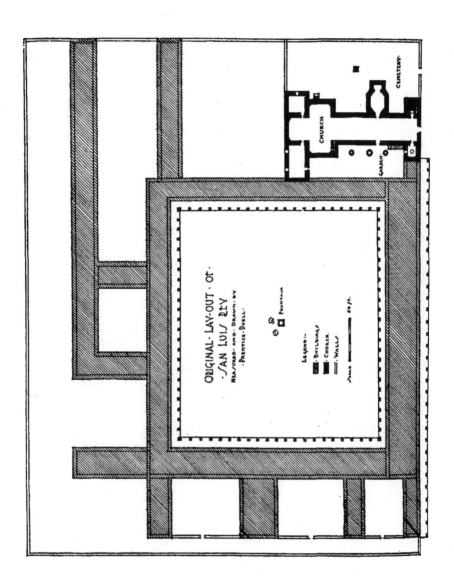

ORIGINAL · LAY-OUT · OF ·
· SAN LUIS REY
MEASURED · AND · DRAWN · BY
· PRENTICE · DUELL ·

LEGEND :-
▨ · BUILDINGS
■ · CHURCH
▪▪▪ · WALLS

⊕ ⊡ FOUNTAIN

SCALE ━━━━━ 50 FT.

CHURCH

CEMETERY

GARDEN

trades at work, presenting a scene not dissimilar to some of the working departments of our state prisons.[7] Adjoining are two large gardens, which supply the table with fruit and vegetables, and two or three large 'ranchos' or farms are situated from five to eight leagues distant, where the Indians are employed in cultivation and domesticating cattle.

"The church is a large stone[8] edifice, whose exterior is not without some considerable ornament and tasteful finish; but the interior is richer, and the walls are adorned with a variety of pictures of saints and Scripture subjects, glaringly colored, and attractive to the eye. Around the altar are many images of the saints, and the tall and massive candelabras, lighted during Mass, throw an imposing light upon the whole.

"Mass is offered daily, and the greater portion of the Indians attend; but it is not unusual to see numbers of them driven along by alcaldes, and under the whip's lash forced to the very doors of the sanctuary."[9]

---

[7] Why that odious word, when ''Industrial Schools,'' ''Manual Training Schools,'' or even ''Factories'' would have expressed the situation truthfully? Robinson borrowed from the mission despoilers. He wrote almost twenty years after his visit, and then from memory, which he freshened up to suit the taste of a period immediately following that of mission spoliation, when the mission despoilers and their friends were still powerful and were held in some esteem, and whom, for one that looked which way the wind of profit was blowing, it was not business policy to antagonize by plain speech on the subject. The missionaries, on the other hand, were dead.

[8] Robinson's memory again failed him. The church edifice is not of stone but of adobe. He was thinking of Santa Barbara.

[9] Robinson must throw in this piece of anti-mission gossip to please the mission despoilers, who were hard pressed for justification of their misdeeds. In a multitude of nearly three thousand white people, let alone half-savage Indians, numbers of young fellows will be found with whom something like law and order can not be maintained without some show of authority. The chief men or alcaldes at the missions exercised it after their own fashion. Similarly, wild youths at schools and colleges have to be lined up. The orderly portion of any community needs no driving. Robinson could have said as much and his book would have gained in value for sane views, which are frequently lacking, notably when he failed to strike a bargain as planned.

"The men," Robinson correctly reports, "are placed generally upon the left, and the females occupy the right of the church, so that a passageway or aisle is formed between them from the principal entrance to the altar, where zealous officials are stationed to enforce silence and attention. At evening again 'El Rosario' is prayed, and the second time all assemble to participate in supplication to the Virgin.

"The condition of these Indians is miserable indeed; and it is not to be wondered at that many attempt to escape from the severity of the religious discipline at the Mission. They are pursued, and generally taken, when they are flogged, and an iron clog is fastened to their legs, serving as additional punishment and warning to others." [10]

It would seem that Robinson had failed to close as good a bargain as he desired at purchasing hides and tallow from Fr. Peyri, who naturally looked to the interests of his Indian community. There is absolutely no evidence that the neophytes under Fr. Antonio were in any way ill-treated. The description given by Duhaut-Cilly in the early part of this chapter tells an altogether different story. Running away or playing truant is a feature encountered in public schools and colleges all over the United States. Nor did the wild ones of this populous community run away because of the severity of the punishment, which was not inflicted save for grave misdemeanors. Their reason for "escaping" was the gratification of their animal propensities. Far worse punishments were meted out at that period, and even much later, among white people who pretended to stand at the head of civilization. Richard Dana [11] describes the brutal flogging of a sailor on board the *Pilgrim*, in 1835, and that for a petty offense against military discipline. Nothing like it was ever practiced in the missions. Robinson must have known of the case. In the English navy to this day, so far as we know, the "Cat o' Nine Tails" is in use. In the English

---

[10] *Life in California*, pp. 36-39.
[11] Richard Dana, *Two Years before the Mast*, pp. 112-118, 122, 123.

army flogging was not abolished till 1881.[12] In the United States Navy, flogging of sailors was in vogue till 1850, while soldiers in the United States Army were flogged as late as 1861, when it was prohibited.[13] Hence criticism of the practice of whipping unruly Indians at the missions comes with bad grace from the mission enemies. The question was sufficiently explained in the second volume of our General History; wherefore it is unnecessary to discuss it here. Let it suffice to note briefly what the American soldiers observed when they reached the San Luis Rey district, 1846-1847, hence after the mission period. Captain A. R. Johnson, who was killed in the skirmish at San Pasqual on December 6, 1846, wrote in his diary, under date of December 2, as follows: "We found Warner's (Ranch) * * * with a hot spring and a cold one on his place. * * * The labor is performed by California Indians, who are stimulated to work by three dollars per month and repeated *floggings.*"[14]

Similarly, Major W. H. Emory, of the same company, on reaching Mission San Luis Rey, says in his report, under date of January 2, 1847: "Most of these missions passed by fraud into the hands of private individuals, and with them the Indians were transferred as serfs of the land. * * * They do the only labor performed in the country. Nothing can exceed their present degraded condition. For negligence or refusal to work, *the lash is freely applied,* and in many instances life has been taken by the Californians without being held accountable by the laws of the land."[15]

That the condition of the San Luis Rey Indians under the management of the friars was not "miserable," as Robinson declares, and that they needed no commisseration at all, but that they were to be congratulated, may be learned from the non-Catholic Alexander Forbes, who as contemporary thought it fair to record as follows: "There are few examples to be

---

12 *The Encyclopedia Americana,* vol. vii, "Flogging."
13 *Messages and Papers of the Presidents,* vol. x, p. 362.
14 *Out West,* June, 1903, p. 746.
15 Emory, pp. 116-117.

found where men enjoying such unlimited confidence and power have not abused them. And yet I have never heard that the missionaries of California have not acted with the most perfect fidelity, or that they ever betrayed their trust, or exercised inhumanity, and the testimony of all travelers who have visited this country is uniformly to the same effect. The best and unequivocal proof of the good conduct of these Fathers is to be found in the unbounded affection and devotion invariably shown towards them by their Indian subjects. They venerate them not merely as friends and fathers, but with a degree of devotedness approaching adoration." [16]

---

[16] Alexander Forbes, *California*, pp. 227, 230.

CHAPTER V.

Governor Echeandia's Animosity.—Turbulent Indians.—Fr. Peyri Discouraged.—Demands Passport.—Echeandia's Reply.—Priests Not Mere Superintendents.—Insufferable Conditions.—Fr. Presidente Duran to Fr. Peyri.—The Founder of San Luis Rey Retires to Mexico.—Neophytes Heartbroken.—Statistics.—Calumnies.—Forbes on Fr. Peyri.—Fr. Peyri to Dr. Anderson.—Indian Students.

B ESIDES being poorly grounded in religious matters, Governor Echeandia belonged to that so-called liberal school of politics which rendered Mexico the most unhappy nation in the world. He came to California as an enemy of the religious who had founded the missions and had made them prosperous. For this reason, and in order to gratify "some prominent Californians who had already had their eyes on the mission lands," as Bancroft puts it, Echeandia, despite the warnings of the Fathers to proceed slowly in this matter, on July 25, 1826, issued a circular emancipating from mission tutelage all the Indians who should be qualified to become Mexican citizens in the military districts of San Diego, Santa Barbara, and Monterey. In 1828 these regulations were extended so as to include the district of San Francisco south of the bay.

This plan, engendered by animosity and greed, was not at all intended to benefit the convert Indians, who were living perfectly happy under the fatherly care of the missionaries. Hence it was a failure from the very beginning, inasmuch as the viciously inclined Indians abused the provisions of the unwise decree and became disorderly, whilst the others were made restive and apprehensive. Those who availed themselves of the license which the Governor's circular insured, fell into excesses and, like the Prodigal Son, gambled and wasted what property they received, so that they found it necessary to beg and steal, as Captain Beechy affirms.[1] Only

---

[1] For references see *Missions and Missionaries*, vol. iii, pp. 239, 241.

one month after Echeandia had published his circular, an Indian of Mission San Luis Rey, in a fit of drunkenness, at Los Angeles manifested the spirit of independence which was springing up among the formerly so gentle and peaceful neophytes. He publicly abused the magistrate, the governor, and the nation. To Alcalde Vicente Sanchez the Indian, whose name was Buenaventura, said: "You alcalde are a son of a prostitute, and the general (Echeandia) is an Englishman. There is no nation, nor anything. In the coming year you all will be killed." [2] In April of the next year many of the convert Indians of San Luis Rey and of San Juan Capistrano refused to work in the fields, so that the guards had to be increased. Echeandia's ideas were bearing bitter fruit early. They created such a change in the neophytes that to a large extent they were never after as contented and submissive as they had been before, so that this Mission, in common with all the others, suffered very seriously, both spiritually and temporally. For want of laborers decay necessarily followed. Nevertheless, Echeandia reported to the Mexican Government that the missionaries monopolized all the land, labor, and products of the country! The motive for this charge is transparent enough—there were those who coveted the land which had been made productive by the missionaries and their willing neophytes under the impression that by all rights, human and divine, the convert Indian owners should enjoy the products of their labor.

As a consequence the buildings could not be kept in repair. Since the Indians had been encouraged to refuse their assistance, the fields could not be cultivated, while the live stock, for want of care, decreased. Still, the Indians, who refused to listen to the enemies of the missionaries and remained faithful, had to labor the more in order to support the hostile government of California! What added to the fire of discontent enkindled in the hearts of the Indians

---

[2] *Cal. Arch., Dep. St. Pap., Benicia*, vol. lviii, p. 464, as per Hittell, vol. i, p. 739.

were incessant military exactions, but not disaffection for the Franciscans. The neophytes observed that these unselfish men suffered even more on account of their loyalty to the rights of their wards. Echeandia and his covetous advisers thought that by belittling the Fathers they could alienate the affections which the Indians had for them and in this way secure possession of the Indian property; the seed of dissatisfaction thus planted took root, indeed, but the crop it produced was not at all to the liking of the mission despoilers.

Fr. Antonio Peyri became so disgusted that he, though seventy years of age and infirm, resolved to leave the Mission which he had founded and reared with so much pain; to bid adieu to the nearly three thousand Indian converts, who all, save a few malcontents imbued with the Echeandia spirit, held him in esteem; and to retire from the country where he had spent the best years of his life. In 1826 he had enthusiastically taken the oath of allegiance to the Mexican Constitution, although nearly all of his brethren more than suspected the animus of its authors and steadfastly declined to commit themselves to it. He had even adopted the new Mexican phrase, "Dios y Libertad," when closing his letters, in place of the time-honored "God keep you many years in His grace." So Fr. Peyri had exhibited himself as a *ciudadano* or true citizen of the so-called republic of Mexico; but in the course of time his eyes were opened to the real aims of those who, like Echeandia, held higher positions. The Mexican decree of March 20, 1829, expelling all men of Spanish birth and under sixty years of age from the Mexican domination and disqualifying others, induced Fr. Peyri to abandon the territory and to return to Spain. He therefore asked the governor for a passport, as the following note testifies:

Comandante General of both Californias, Citizen José Maria de Echeandia. Mission San Luis Rey, August 29, 1829.—According to the Decree of the Supreme Government of the Mexican Nation, dated March 20, 1829, I am comprehended in the expulsion of the Spaniards. From the fair justice of Your Honor I ought to expect that you will deign to remit to me my passport. I earnestly supplicate you that

you will for no reason whatever delay me, especially since I am one
of the oldest missionaries and as yet find myself in condition to endure
the voyage and journey with some little strength, which owing to my
advanced age I might be able to do at another time only with difficulty. God and Liberty.—Fr. Antonio Peyri.[3]

It would have caused a sensation to see the highly re-
spected Father depart at that time. Besides, there would
have been no one to direct the Indians in furnishing supplies
for the military. Plainly, Fr. Peyri must be detained. So
in reply Echeandia wrote as follows:

To the Rev. Fr. Antonio Peyri.—Having read the note of Your
Reverence of August 29, last, in which, because you consider yourself
included in the law of March 20, of the current year, regarding the
expulsion of the Spaniards, you ask me to transmit your passport
without delay, before you become incapacitated on account of your
advanced age to journey by sea or land, I have to reply that, inasmuch
as I have petitioned the Supreme Government of the Federation that
it perpetually exempt Your Reverence from being expelled from the
republic, and in virtue of later orders of said government, I can not
extend to Your Reverence the passport which you asked for in your
said note to which I am replying.—José M. de Echeandia.[4]

That Fr. Peyri was not satisfied shows how deep must
have been his disappointment with the republic to which he
had so cheerfully sworn allegiance. He accordingly wrote
another letter, saying:

To the official letter of Your Honor of the 22d instant, in which you
refuse the passport I asked for in my note of August 29, last, by
saying, etc. (he reproduces the governor's plea), I must explain to
Your Honor that this favor of the two governments must be strictly
understood as always supposing the will of the other party, for it can
not be believed that the liberal system of the Mexican Federation
would curtail to any individual the liberty which the law concedes. I
shall appreciate such a favor, for my will is to retire in order to end
my days in my mother province as an ordinary religious or private
person, and in order to extricate myself from these labyrinths of a
sort of public person. Indeed, I confess that I am no more good for
a missionary and less for managing any mission after having been
in continuous charge for more than thirty-three years and having
passed the sixty-ninth year of my age, which I would have the same

3 *Archb. Arch.*, no. 2,068.   4 *Cal. Arch., Dep. Rec.*, vol. vii, p. 783.

government bear in mind. Under these considerations I repeat my request for the passport while I am still fit and ready to travel by land or sea. Trusting, therefore, in the fairmindedness of Your Honor and in your liberal spirit, I hope you will attend to my reasons and will not deny me the consolation which is so much due to me.—San Luis Rey, September 25, 1829. Fr. Antonio Peyri.[5]

The answer of the governor was as follows:

In my letter of the 22d of the present month, I refused the passport which Your Reverence asked of me in yours of August 29, last, with respect to which you there gave as cause only the general tenor of the Law of March 20 of this year (having thousand exceptions which are public, it would exempt also your person), supposing the manifestation which I made to you in my said note. Now, with regard to your later note of the 25th instant, in which you acknowledge the receipt of mine referred to in the beginning, you reiterate the petition for your passport, basing it on the statement that it is your will and that it is not believable that the liberal system of the Mexican Federation would curtail for any individual the liberty which the law grants, I reply that Your Reverence is absolutely free to petition for your passport; but neither in the Laws of Spain nor in those of Mexico, nor in those of any organized country no matter how liberal, will you find a law in your favor that says you must be given at once the release from the charge of your responsibility before God and man, unless there be some one to be substituted in an orderly or at least reasonable way. Consequently, I conclude by telling Your Reverence that as soon as there is a missionary to receive your mission, I shall willingly extend to you the passport you desire. Dios y Libertad. September 26, 1829. José M. Echeandia.[6]

Fr. Peyri might have retorted that neither in Spain nor in Mexico, nor in any reasonable country, was there a law authorizing the governor to transform priests of the altar into mere superintendents of the farm or stockyard for the benefit of indolent, arrogant soldiers and their families, or that bound the priest to continue in such a position for the sake of such unappreciative soldiers and insolent officials. Nor would Fr. Peyri and all the Franciscans able to travel have remained in California, where subsequently they were treated like menials or tenants at the beck of the adminis-

---

[5] *Archb. Arch.*, no. 2,070.
[6] *Cal. Arch., Dep. Rec.,* vol. vii, pp. 785-786.

trators, had not sympathy for the helpless neophytes detained them. All this reference to responsibility before God and man, Echeandia and his mentors should have made their own rule of conduct; then they would not have dared to deprive the Indians of their property and the missionaries of well-merited respect.

In the end, Fr. Peyri left, although he did not run away from his post, as writers generally declare. We shall repeat the circumstances of his departure as stated in accordance with the manuscript documents reproduced in our General History.

The spirit of insubordination aroused among the neophytes, and the incessant slanders heaped upon the missionaries by Echeandia and the irreligious cabal of young Californians, had rendered conditions at the missionary establishments well-nigh insufferable. Since the Picos, Bandinis, Vallejos, and other confederates blamed the Fathers for all the ills of the country, in revenge for not being free to loot the missions, Fr. Narciso Duran, the Superior of the Missions, resolved to take steps which would withdraw him and his brethren from ceaseless insults, and remove the excuse for hostility to the missions. Accordingly, he wrote to Fr. Peyri, then vice-presidente:

On account of the misfortunes which have occurred, in order to prevent the ruin and desolation which the missions are going to suffer, and because of the horrible oppression exercised upon the missionaries, I have been thinking of personally going to the College at the Capital of Mexico, or of commissioning another religious, who should represent what might procure for us our passports and bring hither secular priests to take over the missions. As I myself can not go, I have thought of Your Reverence. You might surrender your Mission to a Father of San Diego, or to one of the Zacatecan Fathers, without giving any reason save that you have to make a journey, and then you might proceed by way of Lower California.

If on account of some unforeseen circumstances it may seem better to embark with Don Manuel Victoria, and there be no time to await my instructions, you may go in virtue of this letter. You will represent to the College and to the Supreme Government our intolerable oppression, the peril from our cruel enemies, and our inability to continue in the service of the missions owing to our old age, physical maladies, and exhaustion. You will urge that secular priests be sent hither to take the missions from us, and that we be given our passports in order to retire to the College, if the Government should permit, or to Europe. In this case the Government should command that the expenses of our voyage to Europe be paid from the funds of the missions, because these have flourished by means of our toils and of our stipends which we expended on them.

Although, by reason of pressing circumstances and difficulties, this letter leaves here not provided with the required formalities, it is my intention that it should have the same force as though it had been sent supplied with all the customary formalities, and that Your Reverence proceed to execute the instructions contained in this letter with all the necessary authority and permission which are all granted to you in virtue of this letter. Moreover, I declare to you that your services in these missions for the period of thirty-five years are praiseworthy to an heroic degree, and entitle you to all the honors of the Order. May Your Reverence fare well, and let me know your determination. Mission San José, December 17, 1831.[7]

As Fr. Duran's letter was penned at Mission San José, it had to travel overland about six hundred miles to San Luis Rey. When it reached Fr. Peyri, he had barely enough time to make the most necessary preparations before embarking on the American ship that bore the noble and brave ex-Governor Manuel Victoria away to Mexico. The governor had become a victim of the conspiracy headed by Pio Pico, because he would not permit the unscrupulous *paisano* chiefs to seize the property of the missions. Of course, they broached other reasons to cover up their real plans; but, as the sequel demonstrates right here in San Luis Rey, the motive stated was the true one. As directed, without consulting any one, Fr. Peyri gave the Zacatecan, Fr. Antonio Ánzar, who had arrived at the Mission as assistant a few months before from Mexico, the necessary information on the affairs of the Mission, and then secretly hastened aboard the *Pocahontas,* which sailed away from the harbor of San Diego on January 17, 1832. As there was a substitute in the person of Fr. Ánzar, no secrecy was needed, so far as the territorial officials were concerned, although Fr.

---

[7] *Missions and Missionaries*, vol. iii, pp. 409-411.

Peyri left without a permit; but there was need of secrecy with regard to the neophytes, who doubtless would have prevented his departure. A tradition relates that when his beloved convert Indians discovered the absence of their father and guide and began to suspect the truth, five hundred on horseback hurried to San Diego in order to intercept and bring him back; but they arrived only in time to receive his blessing, which he imparted to them from the rear of the ship as it sailed out of the harbor. "I saw them both (Governor Victoria and Fr. Peyri)," Robinson writes, "only a few days previous to their departure, when the tears of regret coursed down the cheek of the aged old friar, as he recalled to mind the once happy state of California. His great penetration of mind led him to foresee the result of the new theory of liberty and equality among a people where anarchy and confusion so generally prevailed, and who, at the time, were totally unprepared for, and incapable of self-government. He chose rather a retirement in poverty than to witness the destruction and ravage that from this time ensued." [8]

According to the official report signed by Fr. Vicente Oliva on December 31, 1831, Mission San Luis Rey was at the time in a most flourishing condition, and had reached the largest number of neophytes actually living at the Mission. Down to that date, from the founding in 1798, as many as 5,298 Baptisms had been administered, mostly by Fr. Peyri himself. Only a few of these were other than Indians. Moreover, 1,391 couples had been joined in Christian marriage, 2,586 Indians had received Christian burial, while 1,493 male and 1,326 female, in all 2,819, Indians lived under the direct care of the missionary. San Luis Rey thus surpassed any other missionary establishment by nearly a thousand souls. The herds and flocks were similarly numerous, there being 26,000 head of cattle, 25,500 sheep, 1,200 goats, 300 pigs, 2,150 horses, and 250 mules. For agriculture the sea-

[8] *Life in California*, p. 131.

son had not been favorable. Nevertheless, from the 552 fanégas of various grain sown or planted, 5,217 fanégas were harvested.

According to Bancroft,[9] the Mexican Government permitted Fr. Peyri to retire with full payment of his past stipend. At the rate of $400 a year, this sum for thirty-five years would amount to $14,000; but Bancroft says that the Father took with him only $3,000 from the Mission funds. This amount he thought necessary to pay the expenses for himself and the two Indian youths, Pablo and Agapito, whom he wished to place at the famous school of the Propaganda in Rome. After that he would scarcely have enough to take him to Spain.

It seems scarcely possible that the *paisano* chiefs and their henchmen, who, through the law that disqualified Spanish-born citizens from holding office, had forced themselves to the front by their bluster and unscrupulousness, should have endeavored to besmirch the good name of the noble priest and missionary. Here are some specimens of which the mission enemies proved themselves capable. Pio Pico, himself of malodorous fame, claimed he had it from Juan Mariner, a Catalonian, whom Fr. Peyri was said to have trusted, that the San Luis Rey missionary took along thirty-two barrels of olives, each of which barrels contained money. Mariano Vallejo, known for his outrageous lies, maintained that Fr. Peyri took along fourteen barrels of flour and that the custom officers at San Blas refused to land the suspicious cargo. Leandro Serrano, who is said to have at one time been mayordomo at Mission San Luis Rey, talked of ten kegs of silver dollars which were passed off for brandy. The enemies of Governor Victoria accused Fr. Peyri of having also contributed large sums of money to support the cause of the unfortunate governor. With such gossip the mission despoilers published to the world only their own

9 *California*, vol. iii, pp. 210, 621-622; *Missions and Missionaries*, vol. iii, pp. 409-415.

methods. Bancroft, who was not at all averse to retailing things disparaging to the Franciscans, nevertheless found the odor of these stories far too strong and therefore closes the enumeration with the remark, "I suppose all this to be unfounded." To the Picos, Vallejos, and others of their ilk in the early days the words of a well-known English writer, Father Frederick Faber, apply with especial force: "A man is always capable himself of a sin which he thinks another is capable of, or which he himself is capable of imputing to another." [10]

Alexander Forbes, an English Protestant, then residing at Tepic, whose strong prejudice against the Catholic Church had not robbed him of common sense, wrote of Fr. Peyri: "I had the pleasure of seeing Father Peyri on his way to Mexico. After a constant residence of thirty-four years at San Luis Rey, he left it stocked with nearly sixty thousand head of domesticated animals of all sorts, and yielding an annual produce of about thirteen thousand bushels of grain, while the population amounted to nearly three thousand Indians! He left also a complete set of buildings, including a church with inclosures, etc. Yet after these thirty-four years of incessant labor, in which he expended the most valuable part of his life, the worthy Peyri left the Mission with only what he judged to be sufficient to enable him to join his convent in the City of Mexico, where he threw himself upon the charity of his Order." [11]

Of Fr. Peyri's movements there are extant some data that will interest his admirers. A German merchant and shipowner, who did a large business with California,[12] writing from Mexico to Fr. Duran on October 7, 1835, informs the Fr. Prefecto that Fr. Antonio Peyri went to Rome, and that there was no obstacle to his return to Mexico if he so desired; but that, the Government treasury having no funds, an order was received on a customhouse, where both Fr.

---

[10] *Conferences*, p. 46.
[11] *California*, pp. 228-229.   [12] Bancroft, v, 764.

FR. ANTONIO PEYRI'S LAST FAREWELL AND BLESSING

Peyri and Fr. José Viader could cash their drafts (for their back stipends, presumably), but only at a discount of 25 per cent.[13]

It is quite certain that Fr. Peyri wrote to the Fr. Prefecto and probably to others in California; but only one such communication is extant. It is addressed to Stephen Anderson, physician and supercargo of the *Thomas Nowlan* and other vessels. The letter reads as follows:

Sr. Don Estévan Anderson.—My very dear friend and esteemed Sir.—In the month of February, 1834, I left Mexico for Europe, and going by way of New York and France, I arrived here at Barcelona, the capital of my province, on June 21, of the same year. I am still here because I have not been able to pass on to my native town, since the roads are infested with rebels and robbers who cause much damage to travelers and defenseless towns. I am, therefore, like one besieged. It is the most prudent thing to remain here until this devouring war dies out, which, although we always have good prospects, we do not know when it will end. My friend, I confess that I have been very much disappointed at having left my California in order to come to my country; for I thought I should find it very quiet and tranquil and persuaded myself that I might rest from my past hardships and close my days in repose, peace, and quietude; but I have encountered such unfortunate conditions as you may have learned from the daily papers. . . . As a result of all this, or because the Supreme Government may have found it expedient, all the friars in Spain were secularized and driven from their cloisters.

I brought with me two Indian youths, Pablo and Agapito, whom you knew already in California. I had the good fortune of being able to place them in Rome at the College of the Propaganda, where they are very contented and which I doubt not they will leave bright men, for they are very talented, and they are very much appreciated by the entire College for being from such distant countries, true Indians, and of good comportment. Would that they continue! For them and for a lay brother, who joined me and whom I brought as far as his Province of Galicia, and for myself, the expenses of the voyage and journey cost more than I had calculated. You know already that my little experience and meeting men with an abundance of bad faith caused a total loss, leaving me no other recourse than Providence, inasmuch as I am lacking the aid and shelter of a convent. How much I remember the abundance of Cali-

---

[13] *De la Guerra Papers*, vi, 147-148, Bancroft Collection.

fornia! ¹⁴ I should like to return thither, and it would be easy for me, because I came here with the passport of the Mexican Government giving me permission for two years; but the doctors forbid me on account of my ill health and advanced age. So there is nothing more

FR. ANTONIO PEYRI, O. F. M.

to do than to make the most of it, and I shall continue as may please God until the dove, that is to say, death arrives.

---

¹⁴ Could Fr. Peyri have seen how his successor, Fr. Ibarra, fared under the "tender mercies" of Pio Pico, he would have congratulated himself for being so far away from the scene of his former blessed activity.

There is not a day on which I do not remember you and Don
Ignacio Mancisidor. Having asked all the Viscayans whom I met,
I spoke of him at the stopping-place of Don Ignacio; but no one could
give me any information. Therefore I beg that when you reply to
me you tell me where he may be, and about his health, etc., as also
about your own, because it pleases me greatly to know of you both.
I wish you both every felicity, and the same I say about Scot.—Antonio Peyri, *en la Fonda de los Tres Reyes*, Barcelona, Cataluña.[15]

Through the Very Rev. Fr. Luke Carey, O. F. M., Rector
of the Irish Franciscan College, we made inquiries at the
College of the Propaganda, Rome, regarding the two Indian
boys whom Fr. Peyri had placed there. In reply we received
the following interesting information in Latin:

"Pont. Collegio Urbano De Propanganda Fide, via Propaganda, 1 Roma.

"Amamix (Victoria) Agapitus, California Mexican, born
at Mission San Luis Rey, August 6, 1820. Entered on September 23, 1834. Studied Grammar in 1834 to 1835. Died
on September 26, 1837, in the College Villa at Tuscalanum,
Montis Alti, and was buried in the subterranean crypt of the
monastery church.

"Tac, Paul, California Mexican, born in January, 1822,
at the Mission of San Luis Rey, Latin Rite. Entered on
September 23, 1834. Studied Grammar, Humanities and
Rhetoric from 1834 to 1840. In the month of December,
1840, he was likewise stricken with a dangerous fever. From
1841 he studied Philosophy. He died the death of the just
on December 13, 1841, with remarkable tranquility and
cheerfulness of mind, from consumption."

The boys are called Mexicans, but they were pure Indians, according to Fr. Peyri. The Baptismal Register would
have the antecedents, but as they are lost, details may never
be forthcoming.

When the preceding remark was already in type, another
search in the two *Padrons,* or Mission Rolls, found at Mis-

---

15 Vallejo, *Documentos,* vol. iii, no. 1, Bancroft Collection.

sion San Juan Capistrano, at last revealed the antecedents of the two Indian youths. Accordingly, we discovered that Agapíto was the youngest child of Vicente Amamix, a native of the ranchería of Pumusi, baptized at the age of eighteen, on July 23, 1805. His wife was Gerónima Asuma, of the ranchería of Quechinga, but baptized at Mission San Juan Capistrano. Their children were Edita, Maria Presentacion, Casilda, Gerónima, and our *Agapíto,* all born at Mission San Luis Rey. Agapíto was baptized on August 6, 1820. His number in the lost Baptismal Register was 3,709.

A close examination of the second of the two *Padrons* resulted in the discovery that Paul was the second of six children, born at Mission San Luis Rey, of Pedro Alcántara Tac, of the ranchería of Quechinga, who was baptized on October 19, 1801. His wife, Ladislaya Molmolix, of the ranchería of Pumusi, was baptized at the age of three years, on July 3, 1804. The children were Dionisia, *Pablo,* Julia, José, Teófila, and José Fermín. Pablo was baptized on January 15, 1822. His number in the lost Register was 3,896.

CHAPTER VI.

ALTHOUGH the Zacatecan Franciscan, Fr. Antonio Ánzar, took the place of Fr. Peyri, he officiated only in his priestly capacity. Fr. Vicente Pasqual Oliva of Mission San Diego came to administer the temporalities of San Luis Rey and he had the honor of drawing up and signing the Annual Reports of 1831 and 1832, the last that were sent to the territorial government.

As the Mission Registers, Baptismal, Burial, and Matrimonial, are lost or stolen, no details can be offered save those found in the Annual and Biennial Reports, which bring little more than figures. They will be found arranged in tabular form at the close of the narrative.

Forced contributions from the Mission to the soldiery continued as before. For instance, on March 2, 1833, Santiago Argüello, comandante of San Diego, asked Fr. Ánzar for supplies for the troops. In reply, Fr. Ánzar wrote on the next day, March 3: "The muleteer Joaquin leaves here to bring the grain from this Mission to the presidio of San Diego. He takes along sixteen fanégas of wheat, but no beans, for there are none even for planting; nor is there as much as a drachm of peas, manteca, soap, tallow, or anything." [1]

In response to another demand from Argüello, Fr. Oliva, a little more than a month later, on April 16, 1833, had to

---

[1] *Cal. Arch., Prov. St. Pap., Ben.*, vol. lxxix, pp. 88-92, 94.

say that there were only one hundred fanégas of wheat at Las Flores, instead of one thousand, and that he could not send the amount of provisions wanted.[2] It will be remembered that supplies were paid with drafts on Mexico, which were so many scraps of paper; nothing was ever realized on them.

Governor Echeandia's machinations in the district of the south had disastrous effects on the Indians. The latter, so peaceful and industrious under mission rule, became turbulent and seriously disturbed the peace of the southern regions. The governor had appointed Portilla commissioner at San Luis Rey for the purpose of emancipating the neophytes. This was in January, 1833. On February 10, Portilla asked for reinforcements in order to check disorders which arose among the neophytes in consequence of the distribution of lands.[3] What the real situation was may be inferred from the letter which, after making the official visitation, Fr. Duran wrote to Governor Figueroa from San Luis Rey under date of July 19, 1833. It reads as follows:

General.—When I arrived here I found Fr. Oliva melancholy and almost crazed on account of the evils and disorders in this Mission. This obliges me to take up the pen to implore the remedy which Your Honor alone can apply. It is this. The unmarried guards or those who have no family must be removed and replaced by married cavalry soldiers under a corporal who deserves confidence. I hear from the Father that the one now at Mission San Diego would be suitable. In this way, and by means of regular correction with the rod, order might be re-established. With my own eyes I see the insubordination of these Indians as to the work that pertains to them. Half of the men do not want to go out to the fisheries. Yesterday, one-half of the teamsters, who were to take the tallow to the harbor, were missing. Today, after I had administered the Sacrament of Confirmation to some children of white people and Indians, I directed them to come to the reception room in order to give their names. The whites, indeed, came; but soon they tired of waiting and left without giving their names. In consequence, it is not known who have been confirmed. In no other place have I seen such rudeness.

The reason for all this is the lack of adequate punishment.[4] Don

---

2 Ibidem, p. 260.

3 See *Missions and Missionaries*, vol. iii, p. 484.

4 Figueroa had forbidden the infliction of corporal punishment.

Pablo de Portilla [5] neither takes action nor allows any action to be taken. The consequence is that the Father is a veritable slave, and the butt of everyone. The said officer is afraid of the Indians, and for that reason he consents to everything.

I confess that I would not in these circumstances take care of the temporalities; because all the year round, from Indian and from non-Indian, it is, ''Father, give me! Father, give me!'' Then to find the Indian not willing to work, and yet having no power at hand to make him work, owing to the lack of a suitable and paternal chastisement, this is nothing less than a condition liable to consume the health and the patience of even a saint.

I have seen myself obliged to tell Fr. Vicente (Oliva), for the sake of animating him, to appeal to Your Honor, and with due respect and submission to expose to you all the evils which the Mission suffers, together with their causes and necessary remedies, even to the extent of delivering the charge of the temporalities, so that Your Honor may entrust them to whomsoever you may find serviceable, unless an end is put to the insubordination of the Indians, which in my opinion has no other cause than the impunity and the bad example of the soldiers on the spot.[6]

A month before, on June 17, Fr. Duran had already written to Governor Figueroa from San Gabriel regarding the state of the missions:

The condition, in truth, is altogether unsatisfactory, especially at San Luis Rey and San Diego, where the attitude of the Indians appears threatening. This last I observed especially at San Luis Rey. I was not at San Diego, but the conditions there are said to be the same. This may be to a certain degree attributed to the immorality and to the bad example of the troops on guard at that Mission, inasmuch as concubinage, gambling with the Indians, and drunkenness are continuous. This enrages and emboldens the Indians to make the attempts they did, and which they appear to be meditating.

I have spoken to Don Pablo about the matter. In substance he replied that, for fear lest the soldiers desert out of pure disgust, since they had served their time, were separated from their families, and were not paid, he could not reduce them to discipline. To me this seemed a tacit confession of the disorder.[7]

Later he tacitly permitted such chastisement. The unruly youthful Indians could not be made to comprehend the wickedness of a misdeed until they had felt it on their person.

[5] Commander of the San Diego presidio.

[6] *Archb. Arch.*, no. 2,151.

[7] *Archb. Arch.*, no. 2,140.—In the same letter, probably having been

Instead of some measures of relief, Figueroa wrote to Fr. Duran on July 15, 1833, that all qualified neophytes must be freed from missionary control. On the same day he issued his *Prevenciones Provisionales* or Regulations for the Emancipation of the Mission Indians. Though good enough in themselves or in theory, they were entirely unsuited for the yet childish neophytes, and were therefore doomed to failure, as the Fathers predicted.

May God grant His blessing, wrote Fr. Duran to Figueroa, which is so necessary; for the ideas of the Indians and non-Indians and those of the government are much at variance. The latter wants the Indians to be private owners of lands and other property. The Indians want the freedom of vagabonds. The others [8] want the absolute liberation of the neophytes, in order that they may avail themselves of their lands and other property, as well as of their persons.[9]

The rapacious enemies of the missions, the same that had cowed Figueroa to issue the emancipation decree and, in the next year, on August 9, to publish the decree confiscating the mission property under the misleading title of secularization, judged the poor Franciscans from their own irreligious point of view. Accordingly, they pretended to fear that some of the Indian property they coveted might escape their grasp through willful destruction at the hands of the missionaries. Claiming that the Fathers were slaughtering cattle in unusual numbers merely for the hides, the young Californians had the legislature pass a law prohibiting this wholesale slaughter. The law was leveled especially at Missions San Gabriel and San Luis Rey. Governor Figueroa, under date of June 16,[10]

---

asked by the governor, he wrote: ''The wine of San Luis Rey is not, in my opinion, the best nor worthy to be offered to a friend.''

[8] He means the young Californians headed by Pio Pico, who had long coveted the land cultivated by the neophytes in charge of the Franciscans. These Regulations of Figueroa opened the door to their greed. See for details *Missions and Missionaries*, vol. iii, pp. 467-481.

[9] *Missions and Missionaries*, vol. iii, p. 481.

[10] *Cal. Arch., St. Pap., Angeles, Off. Cor.*, vol. vi, p. 133. See *Missions and Missionaries*, vol. iii, p. 659.

1834, notified the said Fathers of the decree passed on June 12, and requested them to suspend the slaughter.

On receipt of the order, Fr. Vicente Oliva of San Luis Rey, under date of July 2, wrote to the governor as follows:

My esteemed Friend and Sir:—I received your welcome note dated June 20 together with the Order accompanying the same. Having received the order of the Most Excellent Deputation for the suspension of the slaughter, which is being done at this Mission, supposing that the same order may be interpreted as permitting the slaughter when a necessity is shown, I have to tell Your Honor that I am bound and pledged to the ships for the amount of $16,000, and that I have no other means of satisfying the debt. This slaughter is carried on in an entirely orderly manner within the enclosure of the cattle, and only the old and wild cattle are killed. I have made use of the two neighbors for the reason that this Mission has not a sufficient number of horses to effect the slaughter. I hope you will permit the work to be continued by the two men [11] until the number is complete to redeem my word. I tell Your Honor all this because at the same time the said men are making preparations for branding the cattle and regulating the ranchos. I salute Your Honor most affectionately and wish you every happiness and health. Your constant friend, Fr. Vicente Pasqual Oliva.[12]

In another note of the same date, Fr. Oliva says:

In response to the official note which Your Honor has been pleased to address to me under date of June 16 of the current year, I can not do less than present to Your Honor the following facts: This Mission was in great need of clothing, and not having any other means of covering the debt contracted with various ships, the Mission availed itself of the slaughter of cattle. This is being done by two persons of honorable conduct in every way. They kill only the old and wild or unbranded cattle. Moreover, they use their own horses in the round-up and slaughter, because owing to the lack of horses the Mission could not furnish them. For the same reason, lack of horses, no branding of cattle could take place last year.

If it be not allowed to continue with this slaughter through the said men, who have a sufficient force of horses for this work, then most assuredly my credit and liability will be put in bad light with

---

[11] Pio Pico and his brother. Pio claimed that he had killed five thousand head of cattle, receiving as his share for the labor half of the number of hides.

[12] *Cal. Arch., St. Pap., Missions*, vol. iv, p. 785; *Missions and Missionaries*, vol. iii, p. 660.

those shipping merchants. If it can not be done, I beseech Your Honor to please instruct me as to what means I should adopt to pay the debts.[13]

It is pleasant to state that Governor Figueroa, under date of July 8, readily consented that Fr. Oliva should pay the debts contracted for the sake of the neophytes in the way represented.[14]

According to Fr. Oliva, who wrote on August 8, 1834, from San Luis Rey, the exact number of cattle killed, from the month of May to the end of July that year, was 5,700. This left to the benefit of the Mission 2,850 hides; an equal number went to the butchers for slaughtering the cattle.[15]

At San Gabriel, about the same number of cattle were slaughtered in this year, doubtless for a similar reason. That is all there is to the story that at San Gabriel alone 100,000 head of cattle had been slaughtered in order to secure the hides for the missionaries, who enacted the same "work of destruction at every other mission throughout the territory; and that this vast country," as the veracious Los Angeles author exclaims, "was become a mighty shambles, drenched in blood and reeking with the odor of decaying carcasses." How the whole story is shown to be a mighty fiction, the reader will find in Appendix K of Volume III of our General History.

Fr. Oliva appears to have been on the verge of collapsing; wherefore Fr. Duran, under date of July 22, 1834, informed the governor that he found it necessary to restore Fr. Oliva as assistant of Fr. Martin to San Diego. He would ask Fr. Buenaventura Fortuni to make the sacrifice for God's sake, owing to the necessity.

What worries me, Fr. Duran continues, is the fear that Fr. Buenaventura may lose courage at sight of the great disorder which abounds in that Mission. I am advising him to put himself in accord with Don Pablo, so that they may harmoniously with deliberation and prudence apply a suitable remedy to what may still be remedied; and

---

[13] *Missions and Missionaries*, vol. iii, p. 659. [14] Ibidem, p. 660.
[15] *Cal. Arch., St. Pap., Missions*, vol. x, p. 174.

that, if he should find he can not endure the burden of the temporalities, he should inform me, as in that case I would ask Your
Honor to place a secular administrator in charge of them, so that
the Father, receiving his support, should attend to the spiritual affairs
only.[16]

Such at this time was the situation at San Luis Rey, which
down to the arrival of Echeandia, eight years before, sheltered
a happy and contented family of more than two thousand
Indian converts!

As the years passed on, the lessons taught the Indians by
the mission enemies turned, like a boomerang, on their unscrupulous authors. As early as 1833, Figueroa had named
Captain Pablo de la Portilla of San Diego, the same who
proved treacherous to the noble Victoria, in December, 1831,
comisionado to execute the decree of emancipation at San
Luis Rey. At the time, the neophytes were still faithful to
the missionary Father; for out of one hundred and eighty
families not one would hear anything of the so-called emancipation.[17] The leven of discontent, first introduced by Echeandia, began to act, however, as soon as a hired master was
substituted for the fatherly priest. Fr. Fortuni, who had succeeded Fr. Oliva on September 30, 1834, surrendered the mission temporalities to Captain Portilla, who had been appointed
comisionado or administrator.

Immediately there was trouble. The Indians on joining the
Mission abandoned savage liberty with its licentiousness for
the liberty of the Gospel, which truly sets free; but they had
done this for God's sake and for the sake of their own temporal well-being under the supervision of the unselfish representative of God. They had not intended to labor in order
that other than their own families should enjoy what they
saved through industry and abstemiousness. Therefore, when
they observed how their land acre by acre and whole ranchos
were claimed by white men who had done nothing to render
such land productive, the neophytes refused to throw in their

---

[16] *Archb. Arch.*, no. 2,182.
[17] See Bancroft, vol. iii, p. 332.

Captain Pablo de la Portilla, at San Luis Rey Mission Urges the Indians to go to Work. They Refuse

Saying: "We are free. It is not our pleasure to obey. We do not Choose to Work." Vol. III. Pg. 534.

labor besides, not to speak of a large number whom Echeandia's machinations had alienated from labor under the
Fathers. The consequence was that the salaried administrator
encountered difficulties of which the missionary had known
nothing before the arrival of the would-be liberator, Echeandia. The situation is pictured in a letter written by Portilla only one month after he had taken charge. It reads as
follows:

These Indians will do absolutely no work nor obey my orders. In
consequence, though the season for sowing the wheat is at hand, and
the necessary plows have been prepared, I must suffer the pain of
being obliged to suspend work for want of hands. The men have
mistaken the voice of reason and even of the authority which orders
the work, for they declare they are a free nation (nacion libre). In
order to enjoy their obstinacy the better, they have fled from their
houses and abandoned their aged parents, who alone are now at this
ex-Mission.

I have sent various alcaldes to the sierra in order to see if, with
sweetness and gentleness, we might succeed in having them return to
their homes; but the result was the opposite of my desires. Nothing
would suit them, nothing would change their ideas, neither the well-
being which must result from their good behavior, nor the privations
which they suffer in their wanderings. All with one voice would
shout, ''We are free! We do not want to obey! We do not want
to work!''

This occurrence, which may in the future be of vast consequences,
must be remedied by calling the insubordinate ones to order. Unfortunately, the lack of troops in this military district suspends the
execution of the plan.

The liberation of the young girls from their quarters has caused
considerable havoc. The girls now rove about in the sierras with their
lovers, the prey to concupiscence.

The horses are rendered entirely useless as well, on account of the
multitude of horses which the Indians have taken without permission
for their flights and outings, as also on account of the damage the
rest have suffered for want of pasturage. The same is true of the
mules. The consequence is that I can not undertake many urgent
matters.

The fields are covered with the remains of dead cattle which those
wicked natives kill for the purpose of stealing the hides. In fine,
everything presages the ruin of the country and makes me predict
dire consequences. My fears emanate from the experience which I
acquired in the fifteen years that I passed on this soil and from the
exact knowledge that I possess of its inhabitants. The dispositions

of the government are doubtless laudable. "Liberty in the whole world" must be the voice of every good citizen, but the Indians of California do not possess the civil virtues which are the main support of free nations.

I believed it my duty to communicate this brief report to Your Honor, who is so solicitous for the happiness of these people and in whom they have placed their hopes, so that you may dictate the necessary and expedient measures for the maintenance of public order, God and Liberty. San Luis Rey, December 20, 1834. Pablo de la Portilla.—To Governor José Figueroa.[18]

Figueroa must have winced at reading this tale of misery brought on by his decree of emancipation and by his later decree of confiscation, ere four months had elapsed. The reader is referred to the third and fourth volumes of the General History for details regarding all the former happy convert homes.

However, on January 23, 1835, Portilla could report a bit of consolation to the governor. He wrote that by dint of much persuasion he had succeeded in inducing the neophytes to sow fifty fanégas of wheat, and that at Pala and Agua Caliente planting proceeded orderly. In the same letter, he notified Figueroa that he had received the news of the appointment of Joaquin Ortega as mayordomo of San Luis Rey at a salary of fifty dollars a month and the maintenance of his family. Soon the satisfaction of Figueroa was spoiled, however, when Portilla, under date of March 23, informed him that the Indians did not want Ortega as mayordomo.[19]

The formal confiscation of Mission San Luis Rey was effected when Fr. Buenaventura Fortuni, not as owner but as steward or guardian of the neophytes, surrendered the property to the comisionado appointed by Governor Figueroa. Resistance was useless, and no court of appeal existed to which Fr. Fortuni in the name of the Indian owners could have applied for protection. The transfer was made by inventory, which was signed by Fr. Buenaventura Fortuni and the two commissioners named for that purpose, Pio Pico and

---

18 *Cal. Arch., St. Pap., Missions*, vol. xi, pp. 658-661.

19 *Cal. Arch., St. Pap., Miss.*, vol. xi, pp. 47-49, 52. Ban. Coll.

Pablo de la Portilla, on August 22, 1835. The general summary with the valuation attached was as follows:

Creditos Activos ....$ 49,619.75
Buildings of the Mission....................... 48,000.00
Furniture, utensils in the buildings, implements,
    tools, effects, grain in the warehouses, animals 24,193.75
Church building, 64 by 10 varas, adobe walls, tiled,
    etc. 30,000.00
Sacred vessels, vestments, and other church goods 11,485.50
Ranchos—
    Pala $15,363.25
    Santa Margarita 10,804.50
    San Juan 411.00
    Temécula 3,009.50
    San Jacinto 10,528.00
    San Marcos 321.50
                                 $ 40,437.75

      Total value $203,737.37
      Pasiva or debts........................ 9,300.87

                                   $194,436.50

The church edifice is described in the inventory as a cañon or nave, sixty-four varas or 176 feet long and ten varas or twenty-eight feet wide. The floor is of mortar (argamaza) and the ceiling is composed of boards. It has nine doors and eighteen windows. There are four apartments attached to the church, which serve for chapel or oratory, baptistry, and two for sacristies. The whole structure is valued at $30,000, exclusive of the contents, among which are eighteen statues. There is mentioned also a library comprising 182 volumes and valued at $591. Six bells are valued at $1,060.[20]

The rancho of Las Flores is not mentioned in the Inven-

---

[20] *Cal. Arch., St. Pap., Missions,* vol. vii, pp. 490-539.

MISSION SAN LUIS REY FROM THE SOUTHEAST. FAMOUS CHIMNEY OVER THE COMMUNITY KITCHEN TO THE LEFT

tory, though it is certain that it belonged to Mission San Luis Rey, and that the buildings, including a small chapel, were arranged in the shape of a mission like Pala on a small scale. The reader will remember that the Fathers early protested against the presence of the presidio horses on the pastures of Las Flores. Bancroft thinks that Las Flores was organized into a pueblo with Indians who accepted emancipation from Governor Figueroa in 1833. In May, 1834, the place was represented by the governor as being in a flourishing condition; but in four years, as Inspector Hartnell found, the emancipated neophytes had already rid themselves of half the property. On November 23, 1834, the comisionado, Pablo de la Portilla, reported that on September 30, 1834, Fr. Fortuni had turned over to him the Book of Accounts, according to which various individuals owed the Mission for goods received the sum of $46,613.09 granos, while the Mission owed $14,419.20.[21]

When the property had been surrendered to the salaried administrators now forcibly foisted on the Mission, the respective missionary, according to the decree of confiscation, was to have the choice of the rooms which he wished to occupy. This any reasonable person would find quite proper. Usually these rooms were situated next to the vestry or the church, as the priest's first duty lay there. In various missions this led to trouble. The men who were appointed administrators wanted to lord it over all and, in fact, they not unfrequently treated the priest as a subordinate, and would dispute the right of the missionary to the quarter he had heretofore occupied. Such was the case at San Luis Rey. Disregarding the fitness of things and the clause of the decree, Portilla determined to oust the Father and to intrude himself. Lest we be said to misjudge Portilla, let us hear that personage himself. On May 2, 1835, Portilla from San Luis Rey addressed himself to Governor Figueroa as follows:

---

[21] *Cal. Arch., St. Pap., Missions,* vol. xi, p. 53. Bancroft Collection.

Having assigned for the habitation of the administrator of this ex-Mission the two rooms which Fr. Vicente Oliva occupied, and having in person communicated this arrangement to Fr. Buenaventura Fortuni, this religious absolutely refused to comply, alleging that he can not permit that any one of the rooms of the principal habitation be occupied by any other individual than himself; and that the charge of the keys must be left to him, because thus his prelate had ordained, whose orders he is determined to obey without recognizing any other superior. In view of the opposition and the little will of said relig-ious to preserve harmony with the administrator, who of necessity must live in a place that affords opportunity to care for the interests of which he has charge, I see myself obliged to have recourse to Your Honor, supplicating you to send me the orders which you regard as just on the incident.[22]

Portilla's assertion that it was Fr. Fortuni who would not preserve harmony with him apparently failed to impress Governor Figueroa. Yet the latter feared to offend the officer who had proved traitor to his predecessor Victoria, as he feared to anger any one of the *pasaino* clique. Instead of harshly reproving Portilla for his selfish disregard of proprieties, let alone the decree, which was clear enough on the subject, Figueroa mildly advised the administrator to try to agree with the missionaries "who have the right to select their own residence." [23]

It will be seen that generally the Fathers, from having been founders and guardians of the missions and neophytes, and by right the masters in the house they built, became mere tenants. Even for their board they were at the mercy of the administrators, especially after the death of Figueroa, which occurred the same year, 1835, on September 29, only five weeks after Portilla signed the inventory and thereby became master of Mission San Luis Rey.

Naturally, the mercenaries who took charge of the Mis-sion property could not and would not look after the wel-fare of the Indians with the same solicitude that the un-

---

[22] *Cal. Arch., St. Pap., Missions and Colon.*, vol. ii, pp. 340, 341. Bancroft Collection.

[23] *Cal. Arch., St. Pap., Missions and Colon.*, vol. ii, pp. 340, 341. Bancroft Collection.—Bancroft, vol. iii, p. 624.

salaried missionaries had manifested; but nowhere was the difference so glaring as at San Luis Rey, where the chief conspirator against the missions, Pio Pico, took charge before the end of the year 1835. There is no documentary evidence of his appointment; but it must have been his boon companion in the war on the missions, José Castro, who bestowed upon Don Pio what the latter desired—charge of the great Mission of San Luis Rey, at the time when José Castro succeeded the ill-fated Figueroa as temporary governor of California. What Pico's aims were can be inferred from his own admission. "I was determined," he wrote, "to put an end to the mission system at all hazards, in order that the land could be acquired by private individuals." [24] This was done without regard to the rights of the neophytes. While in charge, Pio Pico early endeavored to secure for himself the rancho of Temécula. The Indians, however, protested, saying it was their property. So for the time being he desisted. Portilla, too, availed himself of the opportunity of securing land already cultivated by the neophytes, and he seems to have prevailed upon the governor to grant it to him. At all events, in October, 1835, the acting governor, José Castro, forbade Pio Pico to disturb Portilla in the possession of the rancho of San José del Valle. [25]

In passing, it may be noted here that in September and October, 1834, a part of the Hijár-Padrés-Bandini colony were entertained at San Luis Rey on their way from San Diego to Monterey. For the details of this huge swindle, which aimed at nothing less than taking possession of the property of all the Indian missions, the reader is referred to our larger work. [26]

In November, 1835, a number of neophytes went to San Diego and complained to the alcalde that they were not given their promised liberty, but that they were severely

[24] See *Missions and Missionaries*, vol. iv, pp. 366-367.
[25] Bancroft, vol. iii, pp. 361, 624.
[26] *Missions and Missionaries*, vol. iii, pp. 507-512.

treated by Pio Pico, who had taken charge of the temporalities of Mission San Luis Rey. The alcalde reported to the governor that the danger was serious.[27] Pico was receiving a dose of the bitter medicine he had given to the missionaries. His troubles continued during 1836; but, unlike the friars, he provoked antagonism by his inconsiderate and high-handed proceedings. In June, 1836, he even imprisoned Pablo Apis, a leader among the neophytes, apparently for no other reason than that they had petitioned for redress of the wrongs they suffered. These Indians, however, had learned how to help themselves. They forced Pico to release the incarcerated Apis, and then both parties went to San Diego to make charges before the alcalde. The latter hardly improved the situation, for he detained Apis and four others under arrest, sent a small guard to San Luis Rey, and urged Pico to be very careful and not lose the crop which the Indians were raising, from which, of course, the supplies for the troops were to be taken! The shrewd official thereupon reported to the governor. "The correspondence," says Bancroft, "is complicated, but no definite results are indicated. Evidently Don Pio was not as popular a manager as had been Fr. Peyri."[28] The reason is not difficult to discover. The unsalaried missionaries managed for the benefit of the neophytes alone, whereas Pico managed for his own mercenary aims. As a curiosity it may be repeated here from Bancroft that in September, 1836, the alcalde was ordered to aid Pio Pico in retaking fugitive neophytes from the gentiles in the interests of religion! When the friars made such demands, they were disregarded ever since the arrival of Echeandia. Pico's motive for retaking the fugitives was that he might not lack laborers.

---

27 Banc., iii, 624.
28 Bancroft, vol. iii, p. 624.

CHAPTER VII.

DURING the years 1837 and 1838, the young California
revolutionists and counter-revolutionists frequently passed
San Luis Rey or, what was worse, stopped there. The impression they made on the Indians and their coming in con-
tact with them could not have benefited the natives. "Sec-
tional strife," says Bancroft, "so fully occupied the minds
of all that the records bear but slight trace of anything
else. At Las Flores even a combat took place, but it was
for the most part one of tongue and pen, though a cannon
was fired once or twice from the corral, doing no harm." [1]

How the saner portion of the convert Indians must have
longed, amidst this turmoil and oppression, for the former
peaceful and happy times, when the patient Fathers were in
charge, may be inferred from this curious and touching
appeal addressed to the governor by a number of San Luis
Rey Indians on August 1, 1838:

> The neophytes of this Mission come before Your Honor with the
> greatest respect and obedience, and represent that we have experienced
> all the evils which have visited us for many years. We have suffered
> incalculable losses, for some of which we are in part to be blamed ·
> because many of us have abandoned the Mission; but this could be
> remedied, Your Honor, by imposing some penalty or punishment on
> those who absent themselves at their own pleasure, and upon those
> who admit them into their houses for work. We implore this of your
> merciful heart. Meanwhile we hope Your Honor will listen to our
> supplication. We plead and we beseech you to deign to attend to
> this earnest supplication, if it seem just and right, to grant us a
> Rev. Father for this place. We have been accustomed to the Rev.

---

[1] Bancroft, vol. iii, pp. 559-562, 624.

Fathers and to their manner of managing the duties. We labored under their intelligent directions, and we were obedient to the Fathers according to the regulations, because we considered it was good for us all. Your Honor, we promise you who has the power that, if our petition is granted, we will work as before with more energy. We hope from the kind disposition of Your Yonor that we shall receive this grace and favor.—Pablo Apis, Diego Peyri, Ygnacio Atulo, Guillermo Apis, José Miguel Gapala, Agustin Talle, Leon Nojú.[2]

Poor simple-minded Indians! How could one of the chief mission despoilers reinstate the missionary, when the unselfish missionary had been evicted for the very purpose of substituting hungry *paisanos?* How could one crow be expected to pluck out the eyes of another crow? Alvarado, however, who then held the office of governor, moved by similar petitions from all over the territory, and eager to save his own name, appointed an inspector of the missions in the person of William Hartnell, an Englishman by birth and withal an honest man who really desired to benefit the poor Indians. His appointment was dated January 19, 1839. He began his investigations at San Diego on May 22,[3] 1839. Early in June or perhaps in the last days of May he was at Mission San Luis Rey. On the situation here he reported that the vineyard of the Rancho de Temécula was in a poor condition, owing to the plague of caterpillars, which caused much damage to all kinds of plants; that the Mission at the time owed $15,000[4] to various individuals, but that the loans made to various parties would about cover this debt. The looms were at work and the administrator was engaged in having frazadas or blankets made to clothe the greater part of the people for the feast of the Patron Saint, August 26.

In the Indian pueblo of Las Flores the natives presented themselves and asked that the live stock be distributed to them, which to that date had been cared for by the community. After hearing the views of the administrator and

[2] *Cal. Arch., St. Pap., Missions*, vol. i, pp. 652-653.

[3] Not August 22, as misprinted in vol. iv, p. 147, *Missions and Missionaries*.

[4] It had only $9,300 debts on August 22, 1835.

of others, Hartnell acceded to the petition. The animals were counted and valued at $867. As there were thirty-three married couples with forty-six children, ten widowers with ten children, and six widows, Hartnell directed that each family receive $20; each widower and widow, $12, and José Maria, by the consent of all other Indians, $7. This left a surplus of $8, which the inspector had divided among the most needy widows. Hartnell warned the Indians, how-

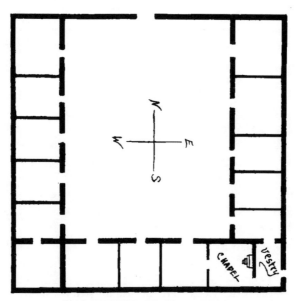

LAS FLORES OR SAN PEDRO

ever, that, at the time when they were freed from the Mission, the government wanted them to improve the property assigned to them, but that, as he had observed, everything in their community was already going to ruin. Therefore, they were to understand that whoever neglected or abused what was now given to him, and did not labor to insure his subsistence, would lose his right to freedom and would have to return to the Mission a second time to work for the community. With this the Indians appeared satisfied.[5]

As yet Hartnell had not detected the misdemeanors of Pico. But daily the Indians felt their menial position more and more. Both reasons may have prompted Pico to write to the inspector immediately after his departure. His letter reads:

San Luis Rey, June 5, 1839. Today I sent twelve barrels of wine and three barrels of brandy to San Diego. I did not send the oil for want of casks. I am going to San Diego in order to see whether I can procure them. If I find some I shall send them at once, as you on leaving this Mission directed me. Do not fail to take steps to have the Indians return to the Mission; for every day they are running away, because they notice that they are not punished at Los Angeles for not having a permit. Hence all are gathering there. Yesterday the mayordomo arrived from the sierra, whither they had gone to haul down timber to repair the buildings. He brought the news that three herdsmen had fled. If the rest who remain see that no efforts are made to return them to the Mission, I shall be left alone, and then the buildings will go to ruin for want of hands.— Pio Pico.[6]

That was what the Fathers had warned the covetous enemies would be the result of their machinations for alienating the neophytes from the obedience they had willingly rendered to the unselfish missionaries. Nevertheless, they had blamed the Fathers for not keeping the missions in repair and the fields under cultivation. The would-be reformers for personal profit were receiving a dose of their own medicine. Nor did Pico care if the Indians did run away from the Mission proper, provided enough hands were left to cultivate the ranchos he was slyly endeavoring to secure, as will appear from the letter of Fr. Ibarra to be quoted later on.

Pico frequently absented himself from the Mission. Doubtless he accounted for it to the satisfaction of Hartnell; for the latter had requested Fr. Ibarra to act as manager

---

[5] *Cal. Arch., St. Pap., Missions*, vol. xi, pp. 334-341.

[6] *Papeles Orig.*, vol. ii, pp. 885-886. Bancroft Collection.

whenever the administrator was absent. Fr. Ibarra referred the matter to Fr. Prefecto Duran, who consented, provided that Fr. Ibarra thereby bound himself to nothing. The consequence was in keeping with the character of Pio Pico. Writing under date of May 7, 1840, Fr. Ibarra says with regard to the subject: "When I was temporarily in charge, I observed what I dare not overlook; but experience has taught me what it is to be exposed to calumny of the worst kind and even after the charge had been proved a calumny." [7]

Fr. Ibarra refers to the few days in July, 1839, shortly after the departure of Hartnell, when he consented to act as manager. Pico later claimed that during an earlier absence much property had disappeared, and he actually had the hardihood to accuse Fr. Ibarra to Governor Alvarado. This was too much for the usual equanimity of the Fr. Prefecto, who better than any one else knew the disinterested integrity of the friars under him. In a letter addressed to Alvarado on October 25, 1839, Fr. Narciso Duran gave vent to his just indignation in this fashion:

The complaints of Pio Pico about the thefts at San Luis Rey have caused me much surprise. What about the hundred yoke of oxen and twelve carts, etc.? Does a friar conceal them up his sleeves that he should be made to render an account of them? It is Pico and not the missionary Father who should be held to answer, for it is he that enjoys the salary and appoints as mayordomos whomsoever he pleases. Formerly, when we managed for the Supreme Government, we did so without giving security. Now, for having, at the request of Señor Pico, taken charge a few days, he wants the Father to render an account! Is that all the compensation said friar is to receive in return? Or is the commotion intended to divert or mislead the attention from the situation for which only Pico and the mayordomos must be held responsible? However, why was this matter not settled when you visited that Mission? Why was it postponed till after your departure? Who, after all, has said that the Father must give an account of what he has not received on security nor could receive, I will not say, to Pico, but even to the government, without the knowledge and permission of his prelate? In order that any one may and should be held responsible for accidental cases, it is necessary that he

---

[7] *Archivo de las Misiones, Papeles Originales*, vol. ii, p. 1,053. Bancroft Collection.

enjoy a salary or is paid for such cases; but no religious can bind his person in such a manner, because he is not free to do so, being subject to his prelate. For all these reasons I have decided to say nothing to the Father, but out of particular friendship for you I have copied your official communication for his information and I am asking him to send his reply to me, which I shall then transmit to you in due time. What eagerness in Pico to drag innocent ones into trouble, when he should be engaged in something better! [8]

Pico was at his old tricks, shifting the blame for his misdeeds on the priests. Fr. Duran penetrated the situation. Unfortunately, Fr. Ibarra's own version is not extant. A later communication is an eye-opener, however. Under date of February 13, 1840, Fr. Ibarra wrote from San Luis Rey to Fr. Prefecto Duran as follows:

Herewith I proceed to show Your Reverence the state of this Mission. Don Pio Pico has solicited the place called Temécula, which is the chief support of this Mission, so much so that without it the Mission can not subsist. I made Don Guillermo Hartnell see as much, in order that he might make representations to the governor. In fact, they were on the point of granting the site to Pio Pico, when I explained the matter to Don Guillermo Hartnell. As soon as the governor had read the report, he said that there was no need for concern, as it had been made plain to him that the place was very necessary to the Mission.

When Pico saw that his scheme was frustrated, he had recourse to other plans which are likewise well outside truth and justice. Indeed, on the night of January 17, when all the alcaldes presented themselves to report according to custom, he told them that an order had come from the governor that all (that is to say, the Indians of the Mission proper, not those of Pala, Themécula, Agua Caliente, etc., many of whom opposed the seizure of their pastures, but in whose name I now speak for all, so that it will be easy to accomplish my object) should ask for their liberty, so that they could go, some to San Diego and others to Los Angeles, etc., after which Pico should have charge of Temécula.

Next day, January 18, an Indian informed me of what had occurred and asked me what I thought of it. I told him that this was very bad, and that I knew nothing of such an order from the governor; and, therefore, in order that no such outrage be effected, all the people should come to me, whereupon I would in their presence speak to Don Pio. However, Pico had the Indians so terrified with

---

[8] *Missions and Missionaries*, vol. iv, pp. 159-160.

threats of floggings, stocks, chains, and imprisonment, that they determined not to approach my apartment.

In the following night, the alcaldes spoke to the Indians for the purpose of having them assemble in the patio next day after holy Mass and to decide to demand their liberty. Nineteen gathered there, but the outcome was not what Pico desired. The Indians offered objections, and so the meeting resulted in nothing.

Seeing that his reasoning had failed to put him in sole control of all the sites and lands belonging to the Mission, Pico at once concocted another plan, which was likewise at variance with justice.

On January 20, Pio Pico set out for Monterey, wishing the Indians to be tangled up in various opinions. On February 7 I asked them how their case stood. They replied that they had already informed Don Andrés (Pio's brother, then in charge) that they wanted to leave the Mission to be free. When I asked them why, they responded by saying, one speaking for all: "Your Reverence sees how we are situated. This man thinks of nothing more than of making us work continually and quickly. For us there is nothing. Our whole toil and labor he exacts for himself. Therefore, we shall go away from here. No more work for him."[9]

To this I responded that they should have patience; that God would remedy it, if it were His will; and if not, they would be recompensed in the other life; that they should learn from me, to whom, as they well knew, nothing more was given than the mere food at noonday and the supper at night, for which they were charging me one dollar every day;[10] that four to five thousand dollars were coming to me, yet I did not insist that I be paid, because I wished that the Mission should be preserved. Therefore, they must have patience until God disposed otherwise.

This, then, Reverend Father, is what happened. Hence it is my opinion that Your Reverence send this letter to Don Guillermo Hartnell and that he present it to the governor, who, it seems to me, will not permit a pueblo libre (free town) at San Luis Rey for the following reasons:

1. These Indians have demanded their liberty, but under deception and like men who are desperate, who can suffer no more, and who will rather abandon the Mission through flight, as have done the

---

[9] "Su Reverencia ve como estamos. Este hombre no piensa mas que hacernos trabajar de continuo y aprisa. A nosotros el nada; todo nuestro sudor y trabajo el se lo lleva. Conque nos pasemos de aqui. No mas trabajar para el."

[10] "que aprendiesen de mi, que bien sabia, que a mi nada me dan mas que la pura comida a mediadia y la cena a la noche, y para esto me cuentan todos los dias un peso."

FR. FRANCISCO IBARRA LISTENING TO THE COMPLAINTS OF THE INDIANS

greater portion, perhaps; so in them the desire for liberty is not the result of free deliberation but only of violence.

2. These Indians, being the minority, can not dispose of the others by prejudicing their rights.

3. There might be some kind of appearance or formality of a deliberate demand if the opinion of all had been called for and taken—that is to say, of all at Pala, Themécula, Agua Caliente, etc. No one from these places knows anything about it, as I have already indicated, and therefore the proceeding is of no value and no weight is to be placed in the demand of the few.

Finally, why does Don Pio want San Luis Rey to be a *pueblo libre?* Because he knows that if here it rains a little more than commonly, all will be *chaguista*, everything will perish; and if it does not rain enough, nothing will be harvested. Therefore he wants to place these unhappy Indians in this arid, salinitrous, and sandy potrero and without any resource whatever! Why does he not want *pueblos libres* at Agua Caliente, Themécula, etc., where the population is numerous, where there is sufficient pasturage, plenty fertile soil, and sufficient water for irrigation? For the reasons stated before.''[11]

In his letter of May 7, 1840, already mentioned. Fr. Ibarra intimates how some property disappeared and why the Picos would saddle the blame on the missionary, whose very presence was obnoxious to them, inasmuch as it at least prevented open robbery. He writes:

In place of repairing the damage done to the Mission it is said of him that he pastured and took away for himself a flock of sheep from the few that had remained. The same I have to say regarding the orders given to the mayordomo. For example, I am allowed to observe when a piece of soap is given to an Indian to wash his blanket, when a pint of wheat is given to a hungry Indian, or when a piece of meat is given to an exhausted courier; but I am not permitted to see how much soap the Picos sell or to witness how much brandy, wine, etc., is taken away, or what the pack mules are burdened with. The mayordomo will tell me that I have nothing to see there; that this is not one of the difficult cases of which the *Reglamento* speaks, when a Father must be present; and thus I am put to shame. If I say nothing, there will be peace; but this is not possible when I have to sign all that he wants me to sign. It is repugnant

---

11 *Arch. de las Misiones, Pap. Orig., Mis.*, vol. ii, pp. 1,021-1,022. Bancroft Collection.

and against conscience, above all for a religious. For this reason I can not agree to it.''[12]

Fr. Ibarra refers to Article 5, 8, and 9, in the *Reglamento* which Governor Alvarado issued on March 1, 1840. These Articles read:

Art. 5. The mayordomos have to take care of everything relative to the advancement of the property under their charge, acting in concert with the Rev. Fathers in the difficult cases which may occur.

Art. 8. They will remit to the inspector's office a monthly account of the produce they may collect in the storehouses, and an annual one of the crops of grain, liquors, etc., and of the branding of all kinds of cattle.

Art. 9. Said accounts must be audited by the Rev. Fathers.[13]

On the same day, May 7, 1840, Fr. Ibarra addressed another letter to Fr. Duran but sent it apart from the other for the reason that he feared the Picos would open it, and then, of course, it would not have left the place. Its contents are astounding. They reveal Pio Pico as he was at the time, and as he remained for many years after the mission period. The wonder is only that he could have enlisted the aid of any decent person in his schemes of ambition and greed. Fr. Ibarra writes:

According to the *Reglamento*, when the Indians are not occupied in working for the community (although this same article was in the former one (Regulation), these caballeros do not care for anything except their own interest and commodity), they are to be paid for particular labor at the rate of $1.20 a day; but this does not suffice for oil nor for paying the hay which they get every day in order to keep in the corrals of the house eight or ten horses and sometimes twenty horses and mules. Whence, then, shall they take the money to pay for their personal expenses, their amusements, and other things?

When I spoke of Las Flores I said to Your Reverence that I had the most solid reasons to offer, but that I did not give them for fear that they would open the letter, and that it would not reach your

---

[12] *Arch. de las Misiones, Pap. Orig., Mis.*, vol. ii, p. 1,053. Bancroft Collection.

[13] See *Missions and Missionaries*, vol. iv, pp. 164-165.

hands. However, I now tell you that, according to the information which I have, Las Flores is a seraglio for the SS. Pico. . . .14. They have their cattle, and they sow their fields when they please. In fine, Las Flores belongs to the Picos; but what kind of *pueblo libre* is that?15

In the previous letter I told Your Reverence that when the Indians informed me that San Luis Rey would be a *pueblo libre*, I said to them that I would then leave for other parts. This they reported to Don Pio. He replied that it was of no consequence if I left, because he would marry them whenever they wished. From this Your Reverence may infer what his doctrines must be when the heart is such, and consequently what the unhappy and wretched state of the soul is like. God behold it with the eyes of mercy, and give them time for repentance.16

The prayer of good Fr. Ibarra was certainly heard by Almighty God as far as time is concerned; for Pio Pico lived fifty-four years longer; but as to his repentance, we are not so sanguine. That he made any reparation even for the slanders he heaped upon the missionaries, let alone other obligations, we have not learned; but then he escaped the poorhouse only through the kindness of an American.

Disheartened, Fr. Ibarra wrote his letters at the request of Fr. Prefecto Duran; for on March 5, of the same year, Fr. Duran wrote to Hartnell:

The friar upon whom I look with most compassion is Fr. Ibarra, who is with Pio Pico. He has complained so much to me during the past summer when he was here, about the despotism and arrogance of Pico, that I saw myself obliged to tell him to draw up a collection of specific cases, so that we may not rely on vague charges; and I told him that he should, through me, ask the government for redress, and, if a remedy was not applied, he should go to San Gabriel in order to give the pueblo of Los Angeles better service. In view of the

14 ''Las Flores es un serrallo para los SS. Pico. En el mes de Noviembre pp. pp., el Señor Don Pio con un sirviente llegó a la ranchería de San Diego como a media noche, y entregó una criatura recien nacida de una soltera de las Flores. Los Picos ocupan la casa del Padre, y el mayordomo ocupa el corral.''

15 Pio Pico, on February 5, 1840, reported to Gov. Alvarado that he had turned over to the Indian José Manuel the property of the pueblo of Las Flores.—*Cal. Arch., St. Pap., Missions*, vol. xi, p. 8. Bancroft Collection.

16 *Papeles Orig. Misiones*, vol. ii, p. 1,055.

wretched state of San Juan Capistrano, and the greatly impaired health of Fr. Buenaventura Fortuni, we are thinking of calling upon Fr. Zalvidea to go and live in his company.[17]

On receipt of the last two letters from Fr. Ibarra, the Fr. Prefecto, on May 14, 1840, sent this indignant communication to Hartnell:

I enclose a letter from Fr. Ibarra, which contains two chief points. The first is that, having been slandered, he, although vindicated, receives not the slightest satisfaction; on the contrary, his adversary triumphs the more. The other is that he is insulted if he takes notice of what is received and of what is expended by the mayordomo (Pico), and thus peace is forfeited. Concerning the first point, the Father has more than sufficient reason for complaint; for, although Pico deserves to be thrashed from head to foot (al Señor Pico se le debe haber expulgado hasta las costuras de la ropa), nothing has been done. As to the second point, the Father is not right, for he should know from the *Reglamento* how to dissimulate, and that he is not obliged to take notice. Hence, he can choose between remonstrating and keeping silence until the *Reglamento* is changed.[18]

The letter referred to in Fr. Duran's communication to Hartnell reads as follows:

J. M. J.—May 14, 1840.—My esteemed Fr. Francisco: I have received your appreciable missive and on this date I forward it to Señor Hartnell. On the two points which it contains, I am telling him that Your Reverence is right as regards the first, because, having been cleared of the calumnies inflicted, no satisfaction whatever has been given to you, while the adversary Pico continues to laugh and continues his transactions; that with regard to the second point, however, Your Reverence is not right; for it will be necessary to ascertain what Mission goods have been disposed of; that would suffice to shut the mouth of the over-bold mayordomo (Pico). This much I say to Your Reverence; but you can do as you please, since I never thought of obliging anyone to subject himself to the *Reglamento*.[19]

It is not pleasant to relate these disagreeable facts; but would it be fair to the slandered missionaries and their persecuted Indian wards to suppress what they suffered at the hands of their oppressors in order not to expose their enemies to condemnation?

---

[17] *Missions and Missionaries*, vol. iv, pp. 179-180. [18] Ibidem, pp. 181-182.

[19] Fr. Duran to Fr. Ibarra, May 14, 1840. *Sta. Barb. Arch.*

CHAPTER VIII.

AFTER perusing the communications of the Fr. Commis-
sary Prefect, Inspector Hartnell hastened down to San
Luis Rey and discovered that Fr. Ibarra's statements were not
only true but did not picture the situation nearly as dark
as it was in reality; for he found that "the condition of
the Indians was pitiable, and particularly so at Pala," writes
Hittell, one of the bitterest enemies of the early missionaries.[1]
"All they had wherewith to clothe themselves," he declares,
"were rags. The women especially, who were compelled to
resort to tule aprons, complained that they had devoted their
whole lives to the service of the Mission, and their only
recompense was barely enough food to support life, naked-
ness and a heritage of misery. All were violently opposed
to the administration of the Picos, and charged them with
all manner of oppression."

This lends color to the statement of a widow who, in
May, 1839, petitioned the prefect of Los Angeles, as the
official placed over the southern district was called, to be
released from the Mission managed by Pico, in order to
support herself and daughters. The poor woman declared
that she was overworked, but that she received no clothing.[2]
Why this same Pico should nevertheless complain that the
Indians were constantly running away, can be explained
only by supposing that he regarded those convert Indians
as his slaves, without any rights whatever. The prefect,
doubtless ignorant of the character of Pico, in June, 1839,

---

[1] *History of California*, vol. ii, pp. 303-304.
[2] Bancroft, vol. iii, p. 624.

actually asked Hartnell to aid Pico in his efforts to recover the fugitive Indians![3]

There were others, however, who appreciated Pio Pico at his true value. In October and November, 1839, Bancroft relates on the authority of Mariano Vallejo,[4] there was trouble between Pico and the administrator of San Juan Capistrano about some cattle at a rancho claimed by both. Hartnell, after investigating the circumstances, decided that Pico should have 4,000 head of cattle and that the other's share should be 2,000 head. At once Pico sent a man to kill his 4,000, and then there were no more left! There is little ground for believing this story, since the particulars are lacking, and Vallejo himself is poor authority; but it goes to show what the fellow conspirators thought of Pio Pico's honesty. With such a man at the helm poor Fr. Ibarra had to live, and upon such a man he was dependent for the little food he needed!

Hartnell saw that there was no possible excuse for retaining Pio Pico in the office of administrator, or mayordomo, as the latest *Reglamento* termed said official. Therefore he appointed José Antonio Estudillo of San Diego. That gentleman, on July 5, 1840, replied to Hartnell, accepting the position, which afforded a salary of $420 a year.[5]

"Pio Pico and his brother Andrés, who was acting under his instructions," says Bancroft, "refused to deliver up possession, and assumed to manage the establishment and its dependencies of Pala and Temécula very much as he pleased. The Picos resorted to various stratagems to avoid relinquishing their hold on San Luis Rey. Hartnell at length applied to the prefect of the department for the necessary force to compel them to obey the orders of the government. This movement had the desired effect, and Estudillo was placed in possession."[6]

The following correspondence clearly shows the hypo-

[3] Ibidem.
[4] Bancroft, iii, p. 624.
[5] *Cal. Arch., St. Pap., Mis.*, vol. xi, pp. 129-130.   [6] Banc., iii, 624.

critical character of Pio Pico, and the trickery he employed to retain the position as administrator of the Mission and Indian property of San Luis Rey; nor did he change his tactics for the better when he secured the office of governor of the territory.

On July 6, 1840, he addressed from Los Angeles the following remarkable letter to Inspector Hartnell:

My dear Sir:—In order to reach San Luis Rey at an opportune time for the purpose of delivering the establishment in the most suitable terms, I hastened my journey and made it with some precipitation until I arrived at this city today. Here I at once learned the date designated for the transfer in spite of my absence. This reason and many others which occurred to save my responsibility compel me to hope that you may come to this place where it is convenient to overcome the difficulties which may present themselves.

The governor verbally told me that between you and me we should compose everything so that every kind of embarrassment might cease. In the face of this I must expect of you that you leave the establishment of San Luis Rey in the condition you find it, and, as I said before, at our interview in this city we shall reach an agreement with regard to the manner in which we have to proceed in this matter.[7]

To this ridiculous proposition the indignant Hartnell replied, under date of July 7, 1840, as follows:

I can not find words with which to express the supreme amazement which your strange letter of yesterday has caused me. In it you tell me that, in order to reach San Luis Rey at an opportune time for the purpose of effecting the transfer of this establishment in the most suitable terms, you hastened your journey with some precipitation until you reached the city. Of course, I do not know the nature of the business which might have detained you so long a time up there; but let it be of whatever nature it may. As already more than a month has elapsed since I set out from Monterey, it seems to me you ought to have calculated that by this time I had concluded the visit to this Mission, as in effect would have been the case if the ship on which I was coming had not delayed so long in reaching San Diego. Yet, in spite of so long a delay, very long before I received your letter, I had appointed José Antonio Estudillo mayordomo of this Mission, and on Sunday last I gave him an opportunity of becoming acquainted with these Indians, who are very much con-

---

7.*Cal. Arch., St. Pap., Mis.*, vol. xi, pp. 8-9. Bancroft Collection.

tented with said appointment. If the stock and other property of the Mission have not yet been delivered, it is because I am compelled by all means to go to Temécula. I have yielded to Andrés Pico to defer the transfer until my return, in order to afford you time to reach here to accomplish this in person.

I can in no manner accede to the request which you make to leave the Mission in the hands in which I found it, and to pass on in order to meet you at Los Angeles. Nor can I imagine how you for a moment can suppose that I, for no apparent reason whatever, should take such an absurd step.

Until now I am still vested with the authority of inspector, and meanwhile I shall exercise the functions of this most odious charge as far as I am able (which I am told will not be long) without any partiality whatever, and in spite of the consequences which may result from the duties which my conscience may dictate. Therefore, I notify you that today I set out for Temécula in company with Don Andrés (Pico). I expect to return by Thursday (he wrote this on Saturday), by which day I shall expect your arrival before turning over the property of the Mission to your successor. However, when that day has arrived, whether you come or do not come, I shall have to comply with my obligations.

As it is quite likely that you will reach this Mission during my absence, I must expect you to make no innovations whatever concerning the Mission until I return.[8]

Two weeks later Pico complained to Manuel Jimeno, the governor's secretary, who acted as governor when Alvarado was incapacitated, that the inspector general had turned over the office of mayordomo before he (Pico) could reach the Mission.[9]

Hartnell, under date of August 26, 1840, relates what occurred at the Mission and its ranchos: On the eighth of that month Pio Pico occupied himself at Mission San Luis Rey in arranging and adjusting the accounts of the subordinate mayordomos. On the ninth, after holy Mass, 168 blankets or shawls were distributed to the Indians; and later Pio Pico spoke to the Indians, telling them that the government had given him the place Temécula, notwithstanding they had always opposed him; that they should appoint four men who, empowered by them, should go to

---

8 *Cal. Arch., St. Pap., Mis.*, vol. xi, pp. 57-59.   9 Ibidem, 50, 53.

Monterey; and that he, too, would go there and show that
the Mission does not need said place. All the Indians replied
that they would not appoint anyone. Hartnell, on the other
hand, told them that he had written to the governor, and
the governor had answered that the matter should remain
in its actual condition until his arrival at Monterey. At
this the Indians expressed great satisfaction. On the 10th
the mayordomos were paid what was coming to them and
Pio Pico began to deliver the property to Estudillo. On
the 11th, Andrés Pico, on behalf of his brother, and Juan
Salazar, in the name of Estudillo, went to San Fernando

THE ANTONIO CORONEL REPRODUCTION OF THE MISSION
IN CARDBOARD

and San Jacinto, and from the declaration of some Indians
it was proved that Carlos Castro had never gone to San
Jacinto and had never counted the cattle of San Luis Rey,
but had just stated what he thought. Nor was this the
only fault he committed in the discharge of the commission
which the government had given him.

On the 17th, says Hartnell, he left San Luis Rey, and then
the Indians of Las Flores presented themselves, complaining
bitterly that the cattle of Pio Pico were doing much damage
to their little farms; for he occupied their whole territory
and even went to stop their water ditch. They pleaded that
the government command him to remove the cattle, for

otherwise they could not subsist. The Indians also wanted the Picos to be forced to vacate the dwellings of which they had possessed themselves contrary to the will of the Indians. On the 18th, Hartnell reached San Gabriel, and on the 19th he received a letter from Santiago Argüello, in which he demanded satisfaction for having been despoiled.[10]

Even after he had been removed from the management of the mission property, and in spite of the opposition of the Indians, Pio Pico in different ways persistently continued his efforts to secure possession of the Temécula Rancho; but, as a report of Joaquin de los Rios has it, "the alcalde of the Rancho de Pala, Nepomuceno by name, told him that the Capitan Juan had consulted his people on the entry of Pio Pico's cattle, and that they were unanimous in replying they would admit neither the persons of the Picos nor their cattle on said land." Rios said he knew that on said rancho the whole people were up in arms; that Capitan Juan had let him know that they were not minded to oppose the authorities, but only to prevent the Picos from taking possession of said rancho. The Indians would not cede their rights, because the rancho of Temécula was the one that produced the most grain for the Mission. Capitan Juan expected a decision on this point from the government; but the people of Temécula, though armed, were tranquil, awaiting the outcome of the matter.[11]

On the other hand, Santiago Argüello, prefect of Los Angeles, writing from Los Angeles to the mayordomo of San Luis Rey under date of September 22, 1840, declared "that on June 2 the government decreed to concede the place called Temécula provisionally to Pio Pico and his brother Andrés. He should place them in possession of said land without making any objection whatever, which had no legal foundation."[12] From what has been said it is

---

10 *Cal. Arch., St. Pap., Mis.*, vol. xi, pp. 166-168.

11 Joaquin de los Rios, November 15, 1840. *Cal. Arch., St. Pap., Mis.*, vol. x, pp. 117-122.

12 *Cal. Arch., St. Pap., Mis.*, vol. x, pp. 125-126.

clear that Argüello must have been deceived. At all events, Hartnell knew nothing of such a grant. Pico was playing a desperate game and he hoped through sheer boldness to gain his point.

Finally, on November 22, Administrator Estudillo and eleven Indians went to Los Angeles, in order to oppose the grant of the land to the Picos, resolved to quit the Mission if the grant were confirmed. Manuel Jimeno, Alvarado's secretary, on December 15, assured the Indians of Temécula that they need not be disturbed. The Indians succeeded in retaining at least partial control of the ranchos of Santa Margarita, Pala, Santa Isabél, Temécula, and San Jacinto, but not much later than 1840, according to Bancroft.

Despite the machinations, unscrupulous greed, and total disregard for the convert Indians, with whose welfare he had been entrusted, Pico yet claimed that the ex-Mission was very prosperous under his "honest and systematic management," but not so under that of his successor. Bancroft, however, quotes one Julio Cesar, who declares that "all the administrators were cruel despots, and Pico the worst of all." [13] The last clause appears, from what has been said, to be no longer open to dispute; but let us hear a foreigner and an eye-witness.

M. Eugene Duflot de Mofras, formerly an attaché of the French embassy at Madrid, under orders from the French Government, visited California in 1841-1842. He reached Monterey on April 13, 1841, and traveled through Northern California. On January 18 he arrived at San Luis Rey and remained there till the 27th. "The buildings of San Luis Rey," he writes, "are the most beautiful, the most regular, and the most solid in whole California." [14]

Of the nearly three thousand Indians, who only ten years before lived here under the shadow of the Cross, Mofras says

---

13 *California*, vol. iii, pp. 624-625.

14 "The missions of the California chain are each and every one a separate jewel, with San Luis Rey the most perfect." (Prent Duel in *Mission Architecture*, p. 29.)

he found only six hundred, and these were distributed over various rancherias.

On the subject of figures, however, Mofras is entirely wrong. It is evident that he relied too much on the *paisanos* for information regarding the past condition of the missions. "In 1834," he writes, "San Luis Rey Mission owned 80,000 head of cattle, more than 10,000 horses, and 100,000 sheep." This is a gross exaggeration, as the reader will learn from the tabular reports annexed near the close of the narrative. "Today (January or February, 1842)," Mofras declares, "the Mission has no more than 600 Indians, 2,000 head of cattle, 400 horses, and 4,000 sheep." Mofras, again relying for what he could not investigate in person on the *paisano* officials, gravely tells us that the Mission manufactured 200 barrels of wine and an equal quantity of brandy. It was said also to have raised as many as 14,000 fanégas of grain, which is also incorrect, even if all kinds of grain are meant. The produce was generally taken to the port of San Diego, to which the road was good. On a grand scale the Mission worked smithies, tanneries, soap factories, carpenter shops, weaving rooms for weaving cotton and woolen fabrics. Hemp also was produced.

"A large salt pit, the salt of which is of brilliant whiteness, is situated one league from the Mission," Mofras continues.

"The principal ranchos of the Mission are Las Flores, San Antonio de Pala, San Jacinto, Santa Margarita, Agua Caliente, San Onófrio, San José, and Temécula. They are nearly all in ruins.

"Two leagues to the north of San Luis Rey lies the Rancho of Santa Margarita, at present in the hands of someone who raises very fine grapes on it. Two leagues beyond this is the great ranch and the chapel of Las Flores, erected upon a little elevation a few hundred yards from the seashore and very picturesque in appearance.

"On the day we visited Las Flores we had occasion to marvel at the extraordinary influence which the religious

still possess over the Indians. In consequence of the perse-
cution which the Mexican authorities set on foot against the
friars, Fr. Antonio Peyri, the founder of San Luis Rey,
had quit California in 1832, personally as poor as he had
come, but leaving the Mission in a most flourishing state.
The Indians, who had all along entertained for that holy
man a respect that bordered on adoration, had with feelings
of deep regret seen him depart, for they well understood
that in him they lost their father and protector.

"A few hours after our arrival at Las Flores, the Indians,
headed by two chiefs, who bore batons as marks of authority, advanced to meet us. They were accompanied by
their families. When, according to their custom, all the
men had come forward to shake hands, the following dia-
logue took place between the first chief and myself:

" 'Captain,' the chief began, 'it is said that you come from
Spain; have you seen the king?'

" 'Yes.'

" 'Have you seen Padre Antonio?'

" 'No; but I know that he is in Barcelona.'

" 'They say that he is dead,' put in the other chief. At
this, the first speaker turned to his companion with an air
of profound incredulity and said:

" 'No, sir, that padre does not die.'

"At San Luis Rey may be seen a painting which repre-
sents Fr. Peyri surrounded by Indian children. When the
natives stop before this picture, they address to it the same
prayers which they direct to the images of the saints that
adorn the church. They have not abandoned the hope of
seeing the Father some day in their midst again.

"I was surprised at the first question of the alcalde asking
information about the king of Spain. The same subject
was the burden of our conversation with him and several
Indians, who spoke Spanish quite well and were very much
Castilian, to use an expression current in the territory.

"The Indians told me of the bad treatment to which they
were subjected by the whites. They complained that the

whites took away the little live stock which had been given to them and turned into pastures for their own herds the lands assigned to the Indians for cultivation. 'You see, Captain,' they said, 'to what misery we are reduced. The Fathers can no longer protect us, and the authorities themselves are robbing us. Is it not painful for us to see wrested from us with violence the missions which we have built; those great herds of live stock which we have raised; and after all, to find ourselves and our families constantly exposed to the worst treatment, even to death? Shall we, then, be at fault if we defend ourselves, return to our tribal relations in the Tulares, and take along all the live stock able to follow us?'

"I advised the Indians to be patient and endeavored to give them hopes, which I was far from entertaining myself. In the depth of my heart I could not refrain from admitting that reprisals from the natives would be a just reparation for the cruel and arbitrary conduct of the whites toward the Indians.

"When the management of the missions was entirely in the hands of the friars, the class of people called *de Razon* were careful not to ill-treat the Indians. It was not till after their authority had been usurped by the civil power that acts of brutality were practiced upon the Indians.

"The natives have kept in memory a sermon which Fr. Peyri preached and in which a passage ran thus: 'In our country here there are two quite distinct races; namely, the barbarians and the semi-barbarians. The semi-barbarians are our poor Indians; the barbarians are the people called *de Razon,* but who are devoid of it (gente que se llama de razon, y que no la tiene). In fact, we find among the natives docility at least and love for work, whereas among the whites we observe only a propensity for sport, idleness, and drunkenness.'

"The plan for vengeance is well laid by the Indians. They commence by stealing the horses of the *rancheros,* well aware that a Californian on foot is unable to pursue

"WE HAVE SEEN FR. GONZÁLEZ DE IBÁRRA FORCED TO SUFFER THE RUDENESS OF COWBOYS".
— MOFRAS.
SEE M. AND M. OF CAL. VOL. IV. Pg. 181.

them. Thereafter, it is easy for them to possess themselves of the cattle and finally to carry off the white women."

If the Indians fared badly, they must have been stunned at the treatment their missionary received, who, for the sake of the neophytes, submitted to the indignities. Says Mofras: "The religious at San Luis Rey is Fr. Francisco González de Ibarra, a Spaniard already advanced in years, who had been able to save some of the fragments of the Mission and to reunite four hundred Indians on the Rancho de las Flores, where they are dwelling together with one white family. The friars of San Luis Rey were reduced to the most deplorable condition. We have seen Fr. González (Ibarra) compelled to sit at the table of the administrator and to endure the rudeness of cowboys and mayordomos, who a few years before esteemed themselves happy if they could enter the service of the friars as common servants." [15]

The poor victim of Pio Pico's misrule and heartlessness, who had resided at San Luis Rey since the year 1837, perhaps earlier, was relieved of his misery some time in 1842, when he succumbed to an attack of apoplexy, it is said, but he probably died from a broken heart. Details of his last illness and death are lacking, because the Registers of San Luis Rey were either stolen or lost.

---

[15] Mofras, *Exploration*, vol. i, pp. 340-347, passim.

CHAPTER IX.

IN March 29, 1843, Manuel Micheltorena, whom the Mexican Government had appointed governor of California,
issued a decree reinstating the Franciscans in their former
positions. Accordingly, by order of March 31, 1843, Administrator José A. Estudillo of Mission San Luis Rey was
directed to take an inventory and to turn over all the
property of the Mission to Fr. José Maria Zalvidea.[1] On
April 22, Estudillo informed the governor that he had com-
plied and delivered all the property and books to the Rev.
Fr. Zalvidea.[2]

Micheltorena imposed a condition, however. . He demanded that by way of a tax the restored missions pay to
the territorial government one-eighth of the total income.
This was much more than the customary tithe, and in the
exhausted state to which the nine years of administrator
rule had reduced the establishments, it was well nigh impossible of accomplishment.[3]

Good Fr. Zalvidea was loath to burden himself again
with the management of the temporalities, and therefore

---

[1] *Missions and Missionaries*, vol. iv, p. 277; *Cal. Arch., Dep. Rec.*,
vol. xiii, p. 92.

[2] *Cal. Arch., Dep. St. Pap., Ben.*, vol. ii, pp. 1,086-1,087; *Dept. Rec.*,
vol xiii, p. 92.

[3] *Missions and Missionaries*, vol. iv, pp. 274-276.

persuaded José J. Ortega to act in his stead. Accordingly, Ortega informed the governor on April 22, 1843, that he had received from Fr. José M. Zalvidea charge of all the interests belonging to the Mission, and that he was forwarding to His Honor the inventory and other documents.[4]

On May 6, 1843, Ortega supplemented his former report by saying that the governor would see from the inventory how little or almost nothing of the property was left; that there was not grain enough on hand to maintain the neophytes for even two months; that there was a scarcity of iron implements and tools and a lack of iron to repair or restore the implements, such as plows, spades, hatchets, carpenter tools, and the forge. Then he continues:

> When Your Excellency considers that the Rev. Missionary Father, as I am working in accord with him, has placed his whole confidence in me to manage all the work and to care for the interests of this Mission; and when I reflect upon such great confidence, I am filled with affliction on finding that there are no resources to enable me to comply with the desires of the Missionary Father and with the wise intentions of Your Excellency. On the other hand, the small number of neophytes who perform the work at this Mission, and the similarly small number at the ranchos outside the Mission, are both lacking sufficient clothing, and since they know that goods are on hand, not a Sunday passes but they come to me and beg for a shirt to cover their nakedness. Will Your Excellency be pleased to direct what I shall do?

In reply, Governor Micheltorena wrote on the margin, under date of May 15, 1843:

> In accord with the Missionary Father you may sell some wine and olive oil in order to procure implements and tools, or you may secure them on credit with the pledge of the Father that the goods will be paid toward the close of the year. With regard to the destitution of the Indians, likewise in accord with the Reverend Father, you may distribute the $800 which this government commanded should be kept on deposit, one-half to the Indians of San Luis Rey, and the other half to the Indians of Pala; but you will transmit to this government an itemized account and the names of the persons to whom the things are to be distributed.[5]

---

[4] *Cal. Arch., Dep. St. Pap., Ben.*, vol. ii, pp. 1,089-1,091.
[5] *Cal. Arch., Dep. St. Pap., Ben.*, vol. ii, pp. 1,083-1,084.

The peace, which the poor neophytes enjoyed in consequence of the restoration of the Mission to the care of the
missionary and his faithful mayordomo, José Joaquin Ortega,
lasted less than two years.   Micheltorena had curbed the
greed of the young *paisano* chiefs and had prevented the
mission property from falling entirely into their hands by
his decree restoring the missions to the management of the
missionaries.   In turn, they formed a conspiracy in which
Pio Pico took the lead.   Micheltorena was driven out of the
country for the same reasons that Victoria had been forced
to leave California.   The conspirators put forth other reasons; but these were only pretexts, as the reader will find
by consulting the fourth volume of the General History.
Pio Pico himself assumed the office of governor, and from
that day the missions were doomed.   He had resolved to
wipe them out in order that the lands might fall into the
hands of white individuals.   He did wipe them out, and
this chief of the missions, San Luis Rey, suffered the same
doom.   Only a few details are extant that dimly show the
wrangle for the property and the disregard for the rights
of the Indians.

Mayordomo Ortega continued in office.   He appears to
have been one of the few who possessed some regard for
the missionaries and their wards; but he was subject to the
territorial government represented by Pio Pico, who resided
at Los Angeles, which he had made his capital.   Whether
Pico followed in the footsteps of Alvarado in disposing of
the mission goods and cattle for the benefit of the troops,
the few documents extant do not demonstrate.   Under Alvarado, orders like the following would reach the missionaries.
On February 11, 1842, Manuel Jimeno, Alvarado's secretary,
directed the person in charge of San Luis Rey to deliver
some cattle to J. Warner.   There is no mention of payment
to the Mission.[6]   On August 12, 1842, Manuel Jimeno

---

[6] *Cal. Arch., Dep. Rec.*, vol. xii, p. 167.

directed the administrator, José A. Estudillo, to seize animals
of the Mission and with them to pay his salary.[7]

From the following items the reader can draw conclusions
also as to the state of the Mission at this time in comparison
with the period when the Franciscans were in charge. On
February 1, 1841, José Estudillo, the mayordomo, reported
receipts for the preceding months to the amount of $19, and
expenditures to the amount of $52; for October, receipts
$24, expenditures $6; for November, receipts $11, expendi-
tures $5; for December, receipts $7, expenditures $4; for
January, 1842, receipts $39, expenditures $302; for February,
receipts $21, expenditures $8.[8]

In March and April, Governor Alvarado, through the
prefect of the southern district, ordered two arbitrators to
the Rancho of Santa Margarita, who should appraise the
property there, which amount the Picos were to pay to the
Indians, after the consent of the latter had been obtained
before a magistrate. The valuation was as follows: Vines,
$3,000; trees, $100; fence, $100; house, $100; total, $3,300.
The result of the whole transaction is not known. The Picos
were not in the habit of paying the rightful Indian owners
for land taken from them.

A significant item is the following. In May, 1841, five
Indians were sent to the judge at Los Angeles for stealing
Pico's cattle, after they had already worked in chains at
the secularized Mission for a month and had received *fifty*
lashes from the mayordomo, who, as Bancroft correctly says,
had no right to punish prisoners, much less in such a brutal
way. It will be remembered that under the missionaries
no Indian received more than twenty-five lashes. Yet the
mission enemies prated about humanity and freedom to the
neophytes! Instead of freedom, repeatedly promised, in
July of the same year, an order was issued to collect all
the scattered Indians without regard to the fact that the

---

[7] *Ibidem*, p. 191.

[8] *Cal. Arch., St. Pap., Mis.,* vol. ix, p. 50. Banc. Coll.—Bancroft, vol.
iv, p. 623.

neophytes had been dispersed through the inhumanity and greed of the *paisano* chiefs and their henchmen.[9]

In 1844 there was little property left. At all events, the mayordomo, Ortega, was tired of his position, as Fr. Duran informs Governor Pico. He writes:

As regards Mission San Luis Rey, taking into consideration that the present mayordomo wishes to withdraw and that a missionary is still there who has some shadow of authority, and considering his difficult position and also that of the Mission, about which I have been informed, my opinion is that, the accounts having been rendered, another mayordomo be appointed by Your Excellency, subject in his accounts and undertakings to the nearest missionary, who is the one of San Diego. I can find no other expedient. Fr. José M. Zalvidea will do a great deal if he attends only to the spiritual matters; but to give him charge of the temporal affairs would be to shorten his days.— Fr. Narciso Duran.—To Pio Pico, Governor, May 16, 1845.[10]

At the time of this writing, Pico was big with an altogether different plan, and only twelve days later he had his so-called Departmental Assembly execute it. This was nothing less than the "Renting of Some of the Missions and the Converting of Other Missions Into Pueblos or Towns." For details regarding this iniquitous measure, for which Pico had no warrant from the Supreme Government of Mexico, the reader is referred to the fourth volume of the General History.[11]

José J. Ortega, the mayordomo, having insisted on his resignation, Juan Maria Marron, it appears, was appointed to take his place until Pico had accomplished his object to the full, as will be seen presently. At all events, Ortega, on July 20, 1845, delivered the mission and property to Marron after the inventory had been drawn up.[12] Marron, whose salary was to be $300, received from Ortega, as the inventory shows, 279 horses, 20 mules, 61 asses, 196 head

---

9 Bancroft, vol. iv, pp. 323-324.
10 Pico, *Documentos*, vol. ii, pp. 46-47. Banc. Coll.
11 *Missions and Missionaries*, vol. iv, pp. 373-375.
12 *Cal. Arch., St. Pap., Missions*, vol. xi, p. 59. Banc. Coll.

of cattle, 27 yoke of oxen, 700 sheep, some implements and other effects of slight value.[13]

Meanwhile, another aspirant for Indian property had been on the alert. This was M. Pedrorena, who demanded the grant of the Rancho of Pala; but on June 26, 1845, Pico notified him that Pala could not be granted to him, because it belonged to the Indians of San Luis Rey.[14] It is scarcely probable that Pico stated the true reason for this refusal. Temécula also belonged to the Indians; but that did not deter him from trying to secure possession of it, nor from doing worse to the whole property of the Indians, as we shall have to relate now.

On October 28, 1845, Pico at last published his illegal decree for the *Sale and Leasing of the Missions,* which the reader will find in the fourth volume of the General History.[15] Regardless of the wishes of the rightful owners, some of the missions were to be sold at auction, and others were to be leased. The renting of San Luis Rey was yet postponed, until certain difficulties, not specified, were removed. It was Don Pio Pico's day of triumph.

Finally, on May 18, 1846, despite the express prohibition of the Mexican Government, dated Mexico, November 14, 1845, Governor Pico sold Mission San Luis Rey, which he had brought to the verge of bankruptcy, and from which he had been discharged for mismanagement of property and ill treatment of Indians. The purchasers were José A. Cot and José A. Pico, who received a full conveyance of the property of Mission San Luis Rey, including the Rancho of Pala, in consideration of $2,000 in silver and $437.50 in grain, to be delivered to the government of Pico, and under

---

13 Bancroft, vol. iv, p. 624.—Compare this with the last report of the Fathers.

14 *Cal. Arch., St. Pap., Mis. & Colon.,* vol. ii, p. 416. Bancroft Collection.

15 *Missions and Missionaries,* vol. iv, pp. 445-450.

INTERIOR OF CHURCH AT SAN LUIS REY MISSION

the condition that they pay the debts.[16]   The sale of this property was later declared null and void by the United States Court, on the ground that Pico had no right to sell it.[17]   With regard to Mission San Luis Rey, it could not be proved that the deed had been made out at Los Angeles, as was claimed.[18]

Fr. Zalvidea survived Pico's decree of confiscation, but he had already grown very feeble in 1843, insomuch that on February 17, 1843, he was unable to acknowledge a letter he received from Fr. Prefecto Duran.   Mayordomo Estudillo wrote in reply and Fr. Zalvidea signed with trembling hand, as is clearly noticeable.[19]   At times, he would rally, however.   It was on such an occasion that he signed and acknowledged the receipt of Fr. Duran's Circular of April 18, 1843, communicating Micheltorena's decree that restored the Missions to the Fathers.   He signed it on

SIGNATURE OF FR. ZALVIDEA

May 8, 1843.   It is the last time he signed his name with a fairly strong hand, as may be seen from the accompanying illustration.   Once more he was called upon to affix his name with the customary acknowledgments to a circular. This was the joint letter of Fathers Duran and Gonzáles, notifying the clergy in the territory that the Rt. Rev. Bishop had appointed them Vicars-General.   It was dated April

---

16 *Missions and Missionaries*, vol. iv, p. 507; *Cal. Arch., Unbound Documents*, p. 278.   Banc. Coll.

17 See *Missions and Missionaries*, vol. iv, pp. 723 et seq.

18 *Cal. Arch., Unbound Documents*, pp. 277-279.   Banc. Coll.—Compare *Missions and Missionaries*, vol. iv, pp. 746-771.—The deed of sale itself is nowhere to be found.

19 *De la Guerra Papers*, Santa Barbara.

20, 1846, and it reached San Luis Rey in May; but Fr. Zalvidea was unable to do more than scribble his name under that of Fr. Esténaga of San Gabriel, whence it had come to San Luis Rey. The letters tell their story plainly enough. Indeed, Fr. Zalvidea passed to his eternal reward only a few weeks later, in the month of June, thus outliving Bishop García Diego by perhaps six weeks and Fr. Duran by about two or three weeks, as the Bishop died on April 30, and Fr. Duran on June 1, 1846.

Henceforth, facts about the Mission are still more fragmentary. When the armies of the United States took possession of the country, Pio Pico, on August 10, 1846, fled from Los Angeles to Mexico. On his way he tarried secretly, for about a month, in the vicinity of Mission San Juan Capistrano and the rancho of Santa Margarita, which he had made his own. On September 7, 1846, he escaped across the border into Lower California.[20] On July 24, before disappearing from California, when the United States authorities had already assumed control, Pico ordered administrator Marron to deliver, by inventory, all the interests, lands, and appurtenances of Mission San Luis Rey in his charge to the purchasers, José A. Cot and José A. Pico.[21] John Forster of San Juan Capistrano claimed that he took possession for the purchasers and then left Marron in charge for Cot and Pico.[22]

In August, Captain J. C. Fremont, whom Commodore Stockton had appointed military commander of California, put John Bidwell in charge. Bidwell himself relates:

I was appointed by Fremont as magistrate of the district of San Luis Rey, and directed to take possession of the Mission and to make an inventory of the property, caring for the same, examining into the title to the property, protect the Indians and so on. During all this time (Flores and Pico revolt, in 1846) my situation at San Luis Rey, without any force to protect me, was by no means comfortable. * *

---

[20] Bancroft, vol. v, pp. 278-279.
[21] *Cal. Arch., St. Pap., Missions*, vol. xi, p. 53. Banc. Coll.
[22] Bancroft, vol. v, p. 620

No neighbor among the California population could be depended on for information or assistance.

The Indians, however, were faithful. It was not long after I went to San Luis Rey before owners of ranches came to reclaim Indians, asking me to command them to return to their service, generally on the ground of indebtedness and of their right to make the demand, because of the laws and customs of the country which obtained under the Mexican rule. The applications were invariably refused by me and highly appreciated by the Indians. In a word, the Indians, by this course, had become my friends and they were friendly to our American cause. They were willing to take up arms and fight against the Californians, upon whom they looked as oppressors; but I had nothing with me with which to arm them.

The Indians at the Mission of San Luis Rey were by no means wild and untutored. They had lived, many, if not most of them, at the Mission from infancy, and had been taught to do all kinds of work by Padre Antonio Peyri, the founder of the Mission. Him they loved with a friendship truly wonderful.

When the achievement of her independence by Mexico brought about a new order of things in California, it required but little sagacity to see the downfall of all those missions, and that in the no distant future. This priest, so loved by the Indians, rather than wait to see the beautiful Mission, which he had erected, destroyed, resolved to leave California forever and return to Europe.[23] But the Indians would not suffer him to go, and they watched him for weeks to prevent his leaving. In a dark night at last Peyri succeeded in eluding the friendly vigilance of the Indians, and embarking at San Diego on board the vessel which was to bear him from the coast. From one who aided him in his escape, it was told that on gaining the high hill in front of the Mission he looked back, knelt down and made a prayer blessing the Mission.

I found the Indians very intelligent; most could speak the Spanish tongue fluently. Some could read. One, a chief, named Samuel, was not only fluent, but eloquent, and no Mexican to my knowledge had so fine a command of the Spanish language.[24]

Bidwell had to retire in October on approach of hostile Californians, who seem to have tarried around the Mission until General Kearny and Commodore Stockton took the

---

[23] The real motive for the departure of Fr. Peyri has been stated in a previous chapter. Fr. Peyri would never have abandoned the Indians, whom he loved as well as they loved him, had not obedience directed him to present the cause of the missions to the Mexican Government.

[24] Bidwell, *California*, pp. 183-187. Banc. Coll.

place in January, 1847. It was during the month of December, 1846, that eleven men were massacred at the Pauma rancho above Pala by a band of Cahuila Indians and some ex-neophytes of San Luis Rey. The Indians were instigated by one William Marshall, who was afterwards hanged for the offense.[25]

The troops of the United States under Kearny and Stockton arrived at the Mission in the beginning of the next year, 1847. Major W. H. Emory, in his description of the march, writes:

January 2.—Six and a half miles march (from Buena Vista) brought us to the deserted Mission of San Luis Rey. The keys of the Mission were in charge of the alcalde of the Indian village, a mile distant. He was at the door to receive us and delivered up possession. There we halted for the day to let the sailors, who suffered dreadfully from sore feet, recruit a little. This building is one which, for magnitude, convenience, and durability of architecture, would do honor to any country. The walls are of adobe, and the roofs of well-made tile. It was built about sixty years since [26] by the Indians of the country, under the guidance of a zealous priest. At that time the Indians were very numerous, and under the absolute sway of the missionaries. These missionaries at one time bid fair to Christianize the Indians of California. * * * The avarice of the military rulers of the territory, however, soon converted these missions into instruments of oppression and slavery of the Indian race. The revolution (confiscation) of 1836 saw the downfall of the priests, and most of these missions passed by fraud into the hands of private individuals, and with them the Indians were transferred as serfs of the land. This race is in that degraded condition throughout California, and do the only labor performed in the country. Nothing can exceed their present degraded condition. For negligence to work, the lash is freely applied, and in many instances life has been taken by the Californians without being held accountable by the laws of the land.

The Mission of San Luis Rey was, until the invasion of California by the Americans, in 1846, considered (by the so-called Californians) as public property. Just before that event took place, a sale was made of it, for a small consideration, by the Mexican (Californian) authorities, to some of their people, who felt their power passing away, and wished to turn an *honest penny* whilst their power was left; but this

---

[25] Banc. v, p. 567.
[26] Just forty-nine years, at that time.

MISSION SAN LUIS REY FROM THE NORTHWEST

sale was undoubtedly fraudulent [27] and will, I trust, not be acknowledged by the American Government. Many other missions have been transferred in the same way; and the new government of California must be very pure in its administration to avoid the temptation which those fictitious sales, made by the retiring Mexican (rather *paisano*) authorities, offer for accumulating large fortunes at the expense of the Government. The lands belonging to this Mission are extensive, well watered, and very fertile. It is said, and I believe it probable from appearances, that wheat will grow in the valleys adjacent without irrigation.

January 3.—After marching a few miles the wide Pacific opened to our view. We passed the Santa Margarita ranchería, once a dependency of San Luis Rey, now in possession of the Pico family. We encamped near Las Flores, a deserted mission (station). Just below it, and near the ocean, is an Indian village.

January 4.—After leaving Las Flores a few miles, the high broken ground projects close in upon the sea, leaving but a narrow, uneven banquette, along which the road winds through a growth of chapparal. Here we met three persons bearing a flag of truce. They brought a letter from Flores, who signed himself governor and captain general of the department of California, proposing to suspend hostilities in California, and leave the battle to be fought elsewhere between the United States and Mexico, upon which was to depend the fate of California. The commission returned with a peremptory refusal of the proposition.[28]

After going nine miles from (Las) Flores, the high land impinges so close upon the sea that the road lies along the sea beach for a distance of eight miles. Fortunately for us the tide was out, and we had the advantage of a hard, smooth road.[29]

About January 22, 1847, Emory, back on his way to San Diego, writes:

We reached the Mission of San Luis Rey, and found not a human being stirring. The immense pile of building, illuminated by the pale cold rays of the moon, stood out in bold relief on the dim horizon, a monument of the zeal of the indefatigable priests by whom it was built. Now untenanted and deserted, it offered no resting place for the weary and hungry, and we rode on, determined to halt at the first place where grass should be in abundance. The road here divided into two branches; one leads to the west by the ranchería of San Bernardo, the other directly to San Diego over the high lands run-

---

[27] Emory is the first to express this judgment in words. It was later ratified by the United States courts.

[28] *Missions and Missionaries,* vol. iv, pp. 567-577.

[29] Emory, 116-117.

ning nearly parallel to the sea coast. * * * The only habitation on the road from San Luis Rey to San Diego is a hut half way, where there is a good spring.[30]

A week later, another body of United States troops took up their quarters at Mission San Luis Rey. This was the Battalion of Mormon Volunteers. Daniel Tyler, their Elder, writes:

> On the first of October, 1847, the Battalion took up the line of march for San Luis Rey, where we arrived about noon on the 3rd. On the 4th, about eighty men were detailed as police to clear up the square and quarters, and make necessary repairs, which was done in good order, making everything look as cheerful and respectable as our dirt floors would permit.
>
> The public square of the Mission, with a large adobe Catholic Church and a row of minor buildings forming the outside wall, contained about four acres of ground, with orange and other tropical trees in the center. The olive, pepper, orange, fig and ornamental trees grew in the garden. There was also a large reservoir, used for bathing, washing clothes and watering the garden. Two large vineyards were also connected with this Mission.

Elder Tyler would preach there on Sundays. The Battalion remained apparently till April 12, 1847, when they marched to El Cajon Pass.[31]

For some reason or other the military commander of the district found it wise to retain soldiers at San Luis Rey. He accordingly despatched the following order to Captain Daniel C. Davis at San Diego:

> Headquarters Southern Military District, California.
>
> Santa Barbara, August 4, 1847.
>
> Sir: You will immediately, upon the receipt of this, post at the Mission of San Luis Rey twenty-seven men of your company, with one sergeant and one corporal, the whole under the command of Lieutenant Barrus, who will take charge of and prevent any depredations being committed upon the Mission property. The detachment will remain at that post until further orders from the district headquarters. You will receive by this mail a garrison flag, which please return receipt for.
>
> J. D. STEVENSON.
> Commanding S. M. District,
> California.

---

[30] Emory, pp. 123-124. [31] *The Mormon Battalion*, pp. 263-264; 267; 277.

Captain Davis in turn issued the following order to Lieutenant R. Barrus:

Military Post at San Diego,
August 9, 1847

Second Lieutenant R. Barrus, Mormon Volunteers, will proceed tomorrow, 10th instant, at 2 p. m., with twenty-seven men and one sergeant and one corporal to San Luis Rey, and take charge of the Mission and all other public property there, and prevent any depredation being committed by the Indians or others upon the same, and will report to me by every mail anything that transpires which at all affects the public good. You will be vigilant and act with prudence and discretion in the performance of your duties. You will make requisition upon the quartermaster for twenty days' provisions. The wagon and team which transports the provisions, etc., you will retain at the Mission until further orders.

DANIEL C. DAVIS,
Captain Commanding,
San Diego.[32]

In July, Governor Mason resolved to establish an Indian sub-agency for the Indians of Southern California, and to locate the agent at one of the missions. At the recommendation of Colonel Stevenson, he named Captain Hunter, of the late Mormon Battalion, sub-agent with headquarters at Mission San Luis Rey. The appointment and instructions were contained in the following communication:

Headquarters, Tenth Military Department
Santa Barbara, California,
August 1, 1847.

Sir: I enclose to you herewith the appointment as sub-Indian agent for the lower district of Upper California, and more especially for the district of the country in and about the Mission of San Luis Rey. This appointment invests you with a wide range of discretionary powers, and Colonel Mason wishes to impress upon you the great importance of your office, and the great good that will result to the people of that district from a prudent and mild, yet determined, course of conduct.

You will establish yourself at or near the Mission of San Luis Rey, and at the earliest moment practicable make a correct inventory of property belonging to that Mission—such as farms, horses, cattle,

---

[32] *The Mormon Battalion*, pp. 328-329.

MISSION SAN LUIS REY FROM THE NORTHEAST

and every species of property; a copy of which inventory you will send to headquarters.

You will then consider yourself the agent for that property, so as effectually to guard it from abuse or destruction, and more especially to see that *no damage or desecration is offered to the church or any other religious fixture.*

You will take a protective charge of all the Indians living at the Mission, and in the neighborhood, to draw them gradually to habits of order. You will likewise endeavor to reclaim such as formerly belonged to the Mission, and persuade them to return,[33] to restore it to its former prosperity. To do this, you can maintain them and their families at the mission, but in no event contract a debt, or go beyond the resources of the property of which you have the charge.

You will make such rules for the government of the Indians as you deem suitable for their condition, so as to prevent their committing any depredations upon others, or leading an idle, thriftless life. You will endeavor to prevent their going about in crowds, and make them receive from yourself a written paper when they desire to go any distance from their houses or rancherías,[34] setting forth that they are under your protection, etc. Much, however, is left to your own good sense and judgment to reclaim the old mission Indians to habits of industry, and, if possible, to draw in the wild ones, too, and protect them in their lives and true interests, and to prevent them from encroaching in any way upon the peaceable inhabitants of the land.

Frequent communication upon all subjects of interest is requested, both to the commanding officer at Los Angeles and to these headquarters. A small force will probably be sent to assist you in maintaining your authority.[35]

Your salary will be seven hundred and fifty dollars a year, payable quarterly to yourself by the quartermaster at Los Angeles.

I have the honor to be your most obedient servant,

W. T. SHERMAN,[36]

First Lieutenant, Third Artillery, A. A. A. G.

J. D. HUNTER, Late Captain, Mormon Battalion,
Santa Barbara, California.[37]

---

[33] Compare these rational directions with the tactics of Echeandia and the young Californians from Alvarado to Pio Pico.

[34] When the friars practiced this system, the mission enemies called it slavery.

[35] An instance, showing that the United States officials actually adopted the mission system in vogue under Spanish rule, except that the salaried agent took the place of the unsalaried friar.

[36] The later General Sherman of Civil War fame.

[37] *Missions and Missionaries*, vol. iv, pp. 594-595.

CHAPTER X.

Gentlemanly Officers. — Governor Mason's Orders. — J. B. Charbonneau, Alcalde.—Indian Laborers and Their Wages.—A Dramshop. —Amazing Account.—Sentenced to Labor for Liquor Debt.— Certificate of Alcalde.—Governor Mason's Proclamation Against Liquor.—A Month of Booze.—Military Correspondence.—Bartlett's Description of the Mission.

IT is worthy of note, and a pleasure for us to relate, that the military officers of the army of the United States, who took possession of California, were singularly free from intolerance and bigotry. Of course, they had orders from President Polk to respect the religious sensibilities of the inhabitants; but, apart from this, they appear to have been true gentlemen, so that the Catholics had no reason for complaint. In fact, the kind and considerate ways of the United States officers and even of the soldiers under them stood out in marked contrast to the overbearing manner of the *paisano* chiefs and of their henchmen. Such treatment as Fr. Ibarra, for instance, experienced here in San Luis Rey at the hands of the Picos would have been out of the question with even the least gentlemanly of the United States officials. As a sample of the consideration the priests met with at the hands of the officers, from the highest to the lowest, the following letter will be enlightening:

Headquarters, Tenth Military Department,
Santa Barbara, California,
August 2, 1847.

Sir: Should any of the Catholic priests come to the Mission of San Luis Rey, either to locate there permanently, or for the performance of any of their religious duties, you will not only cause them to be treated with great courtesy and kindness, but they are to have any of the apartments they desire,[1] and any product of the mission or mission farms for their own use, and the entire management of the

---

[1] With this compare the assumption of the administrator twelve years before. See *supra*, chapter vi.

Indians, so far as it relates to their connection with the Mission and Mission farms, the only object in placing you in charge of the Mission and its property being to guard it from desecration and waste.

I am, Sir, very respectfully, your obedient servant,

R. B. MASON,

Colonel 1st Dragoons, Governor of California.

Captain J. D. Hunter, Sub-Indian Agent, present.[2]

In consequence of this wise and conciliatory policy inaugurated by the United States authorities, peace and confidence prevailed all over the territory. As might have been expected, life at San Luis Rey soon took on another aspect. *Paisano* rule had lain like an incubus on the poor and helpless Mission Indians. Now when they observed that they were to be no longer victimized and exploited for the benefit of indolent and heartless masters, they willingly yielded to the efforts of Captain Hunter for the improvement of their conditions. Under date of January 31, 1848, for instance, the captain reported with excusable gratification that he had been raising a crop of wheat on the mission farm at Pala, and had induced the Indians to do the same on their own account.[3]

According to Bancroft,[4] Colonel Stevenson on September 1, 1847, reported to Governor Mason that the Indians were pleased with the appointment of Hunter as sub-agent, that they had raised grain enough to satisfy their needs, and that their settlement showed more evidence of comfort than most of the ranchos of the rich Californians. On November 24, 1847, Governor Mason requested J. A. Pico to turn over to Hunter any Mission property in his possession, and to furnish an inventory of all such property that might have been at any time in his possession. A week later, on December 1, Mason wrote to Hunter regarding the conciliatory measures to be adopted with J. J. Warner and the

---

[2] Ex. Doc. No. 17, 31st Congress, 1st Session (Halleck's Report, p. 348). See *Missions and Missionaries*, vol. iv, pp. 595-596.

[3] *Cal. Arch, Unbound Documents*, pp. 62-63. Banc. Coll.

[4] *California*, vol. v, p. 621.

Indians whose land Warner claimed, so as to keep the Indians quiet, and leave the question of title for the courts to decide.

On November 24, 1847, when requesting J. A. Pico to surrender the property, Governor Mason sent to Colonel Stevenson a blank appointment for alcalde of the district to be filled out with the name of J. B. Charbonneau, one of the guides of the Mormon Battalion, or with any other name. Stevenson named Charbonneau, who served till August, 1848, when he offered his resignation on the ground that, being a halfbreed himself, he was thought to favor the Indians too much. His resignation was accepted, and Stevenson suggested that the expenses of Charbonneau's office should be paid from the civil fund, since the alcaldes served without pay.[5]

Most probably, Charbonneau was induced to resign his office for reasons other than he offered to the governor. Lately, the Account Book for the year 1847 was discovered at Mission San Juan Capistrano and turned over to the writer through the courtesy of the Pastor, the Rev. St. John O'Sullivan. It contains about ninety folio pages filled with the accounts of individuals who made purchases from day to day at the general store and dramshop of José Antonio Pico at San Luis Rey. The customers appear to have been in most cases Indian laborers whose wages were $3 a month or 12½ cents a day. This, we presume, was given them in addition to board, although there is nothing to show it. Two Americans also appear in the account; but these received $20 a month for helping to construct a building, which fact suggests that they were carpenters. They received their wages in cash. It was different with most or nearly all other workmen. These secured cash only in very small amounts, if at all. The very first individual whose account for 1847 covers more than a page was a

---

[5] *Cal. Arch., Unbound Documents*, pp. 364-365. Banc. Coll. See, also, Bancroft, *California*, vol. v, p. 621.

certain Flujencio. His real name was doubtless Fulgencio. He begins to receive goods from the store and liquor shop of José Antonio Pico on January 8, 1847. This account is so interesting and illuminating that we offer no apology for reproducing it.

1847   Flujencio, su sueldo 3 ps. al mes

		Pesos	Reales
Eno 8............Agte (Aguardiente—Brandy or			
	whisky	......	2
	Agte	......	4
Eno 12...........Bino (Vino—Wine)		......	2
	4 varas manta azul (blue cotton		
	shirting)	......	1
Eno 13...........Bino		......	1
Febr. 1...........Agte			3
Febr. 4...........Agte			6
Febr. 6...........Agte			1
Febr. 7...........Agte			3
Febr. 13..........Agte		1	0
Febr. 20..........Agte			4
	Agte		1
Marzo 19.........Agte			1
21.........Agte			1
Marzo 21.........en plata (silver)............			4
28.........Agte			2
Abril 4...........Agte			2
Abril 10..........Bino			1
Abril 17..........Un queso			2
Mayo 8...........Bino			1
15.........Bino			1
Junio 2...........Bino		1	4
Junio 5...........Agte		1	0
	Un queso	......	2
Junio 13..........Agte		......	3
	Bino	......	?
July 3............Agte			4
	Sigarros		1
July 6............Un cuarto de carne...........			4
July 10..........Bino			7
	en plata	......	4

		Pesos	Reales
July 16........... Agte			1
July 17........... Bino y plata			4
July 19........... Bino			1
July 20........... Bino			1
July 31........... Bino			4
August 7.........Bino			2
en plata			4
August 9.........Una camiseta		3	0
August 12........en plata en S. Diego............			2
en pan			1
Bino			1
August 14........Bino			4
August 21........Bino			4
en plata			2
Se desertó el 22 de idem		12	87½
1846 Sigue Flujencio			

		Pesos	Reales
May 10...........Agte			6
May 12...........Un cuarte de carne..............		1	0
Agte			1
Agte			2
Agte		1	2
Agte			2
Agte			1
May 18........... Agte			1
May 24........... Agte			1
May 31........... Agte		1	0
June 7...........Agte			2
June 11...........Agte			1
June 13...........Agte			2
June 17...........Bino			5
June 27........... Bino			3
July 14........... Bino			3
July 19........... Bino			6
July 31........... Bino			6
August 3.........Bino			2
August 9.........Una Camisa			?
August 11........Bino			3
August 16........en plata		1	0
Bino			2

	Pesos	Reales
August 25........Bino	....	2
August 28........Bino	....	2
August 30........Una Carne	....	1
Flujencio left August 30, se presentó Sept 23 y		
Septiembre 26......Bino	....	6
Octobre 4........ Bino	....	4
Octobre 6........ Bino	....	1
Octobre 9........ Bino	....	1
Octobre 13....... Bino	....	1
Octobre 15....... Bino	....	2
Octobre 16....... Bino	....	2
Octobre 21........ Bino	....	2
Mayo 4.......... Una Frezada el al (?) Al Feno (?)	....	2
	9	62½

Flujencio, Dr.
To Don José Ant. Pico

A. D. 1846
A. D. 1847

Amount of Acct. for years 1846
1847

109.87½
By Services   58.50

Balance due   51.37½ to be paid in work at the rate of
12½c per Day until the debt paid.

P. B. CHARBONNEAU,
Alc.6

This is to certify that Flujencio after a fair settlement it appears a balance due José Ant. Pico of fifty one Dollars and Thirty seven

---

6 It is significant that the following dates were Saturdays and Sundays in 1846 and 1847:—*Saturdays in 1846:* June 13, 27; September 26. *Sundays in 1846:* May 10, 24, 31; June 7; July 19; August 9, 16, 30; October 4. *Saturdays in 1847:* February 6, 13, 20; April 10, 17; May 8, 15; June 5; July 3, 10, 17, 31; August 7, 14, 21. *Sundays in 1847:* February 7; March 21, 28; April 4; June 13.—From this the reader will see that Pico's dramshop was open for the sale of liquor especially on Saturdays and Sundays. Pico's dramshop was located in the front wing of the Mission building of San Luis Rey, three doors from the church.

and a half cents. All Acct. settled before me at this office at St. Louis Rey April 24th, 1848.

P. B. CHARBONNEAU, Alc.

I, P. B. Charbonneau do sentence Flujencio to work in the service of Don José Ant. Pico at the rate of twelve and a half Cents per Day, until he (Flujencio) has paid said debt.

At this Magistrate's office S. Louis Rey
April 24th 1848
P. B. CHARBONNEAU
Alcalde

We can now very well understand why Charbonneau wanted to resign the office of the Justice of Peace. It was distasteful for a decent man to sentence helpless Indians to slavery in order that they might pay for the liquor received in excess of the 12½ cents, their day's wages for labor. If the Indian had a family, what of the wife and children?

How José Antonio Pico figured in order to make Flujencio's debt amount to $109.87½ is incomprehensible. There is nothing more in the book than the wretched liquor accounts of 1846 and 1847, which shows an indebtedness of only $22.50. Nevertheless, the poor Indian is held in slavery until he pays the balance, $51.37½, by laboring at one real or 12½ cents per day! Meanwhile, he will want other goods from the store of Pico and so he will never emerge from debt and from slavery. This is not an isolated case. The book has many similar accounts, though none are as bad as Flujencio's, on whose weakness the dram-shop-keeper appears to have speculated, as many a saloon-keeper did until prohibition stopped the sordid traffic. In consequence of the dreadful havoc that the use of intoxicants created among the Indians, Governor Mason, on November 29, 1847, issued the following Proclamation:

From and after the first day of January, 1848, if any person shall sell, exchange, give, barter, or dispose of, or in any way connive at. selling, exchanging, giving, bartering, or disposing of any spirituous liquor or wine to an Indian, such person shall, upon conviction before an alcalde, forfeit and pay the sum of not less than fifty nor more than one hundred dollars, and be imprisoned for not less than three

FACSIMILE OF CHARBONNEAU'S ORDER

nor more than six months. One-half of all fines recovered under this proclamation shall go to the benefit of the informer, and the other half to the benefit of the town or jurisdiction where the prisoner may be confined; and in all prosecutions arising under this proclamation, Indians shall be competent witnesses.[7]

From this the charge that in many places the rancheros, who were by no means all Americans, paid the Indian laborers in brandy or whiskey is proved beyond a doubt. Nor did the nefarious practice cease with the year 1846. A scrap of paper which lay in the afore-mentioned Account Book of José Antonio Pico, and on which the entries were evidently made by the same hand, dates from the year 1845, before Pio Pico had sold the Mission. This scrap of paper reads as follows:

Orosco el Tejedor (Orosco the Weaver), 1845.

Tiene apercibido	Pesos	Reales
Una botella Aguardiente (one bottle of Whisky-brandy)	1	4
En idem.....Aguardiente		4
Octobre ....Aguardiente		3
En idem.....Aguardiente		1
En 6 de idem....Aguardiente, un cuarto		6
En idem.....Tabaco		2
En aguardiente		2
En 10 de idem...Aguardiente		4
En tabaco		1
En 24 de idem...Bino		3
En idem.....Bino		2
En idem.....Bino		3
En 29 de idem...Bino		1
En 31 de idem...Bino		4
First of November, Sabado, Un sarape de José Maria..	4	0

Despite Mason's proclamation, the Indians and Mexicans secured the liquor. In his whole missionary career, the writer has never heard that a whisky Indian turned in-

[7] See *Missions and Missionaries*, vol. iv, p. 641, where "not less than *three*" (dollars) should read "not less than *fifty*" (dollars).

RESULT OF MISSION CONFISCATION:—INDIANS DRUNK ON THE ROAD LEADING FROM EX-MISSION SAN LUIS REY TO OCEANSIDE. (ACTUAL SCENE.)

former against a liquor dispenser. The engraving accompanying this depicts a scene near Mission San Luis Rey more than forty years after the mission period. The artist vouches for its accuracy, since he himself witnessed the scene. There was a liquor store close by. Every Saturday the poor Indians could gratify their uncontrollable cravings to the last cent. This in a measure accounts for the disappearance of the natives. Happy those Indians who lived in the sierras away from the temptation and from the unscrupulous whisky seller.

The following correspondence explains itself:

> Headquarters, Tenth Military Department,
> Monterey, California,
> December 17, 1848.

Sir:—Your note of this day, asking to be absent for six months from your duties of sub-Indian Agent, is received. The leave asked for is granted with the understanding that Mr. William Williams will take charge of the Mission of San Luis Rey, so that it will sustain no damage, and act as sub-agent for you during your absence.

I am, etc.,

> R. B. MASON,
> Col. 1st Drag., Gov. of Cal.

CAPT. J. D. HUNTER,
  Sub-Indian Agent.[8]

> State Department of the Territory of California,
> Monterey, March 2, 1849.

Sir:—Governor Mason directs that, on the arrival of the United States troops at the Mission of San Luis Rey, the sub-agent at that place will turn over to the commanding officer all public property and official papers in his possession. His pay shall cease on the day of his being relieved from the duties of his office by the arrival of the troops. Very Resp., etc.,

> H. W. HALLECK,
> Brevet Captain and Secretary of State.

CAPT. J. D. HUNTER,
  Sub-Indian Agent,
    San Luis Rey, California.[9]

General Persifor F. Smith, who for a while succeeded Colonel Mason as governor, wrote on March 15, 1849, to Adjutant General R. Jones at Washington:

---

[8] *Halleck's Report*, p. 681. [9] *Halleck's Report*, p. 697.

I propose to place the greater part of the 2d Infantry in the southern part of the Territory, as furthest removed from the mines, and near the frontiers; its headquarters at San Luis Rey, where the buildings of the Mission are most commodious, and the country most abundant in supplies of forage and food; to garrison San Diego, Warner's Pass, the outlet to Lower California and Sonora; and as soon as possible to establish a post at the mouth of the Gila, not only to facilitate traveling to and from New Mexico, but to prepare for the boundary commission. San Luis Rey is well situated to communicate with these places, and to supply them.[10]

The proposition mentioned by General Smith in the above communication was made by Captain Halleck in a letter to Governor Mason, dated March 1, 1849. He wrote:

As there are no barracks at San Diego, it will be necessary to station troops at San Luis Rey, where they will serve the double purpose of a garrison at San Diego and a lookout to guard the several passes from Lower California and Sonora by the Colorado and the Gila rivers. It is said that Don Antonio José Cot has a claim to this Mission under a grant by Pio Pico; but as titles of this kind have already been discussed, it is unnecessary to resume their examination here.[11]

John Russell Bartlett, a member of the United States Boundary Commission, writes, early in May, 1852: "I made a brief visit to the Mission of San Luis Rey, forty miles north of San Diego. This is the latest of all the California Missions, and was founded in 1798. It stands in a rich valley, from one or two miles wide, and is about three miles from the ocean, being separated therefrom by a range of hills. Of all the missionary establishments in the State, this possesses the most extensive as well as the most imposing structure. It is built of adobe, although stone and brick are used in some portions of it. It faces the south, and has a front of 530 feet, the greater portion of which exhibits a colonade of some architectural beauty, although but sixteen or eighteen feet high. On the front is also a church ninety feet in depth, with a tower and dome. North

---

[10] *Halleck's Report*, p. 711. On page 713 he writes in the same letter, ''Lumber sells at $600 per thousand feet.''
[11] *Halleck's Report*, p. 132.

and south, the dimensions are upwards of six hundred feet. This vast space included everything that appertained to the Mission. On the southeast corner is a small Campo Santo. Next comes the church with the priests' apartments immediately adjoining and a small inclosure or garden, shut in by the church walls on one side and by the main building on the other. This garden was handsomely laid out, and still contains a variety of fruit and ornamental trees. In the interior is an open area of the same dimensions, with a beautiful colonade all around. In the center of this was a garden; but the only plant of interest that remains is a pepper tree.[12] This stands in the circular bed elevated four or five feet above the area, and is protected by a wall.

"On the four sides of this extensive area are double rows of apartments, some of which are very large, including reception rooms, dining halls, sleeping apartments, kitchen, etc. In the rear were corrals or inclosures for cattle; so that everything appertaining to this vast establishment might be brought within its walls. It is all in a good state of preservation except the northwest corner of the area, where the roof has fallen in. Some of the cattle yards and stables are also out of repair; but the church, and nearly all the apartments occupied for dwellings, are still habitable. * * * Its ownership will be settled by the Board of Land Commissioners appointed by the United States Government. In the meantime General Hitchcock, commanding the Pacific Division of the U. S. Army, has placed a file of soldiers here, to protect the property and keep off plunderers and squatters.

"I remained here two nights, accompanied by Dr. Webb and Mr. Pratt, artist of the Commission, and was hospitably entertained by the Sergeant in charge; the officer in command being absent in San Diego. In such a place as this, with such a range of buildings and cultivated grounds, a

---

12 It is said that a sailor from Peru, in 1830, brought a sprig of a pepper tree and planted it in the Mission garden. This was the first of its kind in California.

MISSION VIEWED FROM WEST THROUGH ARCH.   THE PEPPER TREE.

prince or a nabob might luxuriate to his heart's content. Nearby is an extensive orchard and garden, inclosed with high walls, and filled with every variety of fruit trees; but the acequias, or irrigating canals, had been neglected, the dams and embankments washed away, and the beautiful gardens and shady walks, where the devotees passed the long hours when not attending to their religious duties, were overflowed. A swamp filled with rushes and rank weeds had taken possession of these walks and groves; and here the screaming heron and other water fowl had their hiding-places.

"The Sergeant, at my request, sent for an old Indian of the neighborhood, who called himself a chief (capitano). On learning that an officer of the U. S. Government wished to see him, he made his appearance with three others of his tribe. The old man presented himself in the dress of a Mexican officer—a blue coat with red facings trimmed with gold lace, and a high military cap and feather. He was quite communicative, and answered my questions readily. In giving me the words of his language, he enunciated them with great distinctness, and would not be satisfied with my pronunciation until all could at once recognize the word. When I had completed my vocabulary, and read off the native words, he evinced great pleasure as he repeated the corresponding word in Spanish, occasionally exclaiming *Bueno* or *Muy Bueno!* He called his tribe the *Kechi.*

"On inquiring as to the state of things when the padres were here, the old man heaved a deep sigh. He said his tribe was large, and his people all happy, when the good Fathers were here to protect them. That they cultivated the soil; assisted in rearing large herds of cattle; were taught to be blacksmiths and carpenters, as well as other trades; that they had plenty to eat, and were happy. He remembered when three thousand of his tribe were settled in the valley, dependent upon or connected with this Mission. Now, he said, they were scattered about, he knew not where, without a home or protectors, and were in a miserable condition. A few hundred alone remained in some villages up the valley, a few miles from the Mission. He spoke with much affection of Father Peyri, its original founder, who had resided here for thirty-four years. At no time, he said, were there more than sixteen Spanish soldiers here, who occupied a building facing the Mission, which is still standing." [13]

---

[13] *Personal Narrative,* vol. ii, pp. 89-93.

CHAPTER XI.

WHAT became of the Indians whom the Franciscan Fathers regarded as their children and treated as their wards? From the General History contained in *Missions and Missionaries of California* the reader will know that, after the United States flag had happily been raised over California, Military Governor S. W. Kearny named two sub-agents for the Indians in the north. They were Captain John A. Sutter, who was appointed on April 7, 1847, "for the Indians living on and near the Sacramento and San Joaquin rivers"; and Mariano G. Vallejo, whose appointment was dated a week later, on April 14, "for the Indians on the north side of the bay of San Francisco, including those on Cash Creek and the lakes." The salary of each sub-agent was fixed at $750 a year.[1]

On August 1, 1847, Governor Richard B. Mason appointed Captain J. D. Hunter "sub-Indian agent for the lower district of Upper California, and more especially for the district or country in and about the Mission of San Luis

---

[1] *Missions and Missionaries*, vol. iv, p. 593.

Rey." The salary was "$750 a year, payable quarterly by the quartermaster at Los Angeles." [2]

The Indians in the north do not concern us here. The reader will find information on them in the fourth volume of the General History. While under the supervision of Captain Hunter the Indians fared well enough; but military rule ceased when California became a State, on September 9, 1850, and then the government of politicians began. It was not favorable to the Indians, since they had no vote and consequently possessed no influence. To relate how they fared under these conditions would fill several volumes. We have no intention of recounting the harrowing descriptions. Those interested may consult the fourth volume of the General History, Mrs. Helen Hunt Jackson's *Century of Dishonor,* her splendid work entitled *Ramona,* and her *Glimpses of California.* The *Annual Reports of Commissioner of Indian Affairs* are also replete with first-hand information from the respective Indian Agents, many of whom were not mercenary. The earliest U. S. Indian Agent of this class who has left us an official report on California, is O. M. Wolzencraft. Writing from Sacramento Valley, California, to the Hon. Luke Lea, Commissioner of Indian Affairs, this official, under date of July 12, 1851, gives vent to his honest indignation in these words:

It would appear that most of the difficulties that unfortunately have occurred between the white and red men have been owing to an improper and shortsighted policy, or rather a want of true policy, with these children of the forest. I am sorry to say that, in many instances, they have been treated in a manner that, were it recorded, would blot the darkest page of history that has yet been penned. Had they even been *foreign* convicts, possessing a full knowledge of the evils of crime and the penalties therefor, and received the punishment that had been dealt out to these poor, ignorant creatures, this enlightened community would have raised a remonstrative voice that would have rebuked the aggressor and caused him to go beyond the pale of civilized man, etc.[3]

---

[2] For his instructions see *Missions and Missionaries,* vol. iv, pp. 594-596.   [3] *Executive Document,* No. 2, *House of Representatives, 32d Congress, 1st Session, Part III, 1851.*

SAN LUIS REY MISSION CHURCH AND MONASTERY AS IT IS TODAY

Apparently, the first agent for the Indians of San Diego and Los Angeles Counties was D. B. Wilson. In the year 1852, he pictured the situation under his jurisdiction so graphically that it is worth the while to reproduce at least the main points of his report. He writes:

San Diego, San Juan (Capistrano), and San Gabriel, in 1784, had a majority of all the neophyte proselytes in Southern California; they were a large majority of all the laborers, mechanics, and servants in Los Angeles and San Diego counties. Today, in 1852, they are only 7,000, not half as many as were left by the mission Fathers eighteen years ago.

All this time they are much given to drink, and while they do not care for it while at work, the habit of drinking Saturday night and Sunday is imperative, and the time is spent in revelry and gambling, of which they are very fond, and in which they stake all they have, often exchanging their clothing. They are willing to work and do only about half as much as a good white man and expect only half as much pay; $8 and $10 per month being wages, and about $1 per day in towns. In some parts of Los Angeles nearly half of the houses are grog shops for Indians.

Under the rule of the missions they were taught to do all the farm work, also the trades, as masons, carpenters, plasterers, soapmakers, tanners, shoemakers, blacksmiths, bakers, millers, brickmakers, cartmakers, weavers and spinners, saddlers, shepherds, vineros, and vaqueros. In fact, they filled all the branches of mechanics then in use here. They taught the Americans to make adobes; they understood irrigation, planting season and harvest. They had a practical knowledge which outlives their teachers. Their women were quick to learn household duties and often married foreigners and Californians, and made exemplary wives and mothers.

At the close of the Mexican War some of these old Mission Indians remained in possession of lands under written grants from the Mexican Government. Some have sold out, others have been elbowed off by white men. All are now waiting the adjudication of the Commissioner of Land Titles. Many of them are good citizens in all respects save the right to vote and be witnesses. They are anxious to hold their title homesteads and resist all offers to buy as steadily as they can. How long their limited shrewdness can match the overreaching cupidity that ever assails them, it is difficult to say.

They lack thrift, incline to dissolute habits, yet plant regularly year by year, and have small stocks of horses, cattle, and sheep. A better crop and more commodious huts, a few chairs, and a table distinguish them from the mountain villages; still they have made a broad step towards civilization. Three years ago they were practically slaves.

American freedom does not profit them. They soon fall into the bad
ways of their Christian (?) neighbors. The Indian has a quick sense
of injustice. He can never see why he should be sold to service for
drunkenness,[4] when the white man goes unpunished for the same
offense and often refuses to pay him for labor in anything but
spirits. I speak this freely of abuses which actually exist. The law
is good enough, except it will not allow an Indian as witness against
a white man. The abuses of the law have been cruel to the Indian
in every country at all times and nearly fatal to him in California.

The chiefs generally understand their affairs very well, and are
keenly alive to the welfare of their people. They punish murder and
witchcraft with death, and if our local authorities should ask it as a
favor they would hang, shoot, or bury alive any notorious horse-thief
or cattle-stealer.

I wish the idea always to be kept in mind touching all these Mission Indians, namely, that they have a common spirit of amenity for
the whites. They want peace with the whites. They are devoted
neither to war nor the chase; they have learned to work for subsistence; they have acquired the idea of separate property in land.
They possess considerable skill in the useful arts. They are at peace
among themselves and friendly to the whites, docile and tractable,
and accustomed to subjection.[5]

Similarly run the reports of all the Indian agents and
Indian inspectors down to our day. The Mission Indians
and their descendants wanted peace; they were industrious;
and they desired to retain only the plot on which they were
born and their dead were buried.

For generations past, Agent Lawson reminded the Government, on
August 28, 1879, many have had their villages on what they supposed
to be "the public domain," and which they believed would ultimately
be set apart for them, but which in almost every instance turned out
to be covered by the ubiquitous "Spanish (Mexican) grant," whose
title has been confirmed to the inevitable "land-grabber." In some
instances, however, they have been accorded the favor of remaining
on and cultivating these lands so long occupied by them. . . . The
Mission Indians are all engaged in agricultural pursuits, either in the
cultivation of the little fields they *call* their own, or laboring for
ranchmen. . . . At some seasons of the year it is impossible for
all to find employment, while at others, such as in the sheep-shearing

---

[4] The evidence that he was sold is in a previous chapter and will
be treated more in detail in connection with Mission San Gabriel.

[5] *Fifty-ninth Annual Report* of the Commissioner of Indian Affairs,
1890, p. 20.

season, they find ample and remunerative employment, and are eagerly sought for by the large ranchmen. They excel all others in this kind of labor. With few exceptions, the Mission Indians are industrious, having always maintained themselves by their own labor. They do not now, and never have asked for supplies of any kind from the government. All they ask is that land be given them upon which they have an opportunity to better support themselves and families. . . . Until my arrival at the agency, wrongs had been practiced upon these helpless people, that was only to be expected by the absence of a duly accredited representative of the government to protect their interests. Taking advantage of their ignorance, their employers, in many instances, practiced the grossest frauds in the payment of their wages. In some instances, goods of one kind or other were given them in lieu of money, at such prices as to make the price of a day's labor to the employer not exceed ten cents. Instances were related to me in which they received their wages in intoxicating liquor, which of course resulted in a drunken debauch, from which they recovered only when the supply was exhausted, to find themselves without the necessaries of life for their destitute families.[6]

Every conceivable trick is resorted to to get labor of this kind as cheap as possible, the same agent wrote on August 17, 1880. The following case was brought to my attention some time ago. An Indian having labored at cutting wood for six days, earned, at the wages agreed upon, the sum of $2.50, received in part payment two bottles of wine, for which he was charged $1, and upon demanding the balance of $1.50 in money, he was ordered to leave the premises. The Indian refusing to go without the money, the man took down his shotgun and discharged a load of buckshot into the Indian's face, destroying the sight of an eye and otherwise disfiguring his face. The next day this employer boasted to an acquaintance how he had settled a bill of $1.50 with an Indian by paying him in buckshot. Subsequently I had the man arrested, and now he claims that he did the shooting in self-defense; that the Indian attempted to kill him.[7]

We have little documentary evidence regarding the book-learning of the Indians under missionary care. The Fathers wisely put more stress on industrial training with a view to teaching self-support. Various Indian agents in their reports are in full accord with this system. For instance, Agent John S. Ward, as late as August 14, 1886, from the

---

[6] *Report Com. Ind. Aff.*, 1879, pp. 14-15.   [7] *Report Com. Ind. Aff.*, 1880, p. 13.

Mission Agency, Colton, California, presented his views as follows:

There are two great elements or principles underlying Indian civilization, and they are education and agriculture. Agriculture is one of the cornerstones of the temple of Indian civilization. The Government acts wisely in giving so much money and so much attention to this subject among the Indians. . . . The Egyptians could not make brick without straw, nor can the Indian be made a successful farmer without the implements. Since I took charge of the agency not a single farming implement has been sent here for the Indians. They made most piteous appeals for wagons, plows, hoes, shovels, and other tools. I have made application for such things, but they have never reached me.

Education, to be useful, should be manifold. The hand and heart should keep pace with the head in development of character, and every system of education which cultures only the intellectual faculties will surely fail in the development of well-balanced useful men and women. To take the Indian boy or girl from their parental hut and teach them, day after day, reading, writing, and arithmetic, without any training in industrial pursuits, is simply to make educated vagabonds of them. While the Indian's head needs training, his hand needs it more. With all his book learning, unless he has been taught to handle the plow, dig a ditch, cultivate, prune and irrigate an orchard, shove the plane or strike the anvil, he is as helpless as a child when thrown out into busy active life.[8]

Similarly, as early as January 1, 1867, Special Commissioner Robert J. Stevens, after investigating the conditions in California, declared in his report: "I cannot better express my opinion on this subject (schools and arts of husbandry) than by quoting the recently declared conclusions of Superintendent Huntington, who has been some six years in charge of the Indians in the adjoining State of Oregon, namely:

The first efforts with an Indian child should be through the stomach; give him plenty of wholesome, nutritious food; then let him be warmly clad. The next step is to teach him to labor, instil habits of industry, and associate him with industrious people. He may then be approached cautiously with books. Such a system, carried out with patient labor and with earnest energy, can be made to improve and elevate the race. Reverse it and put the book in use at the beginning, and the result

---

[8] *Report Com. Ind. Aff.*, 1886, pp. 43-44.

will not only be useless, it will be absolutely pernicious. In a word, the hoe and the broadaxe will sooner civilize and Christianize them than the spelling book.

By reference to the report, Stevens continues, with estimates for 1867-1868 of late Superintendent Maltby, I see that he asked for nearly $12,000 for the support of schools to be established at different reservations. This is, in my judgment, utterly useless until the great mass of the reservation Indians shall have become a little further humanized by systematic labor. He has asked nothing, to my surprise, *for these Mission Indians, who are for the most part amply prepared to receive the benefits of education; and this opinion I understand to be coincided in by the present Superintendent Whiting. In fact, many of them even now read and write, particularly among the aged. They have seen happier times,* which, I trust, may be at least renewed to their children.[9]

It will surprise the reader that especially many of the *aged* Mission Indians could read and write. They must have learned it at Mission San Luis Rey during the administration of Fr. Antonio Peyri, or at the other three missions of the district, though most of them hailed from San Luis Rey. The same Indians were also advanced in agriculture and in the mechanical arts. Here is official recogntion of the Fathers' system, which it will be well for the mission enemies to ponder.

This statement is corroborated by Special Agent J. Q. A. Stanley. Reporting from Los Angeles to the Government under date of August 5, 1866, he writes: "I am sorry to say they (the Mission Indians) have been sadly neglected, although, *in point of intelligence, they are far ahead of any other Indians in California,* and I would recommend that schools be established among them at an early date." [10]

The reason for their advanced state of civilization is frankly acknowledged by various officials, notably by Special Indian Agent W. E. Lovett, who in May, 1865, recounts in a long report the wrongs which the Mission Indians suffered from the whites. He writes:

Under the old system of mission priests these Indians were not

---

[9] *Report Com. Ind. Aff.,* 1867, p. 134.   Italics inserted.
[10] *Report Com. Ind. Aff.,* 1866, pp. 102-103.   Italics inserted.

only self-supporting, but were also a source of revenue. These pious Fathers, however, while they exhibited towards them a friendly care for their temporal, as well as spiritual welfare, were nevertheless strict in exacting obedience, and firm in exercising care and authority over them, their property, and their labor, the Indians simply furnishing the manual labor, while the priests furnished exclusively whatever brain work was necessary. It must be admitted that under the mission system the Indians were far better cared for, and were much happier, more industrious, and less vicious than at present. It is not to be expected that we can ever fully return to the old system; partially, however, we can.

In my opinion, it is necessary that a small appropriation should be made by Congress for the exclusive care and protection of the Mission Indians of the southern counties of California. Such an appropriation could be most judiciously applied in the purchase and proper distribution of seeds, agricultural implements, and clothing. A small portion of the amount appropriated could be very properly expended in preserving from ruin those first landmarks of Christianity and civilization on the Pacific Coast, the mission churches. Nothing would tend more to subdue the evil passions of the Indians than a restoration of those magnificent edifices now crumbling to decay. Many may disagree with me, but I have no hesitation in saying, after observing for twenty-eight years the habits and character of the Christianized Mission Indians in California and New Mexico, that nothing contributes more to do away with crime among them than the influence of good and holy priests.[11]

Mr. Lovett called a meeting of the Mission Indians for May 4, 1865. The following rancherías were represented:

Potrero.—Contains 80 men, 97 women and children, 143 beeves, 145 horses and mares, 16 jacks, 200 sheep, 200 fruit trees, 1,907 grapevines.

San Ygnacio.—15 men, 9 women, 6 cows and horses, 50 fruit trees.

Ancorga (?) Grande.—34 men, 50 women and children, 9 beeves, 16 horses and mares, 700 grapevines, 400 fruit trees.

Temécula.—196 men, 192 women and children, 225 cattle, 150 horses, 163 sheep.

San Luis Rey.—75 men, women and children, 62 beeves, 45 sheep.

Cahuillas.—703 men, women and children, 60 horses, mares and cows.

Coyotes.—80 men, 60 women and children.

La Jolla.—82 men, 98 women and children, 135 cows, 50 mares, 180 peach, fig and pear trees.

Saboba.—60 men and 70 women.

Pala.—73 men, 89 women and children, 56 beeves, 57 horses, 70 sheep, 56 fruit trees.

---

[11] *Report Com. Ind. Aff.*, 1865, p. 123.

MAIN ALTAR MISSION SAN LUIS REY

Pauma.—106 men, women and children, 43 beeves, 14 horses, 46 sheep.

Cholo.—42 men, 67 women and children, 50 fruit trees, 300 vines, 38 oxen and cows, 18 mares.

San Ysidro.—62 men, 97 women and children.

Agua Caliente.—73 men, 75 women and children, 70 peach trees, 2,240 grapevies, 25 horses, 42 cattle.

San Ysidro.—40 men, 50 women and children, 9 horses, 2 oxen, 15 sheep.

La Puerta de la Cruz.—84 men, women and children, 6 cows, 2 yoke of oxen, 5 horses, 6 mares, 50 vines.

Puerta Chiquita.—80 men, women and children, 14 animals of all kinds, 22 peach trees, 30 vines.

Ten rancherías of the San Diego Indians could not attend the meeting on account of the great distance. Their chief, Tomás, reported that they were in about the same state and as numerous as the average rancherías present.[12]

The disproportion between the sexes may find an explanation in a report of Special Indian Agent Lieutenant Augustus P. Greene, dated San Pasqual Reservation, February 20, 1871. He writes of said reservation: "I found the practice of selling young girls to white men prevailed to an alarming extent at this ranchería, so much so that it is almost impossible for an Indian to get a wife, unless he takes one at second-hand." Again with regard to Santa Ysabel the same agent pleads: "I would most respectfully call the attention of the Department to the monstrous practice of depraved white men buying young Indian girls, and that speedy action be taken in the matter." [13]

All manner of crimes have been committed with impunity against these gentle Mission Indians. With indignation Special Indian Agent Stanley adverts to this fact in his report dated at Los Angeles, California, September 30, 1869. "I have been acting as special agent for the Mission and Coahuila Indians five years," he writes, "and during that time have forwarded to the Commissioner of Indian Affairs at Washington detailed reports of the condition and wants

---

12 *Report Com. Ind. Aff.*, 1865, pp. 124-125.
13 *Report Com. Ind. Aff.*, 1871, pp. 341-342, 344.

of the Indians of Southern California * * *. I presume that one reason why nothing has been done for these Indians is, *they have been peaceable and caused the government no trouble,* and consequently they have been almost entirely neglected." [14]

It would be too tedious to quote Indian Agents in detail. They all have the same story to relate from year to year. Yet the descendants of the neophytes remained, what no white people would have done, *peaceable and submissive.* They keenly felt the degradation and wrong, but the lessons of the early missionaries had taken deep root. Through it all they preserved their Faith, albeit there were now no priests to comfort, guide, and protect them. They would gather for religious services in their poor chapels; and in prayers, led by lay readers, male or female, they would present their case to the Father of all.

The report of Agent Augustus Greene, dated August 30, 1870, on two settlements of this kind may be mentioned as showing how uncertain the Indians were of their staying in the inherited homes. He writes:

"San Pasqual Ranchería, on San Pasqual Valley reservation, is located on less than a quarter-section of land; even this is portioned among the (white) settlers, who are only restrained by fear of the government from taking possession at once and driving the Indians therefrom. The (Indian) *population,* present and absent, is 40· men, 46 women, 55 boys, 54 girls—total, 195. *Buildings:* 1 adobe church, 12 adobe houses, 14 brush houses—total, 27. *Crops:* about 700 bushels of corn and a small quantity of beans and melons. *Stock:* 98 horses, 115 oxen, steers, cows, and calves; 143 sheep and goats—total, 356.

Pala Ranchería, on Pala Valley reservation, is located on less than a quarter-section of land. The (Indian) *population* is, present and absent, 40 men, 47 women, 28 boys, and 22 girls—total, 137. *Buildings:* 1 adobe church, 3 adobe houses,

---

[14] *Report Com. Ind. Aff.,* 1868, pp. 193-194.   Italics inserted.

and 15 brush houses—total, 19. *Stock:* 75 horses, 40 oxen, steers, cows, and calves; 100 sheep and goats—total, 215. *Crops* about 1,500 bushels of corn, 40 bushels of wheat, and a small quantity of beans and melons." [15]

At last an effort was made by the United States Government to provide some permanent homes for the Mission Indians. By Executive Order of President U. S. Grant, dated December 27, 1875, public land clearly described was "withdrawn from sale and set apart as reservations for the permanent use and occupancy of the Mission Indians in Southern California." The Indians thereby affected and the reservations named were: *Potrero, Coahuilla, Capitan Grande, Santa Ysabel,* including *Mesa Grande, Pala, Agua Caliente, Sycuan, Inaja,* and *Cosmit.*

On May 15, 1876, by Executive Order of President Grant the following additional tracts were withdrawn from sale and set apart for Mission Indians: *Potrero* (not same as above), *Mission, Agua Caliente, Torros, Village, Cabezon, Village, Village.*

President R. B. Hayes, on May 3, 1877, restored to the public domain the lands designated as *Potrero* (both), but in the same year, on August 25 and September 29, he withdrew other land and set them apart for the use of Mission Indians.[16]

With regard to the character of these lands, Indian-Agent S. S. Lawson, under date of August 20, 1881, reported some interesting information. He says:

By Executive Order, small and isolated reservations have been set apart for the Mission Indians, aggregating nearly 100,000 acres of land—an amount, if of the proper kind, that would be ample for their support; but which, owing to the mountainous and desert character of the country, is practically worthless for the support of so great a number.

It has been by thrift and economy alone that they have been able to maintain themselves, when the seasons have been favorable

---

[16] *Report Com. Ind. Aff.,* 1877, pp. 238-239; 1878, pp. 238-239;
[15] *Report Com. Ind. Aff.,* 1870, p. 93.
1879, p. 218.

and labor available among the whites. What lands they have that admit of cultivation, they plant and sow to the best advantage; but without other sources or means of support, these would, at best, afford a very scanty subsistence. . . . Whether the government will heed the pleas that have been made in behalf of these people or not, it *must* sooner or later deal with this question in a practical way, or else see a population of over three thousand Indians become homeless wanderers in this desert region. . . . *The Mission Indians are as much civilized as the population by which they are surrounded; and if they are not up to the full standard, it is because of their surroundings.*

No active missionary labor is at present conducted among them. The greater portion of them, however, especially the older people, have had, in years past, the benefit of Christian instruction by the Catholic fathers, who conducted the famous missions whose ruins are yet objects of veneration and curiosity. They have orthodox views as to morals, God, and the future life, and it is not unusual to see sacred pictures, the crucifix, and the rosary, adorning the walls of their adobes and lodges. The priest still makes his annual rounds and baptizes the children; but aside from this no missionary work is carried on, their nomadic habits and settlements over an extended mountain and desert country rendering little else practicable.[17]

The right steps were at last taken in 1882. The Hon. H. Price, then Commissioner of Indian Affairs, seems to have felt that the Mission Indians of California had been and still were deeply wronged, and therefore he resolved to apply the proper remedy. However, let him relate his own story:

The injustice done the Mission Indians and their deplorable condition, have been set forth by several commissions and have been treated of at length in various annual reports of this office, especially in those of 1875 and 1880, and Congress has repeatedly been solicited to interfere in their behalf, but without avail.

The situation of these people is peculiar. It is probable that they are entitled to all the rights and immunities of citizens of the United States, by virtue of the treaty of Guadalupe Hidalgo, yet from poverty and ignorance and unwillingness to abandon their custom of dwelling together in villages, under a tribal or village government, they have failed to secure individual titles to their lands, under the public land laws, or under the Indian Domestic Act. Many of these Indians have been driven from lands occupied and cultivated by them

---

[17] *Report Com. Ind. Aff.*, 1881, pp. 13-15. Italics inserted.

GLIMPSE OF INTERIOR COURT OF MONASTERY.
FATHER DOMINIC, O. F. M.

for years, to which they had at least a color of title from the Spanish Government, and the ejectments have often been made with force and violence.

After nearly all desirable land had been wrested from them or "taken up" by settlers, a few small tracts remaining were set aside by Executive Order for their permanent use and occupation, and entries unlawfully made by white men upon such lands have been held for cancellation. The few little villages left to them in the cañons of the mountains, from long years of cultivation have become extremely fertile, and are looked upon with longing eyes by the surrounding white settlers.

In accordance with authority granted by the Department, Mrs. Helen Hunt Jackson, of Colorado, was instructed, under date of July 7, 1882, to visit the Mission Indians in California, and ascertain the location and condition of the various bands; whether suitable land in their vicinity, belonging to the public domain, could be made available as a permanent home for such of those Indians as were not established upon reservations, and what, if any, lands should be purchased for their use. At her request Mr. Abbot Kinney, of California, was authorized to assist in the work. Their final report gives, with great particularity, the condition of each village, recites in detail the wrongs that have been inflicted upon these Indians, and contains numerous and important recommendations for their improvement.

They recommend as the first and most essential step, the surveying, rounding out, and distinctly marking of reservations already existing.

Second. The removal of all white settlers now on such reservations.

Third. In cases where their villages are included in confirmed grants that other provision be made for the Indians, or that they be upheld and defended in their right to remain where they are.

Fourth. That all the reservations be patented to the several bands occupying them; the United States to hold the patents in trust for twenty-five years; a provision to be incorporated in the patent for allotments in severalty from time to time, as they may appear desirable.

Fifth. The establishment of at least two or more schools in addition to the five already in operation at the various villages.

Sixth. That it be made the duty of the agent to make a round of inspection at least twice a year.

Seventh. The appointment of a law firm as special attorneys in all cases affecting the interests of the Indians. This recommendation has already been carried out, Messrs. Brunson and Wells, of Los Angeles, having been appointed assistants to the United States district attorney in such cases, the appointment taking effect on the 1st of July last.

Eighth. A judicious distribution of agricultural implements among these Indians.

Ninth. A small fund for the purchase of food and clothing for the very old and sick in time of special destitution.

Tenth. The purchase of certain tracts of land.

The necessity for the action recommended is given with great clearness and force in each case. With these recommendations, with the possible exception of the last, I fully agree, and will hereafter submit a draft of the necessary legislation. With the measures already taken and with those herein recommended, it is believed that these poor and persecuted people may be protected from further encroachments, and enjoy in some measure the prosperity to which their peaceful conduct under all their wrongs entitles them.[18]

Two years later, Commissioner J. D. C. Atkins had this to say in his official annual report:

The reservations set apart for the Indians in many cases do not include their villages, and in others cover lands claimed, in some cases no doubt justly, by settlers. Unless something is speedily done for their relief, nothing but starvation and extermination await these people, who, by the treaty with Mexico, were received on an equal footing with other citizens of that republic.

The bill for their relief, which was submitted to the Department January 10, 1884, and which passed the Senate July 3, 1884, appears to afford the most feasible and satisfactory solution of the difficulty. This bill will again be prepared and submitted to the Department for transmission to Congress at the coming session.

I give no details as to the wrongs and sufferings of these Indians, because they have been fully set forth in the report on their condition by Mrs. Helen Hunt Jackson and Mr. Abbot Kinney, which was published a year ago, and also in the report of the Senate Committee on Indian Affairs (Report No. 1522, Forty-eighth Congress, second session).[19]

---

[18] *Report Com. Ind. Aff.*, 1883, pp. xlv-xlvi.
[19] *Report Com. Ind. Aff.*, 1885, p. xlviii. See Appendix C.

CHAPTER XII.

NOTWITHSTANDING the recommendations of noble Mrs. Helen Hunt Jackson, and whatever measures the Indian Department took in consequence, the condition of the Indians remained insecure.

The Government has apparently been very generous to the Mission Indians, writes Agent J. S. Ward, on August 14, 1886. It has given them more than twenty different reservations, embracing nearly 200,000 acres; but what a country! After a careful examination of all the land, we do not think there are over 5,000 (five thousand) acres of tillable land,[1] and the best portion of that is now held by trespassers in defiance of the agent and Government. Much of the best land is included within the boundaries of Mexican grants, and the owners of these grants are now endeavoring to eject these Indians by regular process of law. The case of the Indians on the San Jacinto grant has recently been decided adversely to them, and had the proceedings not been stayed by an appeal to the Supreme Court they would have been ejected by the sheriff before this time. Other cases of a similar kind will soon come up in regard to the rights of the Indians on the Santa Ysabel grant and that of Warner's Rancho. The special attorney for the Indians is making an able and vigorous fight for the legal rights of these Indians. From the general trend of the Supreme

---

[1] In his Report of August 17, 1887, Mr Ward declares: "There are not 500 acres of this vast domain on which a decent living can be made without irrigation."

Court decisions it is more than probable that the Indians will eventually be ejected from the San Jacinto, Santa Ysabel, and Warner's Rancho.[2]

The reason for this state of things is explained by Commissioner J. D. C. Atkins in his General Report for the year 1886:

A special attorney has been appointed to defend the rights of the Indians; but there are no funds available for his compensation. The bill for the relief of the Mission Indians (embodying Mrs. Jackson's recommendations), which passed the Senate July 3, 1884, was again passed in that body February 15, 1886, and was favorably reported in the House of Representatives, but received no further consideration.[3]

While Congress did nothing in the matter, the friends of the Mission Indians won a victory over white cupidity. The Commissioner, in his Report for 1888, relates the facts as follows:

For the first time in many years this office is able to report that some progress has been made in establishing the rights of these Indians to the lands occupied by them and their ancestors. On January 31, 1888, the Supreme Court of the State of California rendered a decision in the case of *Byrne* vs. *Alas et al.*, which fully confirms the position of this office, that grants of lands to private parties are subject to the rights of the Indian occupants, and that *such occupants can not be legally ejected.* The decision has so important a bearing on the welfare and protection of the rights of the Mission Indians that I have deemed it best to quote it entire. It is the most valuable thing which has been definitely secured for these Indians since public attention has been turned to their sufferings and wrongs, and had the decision been rendered several years ago it would have prevented no small part of the hardships, cruelty, and flagrant injustice of which the Mission Indians have been conspicuous victims.[4]

The decision of the Supreme Court referred to covers nearly six pages of small print in the Commissioner's Report. Though replete with interesting matter, it is not practicable to reproduce here the entire text; wherefore the reader is referred to the volume quoted. It will be sufficient, if we show the drift of the decision by quoting the last paragraph.

Of course, the possession, when abandoned by the Indians, attaches

---

2 *Report Com. Ind. Aff.*, 1886, p. 45.   3 Ibidem, p. xliii.
4 *Report Com. Ind. Aff.*, 1888, p. lxiv.

itself to the fee without further grant; and this is true whether there be any record evidence in favor of the Indians or not. Their rights exist only so long as they actually occupy the land. So long as the defendants and their ancestors were in possession of the lands in controversy there remained nothing to be done by them under the laws of Mexico in order to confirm their rights, nor was there anything to be done by the Mexican Government or the officers thereof. The rights of the Indians has been completely established. We think that upon the facts agreed to in this case the defendants are entitled to judgment for their costs.

Judgment reversed and cause remanded, with directions to enter judgment in favor of defendants for their costs.

The Commissioner notes that "it is but just to say that Mr. Shirley G. Ward (special counsel for these Indians) was employed for this service by the Indian Rights Association. When, in the Superior Court, judgment had been given against the Indians in·default of defense, the Association, through him, got the judgment set aside and the case restored to the calendar. When tried the case again went against the Indians, and the Association gave security of $3,300 and had the case appealed to the Supreme Court."

This was not the end of Mission Indian troubles. "The first great necessity here," Agent H. N. Rust reported on October 28, 1889, "is a survey and a correct map of each reservation that Indian and white man alike may know their boundaries."[5] The Indian Commissioner declared that "January 10, 1884, a draft of a bill for their relief was transmitted to the Department for submission to Congress, which bill (in its main features) was continuously before that body up to the close of the last Congress. It has been passed by the Senate three times, and as many times has failed to become a law by the non-action of the House of Representatives. The principal feature of this bill was the authorization of the appointment of a commission of three disinterested persons, to arrange a just and satisfactory settlement of these Indians on reservations to be secured to them by patent. This bill will be prepared for submission to Con-

---

[5] *Report Com. Ind. Aff.*, 1889, p. 125.

INTERIOR AND EXTERIOR OF INDIAN CHAPEL AT PECHANGA. FR. O'KEEFE
BLESSING BELL.

gress at the beginning of its next session." [6]　So the fault lay with Congressmen of the Lower House. It is a pity that those Congressmen could not be placed on a sandy reserve like Pechanga for only three months.

In the following year, 1890, on August 8, Agent H. N. Rust reported that there were 2,895 Mission Indians under his jurisdiction.

now scattered over the southern part of California, principally upon nineteen reservations. Many families and groups of families are living isolated in the mountains, where they have been driven by violent white men. Poor and homeless, they subsist principally upon acorns. Others are living near the white settlements, where they secure a better living by their labor. * * * The Mission Indians have arrived at that period in human progress where they should no longer be classed as Indians, but as citizens. They only need land in severalty, with a set of agricultural implements and a general supervision, to make them all self-supporting; then the school would fit them for the duties before them. They are a very quiet, peaceable, confiding people, and as industrious as any people who have so few wants. The teaching of the padres saved them from savagism. Neglect and white men's greed have robbed them of land, and his vices have reduced their numbers from 15,000 in 1834 to 7,000 in 1852, to 3,000 in 1890. No man with a particle of humanity left can meet these people as an agent does without feeling ashamed that as the agent of this good Government, which has forcibly taken possession of this country and assumed the care of this weak people, we should have by neglect and dishonesty of its paid agents reduced them to such abject poverty and helplessness. Our own records of the past are humiliating. Cortés robbed the Aztecs of gold, but left them their land and water. Americans posing as Christians have robbed these poor children of nature, by legal trickery, of their land made sacred by the graves of their ancestors.[7]

Mr. Rust enumerates and describes various reservations. Of Pechanga Village, Temécula Reservation, the scene of a brutal eviction described by Mrs. Jackson in her *Ramona*, he reports:

It is sixty miles from Colton. These people have very little good land and no water. They take their animals one and one-half miles to drink and carry water the same distance in barrels for the school.

---

[6] Ibidem, p. 59.

[7] *Report Com. Ind. Aff.*, 1890, pp. 16-17.

I hope to supply water soon. These people have suffered from bad whites from Temécula. Average attendance at school is 24. The entire population is 133.

Of Agua Caliente (Hot Springs) the same agent reports:

It is one hundred miles from Colton, a possessory right on Warner's Ranch, where Indians have lived since the earliest knowledge of white men. A fine flow of hot and cold water makes it a favorite resort. These people are among our best Indian farmers, living comfortably in good adobe houses. They are now disturbed by threats of ex-Governor Downey, who owns the ranch, to drive them off. Here we need legal defense at once. The school is doing fairly well. Average attendance, 22. Population, 156.[8]

Legal aid was indeed secured for the Indians on Warner's Ranch, and the case finally reached the Supreme Court of the United States. The result was stated to Congress by the Commissioner of Indian Affairs and the status of the Indians affected explained as follows:

The Supreme Court of the United States, in an opinion rendered May 13, 1901, decided adversely to the claim of some Mission Indians to retain occupancy of a tract in Southern California known as Warner's Ranch, or Agua Caliente.

The effect of this decision will be to dispossess about two hundred Indians of the lands they claim to have held for generations. Under the auspices of the Attorney-General, an agreement was reached with the attorneys for the Downey estate, whereby the Indians will be permitted to remain in possession of the lands until the next session of Congress, when, it is hoped, legislation for their relief may be enacted.

As a temporary expedient, all vacant lands in township 10 south, range 3 east, San Bernardino meridian, Cal., were, on June 11, 1901, withdrawn from settlement and entry, and set aside for the use of the Indians until such time as Congress may provide the necessary legislation permanently reserving those lands. It has since been ascertained, however, that the vacant lands in that township are practically worthless, and that such small areas as are adapted for agriculture, will not support more than a few families. It will therefore be necessary for the Government to provide other lands for the Indians affected by the decision, and, as it is reported that they will go from their former homes practically empty-handed and penniless, relief in the way of necessaries of life must needs be afforded them. This matter will be made the subject of a special communication.[9]

---

8 Ibidem, p. 19. 9 *Report Com. Ind. Aff.*, 1901.

The author was at the time in charge of the Indian Boarding School at Banning, California, and he had likewise
spiritual charge of all the Mission Indians to the south as
far as Warner's Ranch, inclusive. The Indians there received the terrible news by a most pathetic letter from the
Indian Agent at San Jacinto. Poor Indians! To whom
could they turn in their affliction? They needed counsel,
indeed, and from whom could they obtain it save from the
priest? So Capitán Blacktooth and Ambrosio, the sacristan
and lay-reader, set out on horseback for Banning, a journey
of two days, and surprised the writer one day in May with
the letter from the Agent. He had as yet received no inti-
mation of what had happened to his mission people. Of
course, nothing was to be done against the decision of the
Supreme Court; but it was imperative to prevent these long-
suffering descendants of the Mission San Luis Rey neophytes,
who themselves had drunk the cup of bitterness to the dregs,
from despairing and committing some rash act.

The Supreme Court had decided (on what basis of justice the Lord knows, we could not and cannot see it) that
the land which their ancestors had occupied from time immemorial, and which the Spanish laws would have declared
sacred to them, belonged to J. Downey Harvey, and that
the Indians must evacuate the place. It was a terrible blow.
We had read of such things having been perpetrated in Ire-
land, but had thought it impossible under the Stars and
Stripes. Not knowing what else to do, the writer provided
the two noble Indians, who still retained full control of
themselves, with money and a letter of introduction and advised them to ride down to Los Angeles, where they could,
with full confidence, explain the plight of their people to the
Chief Pastor, the Rt. Rev. George Montgomery, Bishop of
the Diocese. A month later, at the end of the school year,
the writer accompanied the Indian children of the school,
between 70 and 80 in number, to their respective rancherías,
Warner's Ranch, San Isídro, San Felipe, and Mesa Grande.
At all these places, in neatly decorated chapels, the writer

CAPITAN BLACKTOOTH AND SACRISTAN
AMBROSIO AT THE HOT SPRINGS.

celebrated holy Mass and preached in English and Spanish
to the Indians, who made a holiday of the event. It was the
first time, as far as known, since the days of Fr. Zalvidea
and Fr. Ibarra, that a Franciscan visited those places. He
made a short visit also to San Ignacio, where a few Indian
families lived on well-cultivated patches around a small
chapel.

At Agua Caliente, or Warner's Ranch, the writer spoke
to the Indians on the subject that was naturally the nearest
to their heart just then, and exacted from them the promise
that they would do nothing rash, but would abide by everything the Bishop would advise them to do in the emergency.
Now they could calmly wait for the worst, if no way was
discovered to prevent ejection. They had before their eyes
the bright example of their parents and grandparents, who
had suffered similarly at Mission San Luis Rey.

Naturally, the decision of the Supreme Court created a
wide commotion. There was scarcely a white man, outside
the class that is, owing to utter selfishness and cupidity,
constitutionally unfriendly to the Indians, who did not sympathize with these poor afflicted Mission Indians. Why the
San Felipe Indians should have been compelled to abandon
their adobe chapel and the few huts on the barren hillside,
is a mystery to the writer. They could have been in no
one's way. Shylock demanded his pound of Antonio's flesh;
luckily he was baffled at his devilish game, and instead, secured a ton of contempt. But alas! in the case of the poor
simple-minded Indians there was no Portia to outwit wanton
cupidity.

With regard to the Indians at Warner's Ranch, Mr. Lummis voiced the general sentiment when he wrote:

Some Indians sometimes eat Harvey cattle. Some Harvey cattle eat
the little Indian fields—but that's another story. The clear thing
is that the Indians are the Government's wards and not Mr. Harvey's.
If the Government maintains a Supreme Court so blissfully ignorant
of the laws of Spain as to oust a Spanish grant people whom every
Crown of Spain could not have ousted, it should have the courage of
its convictions and be willing to pay for its luxuries. The Indians

ought to stay where they are—not because it is the best place, but because it is their home and the only place in the world they wish to inhabit. * * * Fortunately the Government—after losing the Indians their land by one of the most incredible laws ever framed by ignorance afar off—feels its responsibility, and is taking steps to make what reparation it thinks it can.[10]

To a reporter of the *Los Angeles Herald*, on November 4, 1901, Rev. Antonio Ubach, pastor of St. Joseph's Church, San Diego, who for about forty years occasionally visited the Indians of Mesa Grande and other Indian stations, expressed himself thus:

It will be the blackest of crimes to turn these Warner Ranch Indians out of their homes. When, in the year 1836 (?), Don José Portella (?) applied to General Micheltorena, then (?) governor of the Californias, residing at Monterey, for a grant of San José del Valle (at present Warner's Ranch), General Micheltorena ordered him to go back to San Diego and get a certificate from Father Oliva, who was to state whether or not there were any Indians living on this grant, Portella came to San Diego, and got a certificate from Father Oliva, who stated that there were a certain number of Indians living at San José del Valle. By virtue of the powers conferred on General Micheltorena by the Mexican Government, and upon the statements by Father Oliva, General Micheltorena gave a grant of San José del Valle to said Portella, with the distinct and expressed proviso that the Indians living upon it then, and their successors, were never to be molested. They were born on Mexican territory, and were as much Mexican citizens as the whitest man up to the present day. When California passed to American rule, it was stipulated by the two governments that the United States Government would abide by all that the Mexican Government had done during the Spanish and Mexican regime. I myself have seen the document of the original grant to Don José Portella, and translated it into the English language.[11]

We have no means of verifying the various statements; but the correspondent must have misunderstood the year of the grant. Micheltorena did not arrive in California till August, 1842. The name Portella is not found in the history of those days. Doubtless Portilla is meant; but then it must be Silvestre de la Portilla, who in 1836 secured the

---

[10] *Out West*, vol. xvi, April, 1902, pp. 409-410.
[11] *Los Angeles Herald Magazine*, November 10, 1901, p. 12.

grant of San José del Valle, not from Micheltorena, however, but from either Gutiérrez or Chico.[12]

The United States Government could not help taking notice of what was going on. Desirous of affording what relief was possible, the Commissioner of Indian Affairs, W. A. Jones, addressed himself to Mr. Albert K. Smiley, who, for having taken an active interest in Indian matters during the past eighteen years, was familiar with the situation. In reply, Mr. Smiley wrote:

You are doubtless aware that about twenty years ago, Helen Hunt Jackson was sent out by the Government to investigate the condition of the Indians of Southern California, and that in her report she called attention to the need of immediate action to prevent the Indians being driven from their lands by grasping white settlers, and to secure for them the permanent possession of the lands they were then occupying. A short time afterward she and Senator Dawes met in Washington and framed a Congressional bill creating a commission with full powers to secure all available lands for the Indians. This bill failed to pass Congress, but about ten years later practically the same bill was passed, authorizing the President and Secretary of the Interior to appoint a commission of three with power to reserve all available lands for the Indians of that section, said reserves to be held inalienable for a period of twenty-five years. I was chairman of that commission, which consisted of Judge Moore of Michigan, Prof. Painter and myself. We labored for two years and secured all available land which was suitable for occupation by the Indians, striking out from their possessions certain barren tracts, which were practically useless, as many Californians were claiming at the time that the Indians already held too much land.

In regard to Warner's Ranch, it was at the time owned by Gov. Downey, who was making every effort to eject the Indians from the property. We endeavored to show him that the Indians were quiet, peaceable and very serviceable to him in carrying on his extensive cattle-raising operations, their services being always available for a moderate sum; and that, therefore, it was not only for the welfare of the Indians, but his own, that they be allowed to remain. His own attorney, Hon. Stephen M. White, afterward United States Senator, heartily joined with us in the effort to give the Indians a title to the land rightfully theirs. Nevertheless, he stubbornly refused to accede to any of our requests, and as our commission had no power to purchase lands, we could only advance the argument of the Indians'

---

[12] See Bancroft, vol. iv, p. 68; vol. iii, p. 612, note.

SAN ANTONIO DE PALA BEFORE RESTORATION BY THE LANDMARKS CLUB, CHARLES F. LUMMIS, PRESIDENT

right to hold the land. For ten years Mr. Downey's heirs have continued to contest their case in the courts, and, although most vigorous efforts have been put forth and thousands of dollars expended by private individuals in defense of the Indians, quite recently the highest court has decided against them, making them liable, at any moment, to be driven from the lands they are now occupying, with no place provided for them. In reaching this decision, I understand that the court takes the ground that the Indians did not appear at the proper places to register their lands at the time that the President called on all those who had been Mexican citizens to do so; that the Indians were so-called Mexican citizens, and that their failure to register made void their claims to the land they were occupying. While technically this ground may be correct, it seems to me that the Government is dealing most unjustly with the Indians, in view of the fact that when California was ceded by Mexico to this Government, the merciful provision was introduced into the treaty that all Indians holding lands therein should maintain possession as long as they resided on them.

This, then, is the existing condition. All the Indians on Warner's Ranch can, at any moment, be made homeless and forced to abandon their lands, their well-built houses, and the graves of their ancestors, with no place whatever to go to for new homes. In view of the fact that it was by its own action that the Government brought this most pitiful state of affairs upon them, it certainly seems that the Government is morally responsible to them to do one of two things: Either purchase from the present owners the land on which they are now residing, or provide for them its equivalent elsewhere. It is my understanding that the Downey heirs are willing to refrain from turning out the Indians until Congress shall have assembled and a fair opportunity be given it to act in the matter, and it is imperative that immediate and effective action of some kind be taken.

It is my belief that the Government can do no better than to attempt to purchase the present quarters of the Indians on Warner's Ranch for their permanent occupancy. In all they occupy but a small portion of the ranch, and I have no doubt some part of their lands can be purchased at a reasonable figure. It is possible that the heirs will demand an exorbitant price for the hot springs on the land, or, perhaps, refuse to sell the springs altogether. But even if these cannot be secured the purchase of the remaining land occupied by the Indians will be of inestimable benefit.[13]

In their insatiable greed, the Downey heirs did demand an exorbitant price—$245,000 for the 30,000 acres comprising the ranch, 28,000 acres of which were worthless, accord-

---

[13] *Los Angeles Times*, November 25, 1901.

ing to Mr. Lummis. Nor would they sell the 900 acres occupied by the Indians, nor any less land than the 30,000 acres.[14]

At the petition of the Sequoya League, of which Mr. Charles F. Lummis was President, the Government resolved to appoint without delay a special commission to investigate the needs of the evicted Mission Indians, and to select a proper location for them, which the Government would purchase, since the successful claimants to Warner's Ranch were impatient and intended to proceed to actual eviction unless immediate provision were made for the Indians.[15]

Meanwhile at Warner's Ranch and other points, Mr. Lummis writes, I had long juntas (meetings) with the Indians. If these harried people could say in Washington what they said to me, and as they said it, they would need no advocate. The unvexed truth, the simplicity, the directness, the earnestness, and yet the perfect self-control of these aboriginal speeches, the dignity of the satire of them—sometimes unconscious, but oftener mildly intentional—would give them distinction in any parliamentary body.

We had no sooner reached the center of the village than we were surrounded by the troubled natives, who were anxious to know their fate. Shortly after lunch we had a *junta* in the schoolroom, which was attended by every man at home—many had gone ninety miles for work at sheep-shearing—and many of the women. It was as decorous and as respectful a gathering as ever assembled anywhere. A similar meeting was held next morning at our quarters. In an hour's direct talk (Mr. Lummis spoke Spanish to them) I told these harried people the exact status of their case in court and at Washington, and advised them to ponder it over night. There was practically no possibility that the Government would purchase their own land for them—since the Supreme Court had held it to belong to the ranch claimants, who refused to sell the nine hundred acres occupied by the Indians, or less land than the 30,000 acres, which was held at $245,000. They would better think over the outside country and decide what they would like best after their old home.

At the second *junta*, for the first time, they "talked back." The case was again put before them. They had had time to think it over —and it is safe to say there was little sleep in Agua Caliente that night. We began in Spanish; but, after a little, a fine-looking young woman came to the front as spokesman, and talked to us in perfectly

---

[14] *Out West*, April, 1902, p. 410; May, 1902, p. 472.
[15] Ibidem, April, 1902, p. 407.

lucid English the answers of her people to my Spanish discourse. They could all understand that; but under the stress of the deep feeling they talked in the Cupeño—for centuries they have called the Hot Springs Cupa; and since long before "American" ever heard of California they have been known to the people who did not evict them as Cupeños—the Cupa folks.

What was said from our side is unimportant. I shall give literally the words of the Cupeños as Mrs. Celsa Apapas spoke them. For she rendered the captain's answers better than he could say them, yet with exact truth to the spirit:

"We thank you for coming here to talk to us in a way we can understand. It is the first time anyone has done so. You ask us to think what place we like next best to this place, where we always lived. You see that graveyard out there? There are our fathers and our grandfathers. You see that Eagle-nest mountain and that Rabbit-hole mountain? When God made them, He gave us this place. We have always been here. We do not care for any other place. It may be good, but it is not ours. We have always lived here. We would rather die here. Our fathers did. We cannot leave them. Our children were born here—how can we go away? If you give us the best place in the world, it is not so good for us as this. The captain he say his people cannot go anywhere else; they cannot live anywhere else. Here they always lived; their people always lived here. There is no other place. This is our home. We ask you to get it for us. If Harvey Downey say he own this place, that is wrong. The Indians always here. We do not go on his land. We stay here. Everybody knows this Indian land. These Hot Springs always Indian. We cannot live anywhere else. We were born here and our fathers are buried here. We do not think of any place after this. We want this place and not any other place."

"But if the Government cannot buy this place for you, then what would you like next best?"

"There is no other place for us. We do not want you to buy any other place. If you will not buy this place, we will go into the mountains like quail, and die there, the old people and the women and children. Let the Government be glad and proud. It can kill us. We do not fight. We do what it says. If we cannot live here, we want to go into the mountains and die. We do not want any other home."

It was not an easy conversation, Lummis continues. There are cases wherein one could conceive of a pleasanter position than that of advocate of the Government attitude toward a people who know nothing of the political machine, but have the old notion that law and equity ought to be identical. It need not be said, of course, to

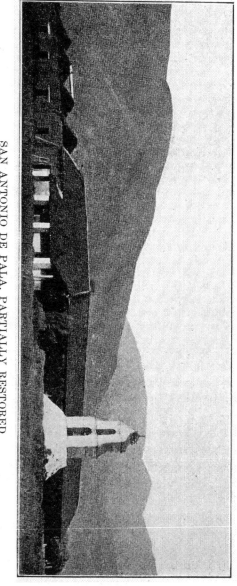

SAN ANTONIO DE PALA, PARTIALLY RESTORED

any student, that no Indian tribe in history ever took such a pro-
cedure under color of peace and law as is now evicting the Cupeños. *
* *

Besides their agriculture and their hot springs, the Cupeños have
other industries of serious consideration. They are skilled basket-
makers. If you would take the "art work" of any community of
American women and compare it side by side in a public exposition
with the handicraft of these women of Warner's Ranch, the civilized
ladies would instantly demand that their "fancy work" be withdrawn
from the comparison. Neither in art, nor in dignity, nor in utility,
could they for a moment afford the test. Some are more expert than
others; but every grown woman in Cupa can make a more artistic
and more valuable article than one American woman in a thousand
can. Besides baskets of all shapes, sizes and designs, made from
three native vegetable products, the Cupeños make a very attractive
and serviceable saddle-blanket or rug of fiber of the yuca or Spanish
bayonet. In both these industries, their hot springs are of the highest value to them for softening the material. Among the minor hardships of the inevitable moving, the loss of the springs alone will be
to the Indians precisely equivalent to taking from a fortunate American woman of today her gas range, her hot-water appliances and her
washing machine, and turning her back to the facilities her grand-
mother had. * * * Certainly if any American community had become used to the utilities of these hot springs—leaving out of count
altogether their medicinal properties and their value as revenue—it
would fight to the last ditch in protest against losing them.[16]

"Through the efforts of the (Sequoya) League," Mr.
Lummis wrote in his *Out West,* one year later, "backed up
by the direct personal interference of President Roosevelt on
several critical occasions, and by the desire of the present
Indian Office to do right, the Government has been enabled
to buy for the Warner's Ranch Indians far more and better
lands than those from which they are evicted." [17]

The Warner's Ranch Indian Commission, composed of
Charles F. Lummis, chairman; Russell C. Allen and Charles
L. Partridge, fully inspected 107 ranchos offered for sale,
that aggregated about 150,000 acres; they made forty-two
engineer's measurements of the flow of streams, and examined the claims of over 100,000 acres in thirty other prof-

---

[16] *Out West,* May, 1902, pp. 472-479.
[17] Ibidem, April, 1903, p. 442.

fers.[18] Finally, the Commission recommended to the Government the purchase of the land around Pala, comprising 3,438 acres, of which 2,028 were arable, 733 irrigable, 650 not yet cultivated, and having a supply the year round of 135 miner's inches. The price demanded was $46,230, or $13 per acre.

Your Commission, the report runs, has not seen anywhere else on its journey such variety and excellence of annual crops; besides oranges, walnuts, apricots, olives, grapes, peaches, pomegranates, pears, etc., corn, beans, onions, potatoes, lettuce, radishes, turnips, etc., surpassed any other seen during the trip. Wheat and barley and oats were up to the best seen by us. This valley of Pala has been the home of the Indians from time immemorial. It was selected three-quarters of a century ago by the Franciscan missionaries (of San Luis Rey) as a site for a (sub) mission; and it is notorious that in the more than thirty selections made in California by these pioneers, not one was a blunder. The mission sites are, to this day, and without exception, conceded to be the pick of California. This Mission (Pala) has never been abandoned, but had fallen into disrepair It is now being repaired by the Landmarks Club, and will have regular church services. The Warner Ranch Indians belong to this diocese There are about ten Pala Indian families still at Pala, on reservations and homesteads. The purchase of this valley by the Government for a reservation would practically unite the Warner's Ranch, Pala, Pauma and Rincon reservations. Pala has a daily mail; is twenty-four miles from Oceanside, twenty miles from Mission San Luis Rey, sixteen from Fallbrook, twelve from Temécula, six from Pauma Indian village, twelve from Rincon Indian village, eighteen from Pechanga, eighteen from La Joya, and thirty-five miles by the road over Mt. Palomár to Warner's Ranch, or fifty-five miles by an easier road.[19]

The Government adopted the recommendation of the Commission, and then directed the removal of the Indians to Pala. That was a critical matter. Fòrtunately, sympathetic and experienced men were chosen to accomplish the wretched and ungrateful task. "The eviction," Mr. Lummis wrote, "might be as tragic as the historic cases of Temécula and otherwhere, but for one thing, and that one thing is that the Indians have, within their own better-balanced heads, not

---

[18] *Out West,* April, 1903, p. 443.
[19] Ibidem, pp. 449-450.

only such a respect for authority as no American community can even comprehend, but a serious amount of that horse-sense which seems to be divinely withheld from volunteer (newspaper) correspondents." [20] Mr. Lummis overlooked the one thing at the bottom, which enabled these poor Indians to bear up against despair and to choke down the rebellious spirit that would fain have given vent to impotent rage and un-Christian words, and to submit to what Divine Providence ordained for their benefit; for unknown to them, the Father of all was leading them, through the machinations of evil men, to where they would fare much better temporarily and spiritually. That is what sustained them— their undying Faith, instilled into their hearts chiefly by the Fathers of Mission San Luis Rey.

"Pala," says Lummis, "is a word of the Luiseño (San Luis Rey) Indian language, and means 'water,' or 'place of water.'" [21] To this place, then, the household and property of the Indians was finally transferred in Government wagons under the gentle and prudent supervision of U. S. Inspector A. E. Jenkins, assisted by Indian Agent L. A. Wright. This took place in the second week of May, 1903. Some of the Indians took to the mountains rather than give up their old home; but later they voluntarily joined their tribe at Pala, with the exception, it is said, of an old woman named Manuela, who could not be found.

Early in September, 1903, Agent L. A. Wright, with eighteen wagons, appeared at the poor little hamlet of San Felipe or Ciénega, for which, according to Lummis, the Indian name was We-nelch. "Their case was conjoined to that of the Warner's Ranch Indians, and the Supreme Court carried against them the same verdict of eviction." On the fourth day, thirty-five exiles reached Pala, where quarters were assigned to them. All the evicted Indians were then set to work erecting their houses of lumber, meanwhile liv-

---

[20] *Out West*, April, 1903, p. 499.
[21] Ibidem, May, 1903, p. 593.

SAN ANTONIO DE PALA AND INDIAN VILLAGE IN 1904

ing in tents, digging and cementing irrigation canals. For this work they received $2 a day, besides rations, until they could subsist on their crops. They have additional advantage, says Lummis, of aloofness from elbowing whites—and the class that largely frequented the Hot Springs at their old home.[22]   Thus, in brief, terminated the tragedy of the eviction of the Warner's Ranch and San Felipe Indians, a theme for a first-class drama.[23]   For a complete description of the evictions the reader is referred to the issues of *Out West.*

---

[22] *Out West,* July, 1903, p. 41.

[23] Ibidem, October, 1903, pp. 420-421; November, 1903, pp. 485-491.

CHAPTER XIII.

THE reader will doubtless welcome biographical sketches
of the Franciscan missionaries who departed this life at
Mission San Luis Rey, or who, after serving there, retired
to the Mother College of San Fernando, in the City of
Mexico.

Fr. José García's antecedents are not known. He left the
College of San Fernando for the missions of California on
February 3, 1800, in company with Fathers José de Miguel,
Martin de Landaeta, and Domingo Yturrate. Having arrived at Monterey in August of the same year, he appears
to have been at once assigned as assistant to Mission San
Luis Rey, where Fr. Antonio Peyri was already engaged in
apostolic labors. On his way down, overland, Fr. García
probably visited the various missions located on the camino
reál. At least, the Registers show that he officiated at San
Carlos in September, 1800, and on November 9 following at
San Fernando. In 1803, on April 15 and 30, he administered Baptism at San Juan Capistrano. Of his activities at
San Luis Rey scarcely anything is known. Together with
Fr. Peyri he signed the Biennial Reports for 1799-1800 and
1803-1804. He visited San Diego Mission and baptized there
on February 2-5, 15-18, and September 9-10, 1807. Once he
also officiated at a Baptism in the presidio chapel. His name
appears for the last time in the Baptismal Register of Mission San Diego, probably just before embarking for Mexico,
on September 18, 1808. The entry bears number 3534. Ill
health was the reason for retiring, for which, of course,
he received the requisite permit from both Fr. Presidente

and Governor Arrillaga. For his signature see Chapter II.

Fr. Domingo Carranza arrived from the College of San Fernando with seven companion friars and landed from the *Concepcion,* if we may believe Bancroft,[1] at Santa Barbara on May 7, 1798. He seems to have been at once assigned to Santa Cruz Mission by Fr. Presidente Lasuén. On his way up the country, he officiated at Mission San Antonio on August 6, and again on October 8, 1798. His first entry in the Baptismal Register of Santa Cruz is dated October 26, 1798. At this mission he labored till 1808, when he was

SIGNATURE OF FR. CARRANZA

transferred to Mission San Luis Rey. Fr. Carranza assisted Fr. Antonio Peyri till late in 1810, when, having served more than the required ten years, he obtained from Fr. Presidente Tapis the permit to retire, and on October 29 from Governor Arrillaga the passport. He departed for Mexico from San Diego, where he baptized for the last time on November 25, 1810. He reached San Blas with Fr. Santiago, but no sooner had they landed than both were made prisoners by the insurgents and sentenced to death. The sentence was not executed, however, and both friars presumably reached their destination.

Fr. Jayme Escudé was born at the Villa de Gandesa, Catalonia, in July, 1779. He received the Franciscan habit on November 18, 1799, in the Convento de Recoleccion at Tatosa. After finishing his studies and having been ordained priest, he applied for the missions in America. On March 29, 1810, he embarked at Cadiz for the Apostolic College of San Fernando, Mexico. Early in July, 1811, he set out with five companion friars for the missions in California;

---

[1] *California,* vol. ii, p. 108.

but they were delayed at San Blas by the insurrection then prevailing in Mexico. The little party proceeded on their way to Acapulco. When they arrived there, a pestilence once more delayed them. Fr. Oliva was stricken with the fever and had to remain behind, when at last an opportunity offered to sail across the gulf to Loreto. Here Fr. Escudé and his four companions arrived on April 23, 1812. In May they began the weary overland journey to San Diego, where Fr. Escudé and Fr. Nuez arrived about July 15, not, as Bancroft says, July 7. Fr. Escudé went to San Luis Rey and stayed there several months. Thereupon he was directed to proceed to Mission Santa Cruz, where Fr. Andrés Quintana had been murdered shortly before, on October 12. Fr. Escudé took ship probably at San Diego. At all events, his name never appears in any of the Baptismal Registers of the missions along the camino reál. His first entry in the Baptismal Register of Santa Cruz is dated June 5, 1813.

SIGNATURE OF FR. ESCUDÉ.

but he doubtless arrived there long before that date. Fr. Prefect Sarría describes him as a zealous missionary of edifying conduct. By order of Fr. Sarría, Fr. Escudé visited the savages in the interior of the country, presumably to find a site suitable for a mission or to ascertain the temper of the pagans toward Christianity; but Fr. Sarría offers neither dates nor details. Fr. Payeras reports that Fr. Escudé is capable and worthy to be placed in charge of a religious community. The last entries of Fr. Escudé in the Baptismal Register of Mission Santa Cruz are numbers 1727-1744, dated February 7, 1818. A few months later, he accompanied Fr. Sarría on his official visitation tour through the missions lying southward. We find him

as "Secretario de la Visita" signing the *Auto-de-Visita* with
Fr. Sarría at Mission San Miguel on June 18, 1818, and
at most of the missions until July 17, 1818, at San Juan
Capistrano. From there both went to Mission San Luis
Rey. Here Fr. Escudé remained to take the place of Fr.
Ramon Olbés, who had been transferred to Santa Cruz.
At Mission San Luis Rey, Fr. Escudé exercised his wonted
zeal as assistant to Fr. Peyri till 1822. He signed the An-
nual and Biennial Reports of the Mission, together with Fr.
Peyri, for the years 1818, 1819, 1820, 1821. In 1822, he
returned to the College of San Fernando.

Fr. Antonio Peyri, the founder of the Mission, penned a
brief autobiography reaching to his arrival at San Luis Rey,
on the second page of the front fly-leaf of a book in pig-
skin covers and entitled *Directorio Moral, por Fr. Francisco
Echarri, O. S. F., Tomo II, Madrid, 1790*. It was discovered
in the library of the Franciscans at San Luis Rey and copied
by the writer on October 9, 1912. The translation reads
as follows:

"In the year 1769, on January 8, I was baptized in the
church of the illustrious Villa de Porrera, in the Archdiocese of Tarragona, Catalonia; and in the same church, on
October 30, 1772, I was confirmed. In said Villa de Porrera I lived till the year 1775, when I proceeded to Vinols,
a place in the same archdiocese. Here I remained till the
following year. Then I returned to my native place and
stayed there till the year 1778, when I departed for Lleysa,
a town in the same archdiocese. Here I was till 1781,
when I again returned home and stayed there till the year
1784. Next I went to Cornufella, a town in the same archdiocese. After having lived there to the year 1787, I went
to the Villa de Reus in order to take the holy habit of the
Seraphic Order, which occurred on October 21, of the
same year. On October 22, 1788, I made my profession in
said Order, and immediately I was sent to Esornalbou in
order to pass the year there as cleric. At the end of this
year, I was sent to the city of Gerona, where I remained till

the year 1794, when I received the Patente for new Spain
(Mexico). In said city of Gerona I received all Holy Or-
ders: the four Minor Orders on December 19, 1789; the
Subdeaconship on February 27, 1790; the Deaconate on
April 9, 1791, and the Priesthood on March 16, 1793. I
celebrated the first holy Mass on April 1 of the same year.

"I set out for New Spain from said convent in 1794,
on September 14. On the 24th I left Barcelona and, passing through Madrid on October 25 of the same year with
my companion, Fr. José Viader, I reached the Port of
Santa Maria. There we were detained until May 8, 1795,
when we embarked (at Cadiz) with twenty other religious
and reached Vera Cruz on July 26 of the same year. After
having rested there a few days, we set out for the College,
where we arrived on August 23 of the same year. There
we remained until March 1, 1796, on which day, with four
companions, I set out for California. With this end in
view we reached San Blas after a journey of a month. We
embarked in the Port of San Blas on April 5 of the same
year, and disembarked in the Port of San Francisco on June
18. After I had rested there for fifteen days, I started out
for Mission San Luis Obispo, where I arrived on July 19,
1796, On April 15, 1798, I was destined for the founding
of San Luis Rey, which was accomplished on June 13 of
the same year, and at said Mission I stayed as missionary
with Fr. José Faura." This brief autobiography of Fr.
Antonio Peyri bears no signature; but the handwriting is
unmistakably his.

On November 5, 1817, Fr. Comisario Prefecto Sarría,
reporting about Fr. Peyri to the Missionary College of San
Fernando, Mexico, writes: "He enjoys the merit, not only
of being the founder of Mission San Luis Rey, but also of
having laudably served it for the long period of nineteen
years, and of having advanced it greatly by his personal activity and diligence. A year and some months ago, with
the permit of the government and with mine, he built a
chapel about seven leagues east of the Mission, under the

title of San Antonio de Pala, Pala being, in the language of the Indians, the name of the site.   At this Mission he is ordinarily occupied, but at times returning to the chief Mission.   In a short time, already a good harvest has been gathered, thanks be to God; and while the personal merit of

SIGNATURE OF FR. PEYRI

said Father keeps on growing, it is hoped that even much more will be accomplished toward the conversion of those savages to holy Church."

At first, unlike all other Spanish Fathers in the California Missions, Fr. Peyri was an enthusiastic supporter of the ephemeral new Constitution of Mexico.   This elicited from him an effusion which flowed directly from his heart, but not from his head.   In reply to the demand for the oath of allegiance to the Constitution concocted not by the people of Mexico, but, as Fr. Duran wrote, by a handful of politicians, Fr. Peyri, writing under date of June 7, 1826, said: "I swear to uphold the Constitutional Act and the Constitution of the United States of Mexico, adopted October 4. 1824, and congratulate myself for offering an oath which in itself unites the happiness of the nation, and I assure you that my recognition of it is and always has been without vacillation."   He likewise adopted the new mode of concluding letters and documents with *Dios y la Ley*, instead of the beautiful and time-honorèd *Dios le guarde muchos años— God keep you many years.*[2]

To his deep regret, however, Fr. Peyri soon discovered that he had placed too much confidence in Echeandia and in those who sent him to misgovern California.   Only three months and two weeks after taking the afore-mentioned oath of allegiance, on September 26, 1826, he asked Echeandia

---

[2] *Archb. Arch.,* no. 1,830.

for the passport and for the annual stipend, that he might be able to subsist until he reached Europe, where he wished to spend his last days.[3]

The zealous and most practical of the missionaries continued in charge of San Luis Rey just six years longer, when, governmental interference threatening to destroy the work he had so laboriously constructed, he withdrew to Mexico and later to Spain. During his administration of thirty-four years, Fr. Peyri erected and successfully managed the largest and most populous Indian mission of both Americas.

Fr. Francisco González de Ibarra (Ybarra) was born at Viana, in the Province of Navarra, Spain, in 1782, and became a member of the Franciscan Province of Burgos. When he joined the Order is not known. Having volunteered for the missions in America, he was permitted to cross the ocean and join the College of San Fernando, Mexico. This was in 1819. The next year he was sent with the three Fathers, José Altimira, Thomas Esténaga, and Blas Ordaz, to California. They disembarked at Monterey from *El Señoriano* and the *San Francisco Xavier* or *Alcion*, on August 8 and 9, 1820. Fr. Ibarra was assigned to Mission San Fernando. Forthwith he departed overland for his field of labor. Here he baptized for the first time on November 5, 1820. It is entry number 2433. He served at this mission till about the middle of 1835, officiating there for the last time at a Baptism on June 19, 1835. Under date of June 26, 1826, he replied to Governor Echeandia's demand for the oath of allegiance to the Mexican Constitution as follows: "I oblige myself to guard and observe said Federal Constitution whenever it is not contrary to my conscience and religious character." Under the rule of the administrators, Fr. Ibarra, then at Mission San Fernando, became distracted and fled to Sonora without waiting for the permit of his Superior, Fr. Duran. His last entry in the Baptismal Register, as said before, is dated June 19, 1835.

---

[3] *Archb. Arch.*, no. 1,838.

Fr. Duran fully understood the circumstances under which he had left, and accordingly wrote to the Fr. Guardian of the missionary college: "Out of compassion, I sent the permit, lest he be regarded as an apostate from the Order." Fr. Ibarra returned to California, however, in time to prepare for death and lay to rest Fr. Pedro Cabot, which event took place on October 12, 1836. Bancroft finds no trace of him after that till the year 1839, when he is said to have taken charge of San Luis Rey. It is almost certain that in July, 1837, Fr. Ibarra took the place of Fr. Buenaventura Fortuni, because the latter, in July, 1837, succeeded Fr. Ordaz at Mission San Buenaventura. Inasmuch as the Mission Registers of San Luis Rey have been stolen and most probably destroyed, it is impossible to determine with certainty when Fr. Ibarra came to San Luis Rey. It is quite certain that he succeeded Fr. Fortuni. As a visitor to Mission San Diego we find him baptizing "in the chapel of the Port of San Diego" on December 11, 1837, and again on September 7, 1838. This confirms our view that he was

Fr. Juan² Gonzalez P. Ybarra,

SIGNATURE OF FR. IBARRA

stationed at San Luis Rey after Fr. Fortuni from July, 1837. In January, 1839, he makes two entries in the Mission Register of San Diego. At San Luis Rey the poor missionary fared even worse than at San Fernando, as the reader will have learned from chapters VII and VIII. Bancroft notes that he was well liked by the Indians for his sunny disposition and plain, unassuming manners, for which latter trait they called him, in their language, *Tequedcuma.* He is said to have died from apoplexy; but it is more probable that grief and lack of nourishment brought on his death, which occurred some time in 1842. Very likely, Fr. Oliva came up from San Diego to assist his dying fellow missionary, or at least to give burial to his mortal remains. Perhaps, too, like several other Fathers who had been most solicitous that none of their flock die without the Sacraments, Fr. Ibarra was called upon to make the last supreme sacrifice of passing from this world without those consolations of Religion. The body was doubtless interred in the sanctuary of the mission church at San Luis Rey, although in the absence of the Burial Registers absolute certainty and details cannot be had. From an old settler, Silvester Marron, who declared that he had lived at or near San Luis Rey since 1841, we learned some interesting items about Fr. Ibarra. According to Mr. Marron, Fr. Ibarra was a man short of stature, very old, and with white hair. He maintained also that it was Fr. Zalvidea who gave burial to the deceased Fr. Ibarra, and that the body was interred in the sanctuary on the epistle side of the main altar.

Fr. José Maria Zalvidea was one of the few Vizcayan friars who came to California, most of the others being Catalonians. He was born at Bilbao, Vizcaya, on March 2, 1780. He received the habit of St. Francis in the Convent of Mamos, the house of recollection for the Province of Cantabria, on December 13, 1798. On April 12, 1804, fortified with the blessing of his Superior, he set out from that retreat to devote himself to the missions in America, and arrived at the College of San Fernando, Mexico, on September 10 of the same year. In March, 1805, he was sent to California and he arrived probably at San Diego the following August. He was assigned to Mission San Fernando, where he baptized for the first time on February 1, 1806. The Baptism was entered under number 1564. His last entry there is dated August 31, 1806. During July and August of that year he accompanied an expedition in search of sites for new missions, of which expedition he kept a diary.[4] He was then transferred to San Gabriel, where he entered his first Baptism on December 19, 1806. At this

---

[4] See *Missions and Missionaries*, vol. ii, pp. 679-681.

Mission Fr. Zalvidea manifested such efficiency that Fr. Vicente de Sarría, then Comisario Prefecto, wrote of him to the Fr. Guardian of San Fernando College: "He is, in my judgment, one of the best laborers in this country. His merit is eminent for indefatigable zeal in teaching, instructing, and spiritually advancing the neophytes, not leaving them even to the last moment of his life; for the circumstance that is most remarkable—the great number who belong to his mission; for the knowledge he has acquired of the language, and for his solicitude for and adherence to the fulfilment of other obligations, not only of his personal religious obligations, but also of those which in his ministry bind him to the people of the Pueblo (of Los Angeles), distant three leagues from the Mission, and of other various rancherías in different directions."

This enthusiastic commendation from the saintly Fr. Sarría was corroborated by the report which his successor, Fr. Mariano Payeras, made to the Fr. Guardian three years later. He writes: "His merit is distinguished for activity in and application to whatever branch this ministry in California embraces. His aptitude, if it were but accompanied by complete health, is equal to every similar ministry among faithful and unbelievers, and likewise is he capable for all the offices it may be the wish to entrust to him; but he already suffers breaks in his health," which was owing to the fact that Fr. Zalvidea did not spare himself in the performance of his duties. To prevent a total breakdown, his Superior transferred him to the much less laborious Mission of San Juan Capistrano. Here his first entry in the Baptismal Register is dated March 4, 1826. He was alone at this Mission from January, 1831, till nearly the end of 1842, when he was transferred to San Luis Rey. His last Baptism was administered on November 25, 1842, and it bears number 4586. He passed to his eternal reward in 1846; the month and day of his death are not known. As Fr. Oliva of Mission San Diego departed for San Luis Rey in June of that year, we are inclined to believe that it was to assist the dying Fr. Zalvidea. A statement of Bancroft goes far to demonstrate that the holy death of the veteran missionary occurred at the end of June or July. He relates that it had been the plan to remove Fr. Zalvidea to San Juan Capistrano that he might receive the proper care, corporally and spiritually. The historian, doubtless on the word of witnesses still living when he wrote, says that "Fr. Zalvidea refused to quit San Luis Rey, where he believed his services to be needed; but finally it was thought best to remove him to San Juan. • A cart was prepared with all possible conveniences, by advice of Fr. Oliva and Miss Apollinaria Lorenzana, who had nursed him for some days. The night before his journey was to be made Fr. Zalvidea died. He was buried in the mission church at the left side of the altar. He was doubtless in those days a model missionary." Bancroft further writes: "In political controversies he took no part; but in 1829 (it must be 1826) he expressed his willingness to swear allegiance to the Mexican Republic (rather, to the Constitution of October 4, 1824), so far as was consistent with his state of life. He was well versed in the native tongue in which he was accustomed to preach at San Gabriel." [5]

According to the afore-mentioned Mr. Marron, whom the writer had the good fortune of interviewing, Fr. Zalvidea was very tall and strong. He would always be reading; even while walking. On one occasion, he was walking, book in hand, in the front corridor near the church. Suddenly he threw the book in a certain direction, exclaiming, "Va-te, Satanas!" He had seen the devil, the witness declared, and therefore threw the book at him. Fr. Zalvidea was not insane at all, but very pious and holy. To practice mortification, around his waist next to the skin, he wore a cincture of horse hair. This was discovered after his death. A similar band he wore around his legs above the knees. This, too, was discovered after his death; for when he had died,

5 Bancroft, vol. v, pp. 621-623.

INTERIOR OF THE CHAPEL AT PALA AFTER RESTORATION BY THE LANDMARKS CLUB

everybody wanted a relic of him; so they began to cut bits from his habit, beginning from the bottom, which in this way disappeared to the legs, so that the rope was discovered. All loved him for his holiness. He cared nothing for money. If any one ordered a holy Mass to be offered up, he would take the stipend, but at the first opportunity he would give it to some Indian. Fr. Zalvidea preached in the Indian language from the pulpit that may still be seen in the church. His body was buried by Fr. Vicente Oliva of San Diego, who then moved to San Juan Capistrano. The body was laid to rest on the Epistle side of the main altar, but near the wall, next to Fr. Ibarra's body. Rev. Father Mut of San Juan Capistrano exhumed the remains and had them placed in a new coffin.

This last statement is corroborated by Mrs. Maria González, the wife of Nicholas González. She says that she was present when, in October or November, 1884, the Rev. Fathers Ubach, Mut, and Mora (later Bishop Mora) came to San Luis Rey and on Saturday, in the presence of Silvester Marron and others besides herself, had two Indians raise the body of Fr. Zalvidea, which had been interred under the choir loft in front of the baptistry. The coffin had been obtained in San Diego and it was still in good condition. The body, which was not at all decomposed (nada corumpida), was placed in a new coffin and then they bore it in procession, all holding lighted candles, to the grave prepared for it in the sanctuary on the Epistle side of the main altar, before the door to the sacristy. Rev. Antonio Ubach of San Diego celebrated holy Mass near the pulpit, because the main altar was in ruins. Father Mut also celebrated holy Mass at the same place and for the same reason. Father Ubach had charge of the Mission then. He would celebrate holy Mass on the first Sunday of the month. When he could not come, Father Mut, from San Juan Capistrano, would take his place.

From Mrs. Margaret Pico, daughter-in-law of José Antonio Pico, who was the senior brother of Pio Pico, we have other items of interest and value. According to her, Fr. Zalvidea died in a room near the church. Santiago, an Indian boy, served him when he was ill. The good Father was crippled in his legs and sick a long time. He told Santiago the night before his death that he might go, as he would be called when wanted. That night the saintly missionary passed away. He was found dead the next morning, holding a crucifix in his hands. His breviary lay open over his heart. He died in his Franciscan habit. Mrs. Pico, a lady apparently of superior intelligence, likewise thought that his death occurred in summer, which again corroborates our surmise that Fr. Zalvidea departed this life in June and that Fr. Oliva gave burial to the body and then went to San Juan Capistrano without returning to San Diego.

William Heath Davis relates that when he and James McKinlay were passing north once, they stopped at San Luis, and there found Zalvidea, "strong and healthy, although about eighty years of age. He spent most of his time in walking back and forth in the spacious piazza of the Mission, with his prayer-book open in his hand, saying his prayers, hour after hour. I stood, therefore, some time observing him, and every time he reached the end of the piazza he would give me a little side glance and nod of recognition, and say 'Vamos si, señor' a number of times in succession. Whenever he met me or anyone else through the day or evening he would make the same greeting, and never anything else. If anyone spoke to him he would listen attentively until the speaker had finished, apparently hearing and understanding everything that was said, but he made no reply other than the words I have quoted. During such interviews he would never look a person square in the face, but always gazed a little on one side, round a corner as it were. One might have supposed he was demented from this singular conduct. I inquired if this was so of Mr. McKinlay, who had known him for ten years or more, and he replied that he was always the same; that he was so absorbed in his devotions that he did not care to hold any intercourse with the world or converse on worldly topics, but gave his whole life and attention to religion.

"Father Zalvidea was much beloved by his people, who looked upon him as a saint on earth, on account of the purity and excellence of his character. Among his eccentricities was his custom at meals of mixing different kinds of foods thoroughly together on one plate—meat, fish, vegetables, pie, pudding, sweet and sour—a little of everything. After they were thoroughly mingled, he would eat the preparation, instead of taking the different dishes separately, or in such combinations as were usual. This was accounted for as a continual act of penance on his part. In other words, he did not care to enjoy his meals, and so made them distasteful, partaking of food merely to maintain existence. Whenever any ladies called on him, as they frequently did, to make some little present as a mark of esteem, he never looked at them, but turned his face away, and extending his hand to one side, received the gift, saying, 'Vamos, si señora; muchas gracias.' He never offered his hand in salutation to a lady. At times, in taking his walks for exercise in the vicinity of the Mission, the priest was seen to touch his head lightly on either side with a finger, throw his hand out with a quick, spasmodic motion, and snap his fingers; as if casting out devils. On such occasions he was heard to exclaim 'Va-te, satanas!'—some improper thought, as he conceived, probably having entered his mind." [6]

"He paid no heed to warnings of danger," Bancroft writes, "and on several occasions wild cattle charged upon him without harming him or evoking anything but a slight reproof for throwing dirt upon his book. He made frequent use of the scourge, and wore belts with iron points penetrating the flesh. In his last months he would have no watchers at night, and was always found covered with blood from self-inflicted wounds in the morning. Yet even in the midst of all this madness (?) in devotional matters,

6 G. W. James in *Old Missions*, pp. 108-111.

SAN ANTONIO DE PALA FROM THE REAR

he showed himself to have a clear head and the most practical and liberal ideas on all other subjects. He was a tall
man, of fine presence and fair complexion; always courteous
in his manners, with a smile and a kind word for all, and
never annoyed by the presence of others even in his mad-
dest (?) moments. He was skilled in the native tongue, in
which he used to preach on Sunday at San Gabriel. There
is no evidence that he ever had an enemy, or said an unkind
word to any man. He refused to quit San Luis Rey, where
he believed his services to be needed; but finally it was
thought best to remove him to San Juan Capistrano. A cart
was prepared with all possible conveniences, by advice of
Padre Oliva and Apollinaria Lorenzana, who had nursed
him for some days (?). The night before the journey was
to be made, Zalvidea died. He was buried in the mission
church, at the left of the altar. The date is not known, but
apparently early (?) in 1846." [7] For his autograph see
Chapter IX.

After Fr. Zalvidea's death, in 1846, San Luis Rey was
attended from San Juan Capistrano, or rather, it seems, the
people took the children there for Baptism. The United
States military had taken possession of the mission buildings of San Luis Rey in March, 1847, and remained there
till 1850 or later. At all events, Fr. Oliva, then stationed
at San Juan Capistrano, did not at any time live at San
Luis Rey. At this time, however, the mission books of San
Luis Rey must have been still existing, for no entries were
made in the books at San Juan Capistrano or at San Diego.

When Rev. Antonio Ubach arrived at San Diego, he had
charge also of San Luis Rey; but where he made his entries
for the Indians of the interior is not known. Rev. Father
Mut of San Juan Capistrano later visited the place occasionally; but no priest was stationed at San Luis Rey until

---

[7] Bancroft, vol. v, pp. 622-623. The inserted question marks are
ours. More details on this noble missionary will be found in connection with the narrative on the missions of San Gabriel and San Juan
Capistrano.

the Mexican Franciscans reopened the Mission for themselves in 1893. Father Mut entered all Baptisms at San Juan Capistrano.

According to the Official List, issued annually by the Fr. Presidente, and according to the Annual Reports, signed by the resident missionaries, the following Franciscans were stationed at Mission San Luis Rey:

Fr. Antonio Peyri, June, 1798, to January, 1832.

Fr. José Faura, July, 1798, to May, 1800.

. Fr. José Panella, in 1802.

Fr. José García, August, 1800, to August, 1808.

Fr. Domingo Carranza, August, 1808, to November, 1810.

Fr. Estévan Tápis, 1810 to 1811.

Fr. Gerónimo Boscana, June, 1811, to May, 1814.

Fr. Francisco Suñer, May, 1814, to September, 1816.

Fr. Ramon Olbés, May, 1816, to June, 1818.

Fr. Jayme Escudé, March, 1818, to ...., 1822.

Fr. José Joaquín Jimeno, October, 1827, to .... 1830.

Fr. Antonio Ánzar, July, 1831, to April, 1833.

Fr. Vicente Oliva, 1832 to 1834.

Fr. Buenaventura Fortuni, April, 1833, to June, 1837.

Fr. Francisco Ibarra, ..., 1837, to December, 1842.

Fr. José Maria Zalvidea, December, 1842, to June, 1846.

Doubtless other Fathers occasionally officiated at San Luis Rey; but in the absence of the usual mission records, their names cannot be given. Fr. Jayme Escudé appears in the *Lista* for 1812 as third or supernumerary priest. He had just then come from Mexico; but he signs no reports. Fr. Estévan Tápis, on the other hand, signs the report for 1810 as senior Father with Fr. Peyri, on January 1, 1811. Fr. Tápis, in fact, was Presidente at the time, and for want of missionaries was taking the place of Fr. Carranza, who had departed for Mexico. He remained probably till the arrival of Fr. Boscana; in fact, he signs a letter at San Luis Rey on June 6, 1811.

CHAPTER XIV.

WHAT has been said of Mission San Diego regarding agriculture and stock raising applies to a certain extent also to Mission San Luis Rey. The latter establishment was in a district more favorable to agriculture. Still, the Fathers here, too, had to learn by experience. There were years of drouth and years of floods; and both taught the missionaries where to plant with the greatest advantage. As at San Diego, a great many Indians were permitted after their conversion to live in their native rancherías. The *Padron* of the first year brings a list of the neophytes who lived away from the immediate supervision of the Fathers; but here the disastrous results were not so manifest as at San Diego. Fr. Peyri had wonderful control over his converts and had safeguards thrown around them that were not so feasible at the other mission. San Diego Mission lay too near the presidio with all its evil influences aggravated by the frequent visits of sailors from other countries. Happily, San Luis Rey was out of reach, so that Fr. Peyri's task was much easier.

Fortunately, the Annual Reports of the Mission on matters of agriculture and live stock are almost complete to the year 1832, inclusive, and thus cover the entire period of Fr. Peyri's activity. From these we have compiled the accompanying tabular lists, which clearly tell the story at a glance. They show that Mission San Luis Rey surpassed all other missionary establishments as to live stock, but that Mission San Gabriel was more successful in agriculture. In the religious or spiritual order, San Luis Rey ranks among the first, having enrolled 7,061 converts by October 1, 1843.

MATERIAL RESULTS AT MISSION SAN LUIS REY—AGRICULTURAL PRODUCTS

Year	Wheat		Barley		Corn		Beans		Peas		Lentils		Garbanzos		Habas		TOTAL			
																	Fanegas		Bushels	
	Plant	Harv.	Plant	Harv.	Plant	Harv.	Plant	Harv.	Plant	Harv.	Plant	Harv.	Plant	Harv.	Plant	Harv.	Plant	Harv.	Plant	Harv.
1798	40	.....	14	.....	.....	.....	.....	.....	.....	.....	.....	.....	.....	.....	.....	.....	54	.....	90	.....
1799	40	800	14	400	3	150	1	20	.....	.....	.....	.....	.....	.....	.....	.....	58	1370	97	2283
1800	80	1000	7	60	3	20	.....	.....	.....	.....	.....	.....	.....	.....	.....	.....	90	1080	150	2800
1801	80	700	50	1000	4	250	4	70	.....	.....	.....	.....	.....	.....	.....	.....	138	2020	230	3366
1802	100	1200	32	500	3	280	3	50	.....	.....	.....	.....	.....	.....	.....	.....	138	2030	230	3393
1803	101	1300	40	1300	4	500	3	70	.....	.....	.....	.....	.....	.....	.....	.....	148	3170	246	5283
1804	104	2500	70	1700	4	700	4	70	.....	.....	.....	.....	.....	.....	.....	.....	182	4970	303	8283
1805	.....	.....	.....	.....	.....	.....	.....	.....	.....	.....	.....	.....	.....	.....	.....	.....	.....	.....	.....	.....
1806	106	2000	100	3200	5	500	5	110	.....	.....	.....	.....	.....	.....	.....	.....	216	5810	360	9516
1807	110	450	102	2200	6	700	5	60	.....	.....	.....	.....	.....	.....	.....	.....	223	3410	372	5683
1808	150	3000	100	3500	6	600	6	150	.....	.....	.....	.....	.....	.....	.....	.....	262	7250	436	12083
1809	135	800	100	400	6	700	4	24	.....	.....	.....	.....	.....	.....	.....	.....	245	1924	408	3206
1810	150	1400	100	1400	8	1200	¾	30	.....	.....	.....	.....	.....	.....	.....	.....	262	4030	436	67116
1811	175	3500	130	3800	8	1200	6	35	.....	.....	.....	.....	⅓	18	⅓	13	320	8566	585	14276
1812	250	2500	130	2100	10	1800	6	160	.....	.....	.....	.....	⅓	5	½	18	397	6583	662	10972
1813	250	1100	100	900	13	2300	5	100	.....	.....	.....	.....	¼	5	10	18	378	4423	630	7392
1814	270	2556	141	2400	8	1200	4	70	.....	.....	.....	.....	½	25	¾	11	424	6262	706	10437
1815	309	2780	119	2045	8	900	4	80	.....	.....	.....	.....	½	31	7	32	448	5868	747	9776
1816	351	1500	201	2000	10	800	4	60	.....	.....	.....	.....	½	30	4	12	571	4402	952	7337
1817	388	6200	200	4000	10	3000	5	300	.....	.....	.....	.....	.....	.....	.....	.....	603	13500	1003	22500
1818	350	4500	225	4015	11	3100	7	350	1	40	.....	.....	1	12	1	15	596	12032	973	20053
1819	380	4300	225	4700	15	3060	8	425	1	43	.....	.....	1	7	.....	.....	630	12535	1050	20892
1820	250	3500	100	600	16	4500	9	250	1	30	.....	.....	1	10	.....	.....	377	8890	628	14816
1821	350	4500	200	3000	12	3500	12	712	1	40	.....	.....	1	39	1	15	577	11806	962	19676
1822	230	2150	0	0	12	3700	10	350	1½	43	.....	.....	1½	31	2	30	257	6304	428	10507
1823	300	116	70	0	14	3900	10	174	1	25	.....	.....	1	19	2	34	398	4268	663	7113
1824	300	2000	150	1800	14	3500	8	180	1	42	.....	.....	1	6	1½	34	476	7562	760	12602
1825	400	4500	200	2700	10	300	10	500	1	40	.....	.....	1	12	1½	45	624	8097	1040	13495
1826	300	800	150	2900	16	3015	10	150	1	25	.....	.....	1	8	1½	32	480	6930	800	11550
1827	350	1400	150	3000	20	4500	10	500	1	3	.....	.....	1	12	1	18	533	9433	888	15722
1828	350	2235	170	2500	20	4536	10	600	½	3	⅙	3	1	22	1	0	553	9899	922	16497
1829	300	200	100	300	20	5500	10	300	½	10	½	5	1	22	½	8	433	6345	723	10575
1830	325	4065	150	3015	20	3014	10	234	½	3	½	2	1	22	½	4	508	10359	847	17265
1831	320	1800	200	1200	20	2000	10	200	½	2	½	2	1	10	½	3	553	5217	922	8695
1832	340	2500	230	1200	15	300	13	35	⅔	6	1⅙	1	1	1	½	0	602	4043	1003	6738

It may be justly reckoned as the greatest achievement of the old Franciscan missionaries that they succeeded not only in gathering, retaining, and supporting so many Indian converts at the mission establishments, especially at the much harrowed Mission San Luis Rey and its sub-stations, but also in grounding their neophytes so firmly in the two main features of civilized life—religiousness and industry. Anyone who knows what the native Californians were previous to the advent of the missionaries must admit that they demonstrated absolutely no sympathy for manual labor, and that as to religious convictions they possessed none whatever. Today, on the contrary, all who have become acquainted with the descendants of the Mission Indians are lost in astonishment and do not hesitate to acknowledge that "these Indians (now at Pala) are quiet, unobtrusive, law-abiding, honest, clean, thrifty, holding in respect the marriage tie; their women are chaste. They are religious, following the observance of their Church under many difficulties." [1]

In the summer of 1901, the year of extreme want, the Rt. Rev. Joseph H. Johnson, Episcopal Bishop of Los Angeles, together with the Rev. B. Restarick, Episcopal minister of San Diego, went among the Mission Indians for the purpose of learning the truth about them. "The Rev. Mr. Restarick, after giving most harrowing details, stated that the worst had not been told, which, if he could write as actually seen by them, could scarcely be understood. The reverend gentleman reported that they found everywhere amongst them (the Indians) extreme poverty, and consequent suffering; that they worked eagerly and cheerfully, when work is given them, work as faithfully as white men. Prominent and reliable men had said to them that they had employed Indians for forty years. . . . Among many other instances of the kind which these reverend gentlemen reported as having seen in their trips, was that of Joaquin Pipa, captain of the Inaya Indians, who are now moved to

---

[1] *Los Angeles Herald Magazine*, Nov. 10, 1901, p. 12.

Anahuac because a cattleman wanted their land at Inaya. There are forty-four people on the reservation. They have no cattle. Joaquin Pipa had a house of one room, and fourteen inhabitants, viz: his father and mother, a very old and very sick uncle, his wife and six children. There was

SPIRITUAL RESULTS AT MISSION SAN LUIS REY

Year	Baptisms Indian	Baptisms White	Marriages Indian	Marriages White	Deaths Indian	Deaths White	Confessions	Communions	Confirmations	Viaticum	Neophytes Male	Neophytes Female	Total Number of Neophytes at Mission
1798	210		34		5						103	100	203
1799	284		55		22								279
1800	371	4	78	2	56						170	167	337
1801	477		99		80								452
1802	568	1	113		104	2					256	276	532
1803	670		135		132								615
1804	744		153		189						308	328	636
1805													
1806	1157	3	255		332						487	475	961
1807	1235		270		362								1025
1808	1347	6	288	2	398	2	106	3			578	532	1110
1809	1393		304		432		10						1121
1810	1831	2	378		474	1	25				778	739	1517
1811	1966	2	428		517		116	3			819	782	1601
1812	2158	1	484		575	1	105				874	859	1733
1813	2282	2	513		641	1	140				924	891	1815
1814	2402		529		714		185				942	904	1846
1815	2484		549		775		376				949	917	1866
1816	2537	1	561		841	1	500				971	942	1913
1817	3005	2	586		952	1	1100				1149	1120	2269
1818	3086	1	641		1055	1	952	1		13	1157	1089	2246
1819	3560	8	809		1190	3	1103	5		16	1320	1265	2585
1820	3727	3	866		1314		1109	10		19	1339	1264	2603
1821	3890	4	899	1	1409	3	1115	7		8	1358	1273	2631
1822	4022	2	922		1506	1	1120	8		3	1377	1286	2663
1823	4258	5	995		1669	1	932	7		2	1418	1303	2721
1824	4409	4	1026		1770	2	?	?		?	1445	1322	2767
1825	4511	2	1061		1899	1	730	10		5	1443	1313	2756
1826	4723	5	1111	1	1979	1	683	4		3	1509	1360	2869
1827	4816	5	1129		2252	1	680	4		0	1428	1257	2685
1828	4991	3	1172	1	2372	1	692	6		0	1464	1272	2736
1829	5094	2	1229		2465	1	?	?		?	1470	1274	2744
1830	5188	4	1264		2526	1	579	7		0	1480	1296	2776
1831	5295	3	1301		2586		624	2		0	1493	1326	2819
1832	5397	2	1335		2716	2	?	?		?	1491	1297	2788
1843	7061	?	?	?	?	?	?	?		?	?	?	?

one old cot and a few rags on the earth floor. The Rev. Mr. Restarick wrote thus of the case, which is only typical of many others.

" 'Why don't you work ' I asked of the captain. 'Where?' he asked. There was sometimes woodchopping, but there was not work all the time. He was not bitter, but he seemed to have given up all hope, if he ever had any. Yet at Julian they said he was the best worker on the reservation. . . . It was the same old story about land. The land they lived on was not reserved; white men got title to it and they had to move off. Some of them used to live at Comista, some at Inaya; now they all lived here at Anahuac, for Inaya, I found, now belonged to a cattleman."

Despite this extreme poverty these poor Mission descendants did not forget the Faith they had inherited from the missionaries, a fact at which the Rev. Restarick wonders not a little. He writes: "The captain took us to the church, for these Indians, poor as they are, and having had no visit from a priest for 'many, many years,' meet on Sunday for prayers, and a young woman leads the people. The captain reverently entered the church and we after him. The little altar was of adobe, with tin candlesticks and a few poor outer ornaments. It was all clean and orderly. *It occurred to me that few Protestants*, isolated as these people have been, with no visit from a minister, under hopeless conditions, would have maintained their religious rites.

" 'Were there not many more Indians here years ago?' I asked.

" 'Yes, many.

" 'Where are they now?'

"The man pointed over to the graveyard, marked with Crosses. 'There,' he said, 'are forty-three of them. Over in Comista there are more.' " [2]

That was written nineteen years ago. The conditions have changed since then. The Indians have been allotted lands in reservations, and there will be no more evictions. Today they are prosperous because they are industrious; and as in adversity so also in prosperity, they cling to the Faith instilled into their forefathers by the missionaries of San Luis Rey and San Diego. There are churches on all

[2] *Los Angeles Herald Magazine*, pp. 12-13.

MATERIAL RESULTS AT MISSION SAN LUIS REY—LIVE STOCK

Year	Cattle	Sheep	Goats	Pigs	Horses	Mules	Tota
1798	162	600	....	....	28	10	800
1799	266	1000			102	11	1379
1800	450	1600			146	14	2210
1801	500	2000			180	16	2696
1802	1400	2700			226	18	4344
1803	2200	4400			256	23	6879
1804	3000	6460			276	28	9764
1805	....						....
1806	4025	11043		36	584	42	15730
1807	4400	13500		26	625	55	18606
1808	4800	15060		32	633	70	20595
1809	4800	14500		36	663	76	20075
1810	5000	11000		40	665	84	16789
1811	7000	13000		45	730	106	20881
1812	8300	14000		74	710	95	23179
1813	8400	12000	15	68	700	105	21288
1814	8500	12050	49	170	820	124	21713
1815	10282	14500	98	305	1000	138	26323
1816	10070	15000	....	200	940	155	26365
1817	8200	8000	....	250	900	170	17520
1818	9280	12300	300	356	1059	162	23457
1819	10508	12503	405	372	1161	151	25100
1820	10500	12800	525	316	1192	160	25493
1821	11750	15025	532	220	1450	157	29134
1822	14340	20230	625	125	1650	162	37132
1823	14500	20500	635	87	1285	129	37136
1824	14556	21507	656	125	1305	142	38291
1825	15572	22056	764	160	1260	130	39942
1826	20312	26215	1014	215	1425	204	49385
1827	22610	27412	1120	280	1501	235	53158
1828	25754	28913	1232	295	2226	345	58765
1829	25500	25000	1250	300	2150	250	54450
1830	25510	25136	1235	287	2210	258	54636
1831	26000	25500	1200	250	2150	250	55350
1832	27500	26100	1300	300	1950	180	57330

the little reservations, where divine services are regularly held by a priest of the diocese especially assigned to them.

Another glowing tribute to the work of the Catholic missionaries who first brought Christianity and civilization to the Pacific coast is that of the Hon. Franklin K. Lane, until recently Secretary of the Interior. Depicting what the Franciscans achieved for the development of California, he writes: "California was peopled by the Indians first and followed by the Padres, and it is a strange thing that wherever the Catholic Church has gone in that State you will find a most fertile spot. The rich centers of California are all gathered around those exquisite missions which those beloved Fathers taught the Indians to build.

"The Mission Fathers brought with them the art of irrigation which was a new art to this country; and they brought

their sprigs of vine and of orange and of fig and laid the
foundation for the wondrous productions of that State. So
that today you will find the very northernmost part—
Klamath Lake, on the edge of Oregon—down to the Imperial Valley in the south, the lands of California watered
and made as fertile as the valley of the Nile."[3]

---

[3] See *National Geographical Magazine*, June, 1920, p. 498.

CHAPTER XV.

IN ACCORDANCE with strict regulations, every mission in California kept the following books:
(1) Register of Baptisms; (2) Register of Marriages; (3) Register of Burials; (4) Register of Confirmations; (5) *Padron* or Register of all neophytes, and the (6) *Libro de Patentes,* in which were transcribed Circulars of Superiors, Pastoral Letters of the Bishop, and Decrees of the King. These books usually contained about 150 to 200 blank folios. They were bound in flexible leather; generally one of the covers overlapped the front edge of the book and it was fastened to the other cover by means of leather strings.

As to Mission San Luis Rey, the first four books mentioned above are missing. On January 25, 1848, Miss Apolinaria Lorenzana, who had charge of the linen church goods of Mission San Diego, but who withdrew from there when Fr. Vicente Oliva retired for a while to Mission San Luis Rey, later to Mission San Juan Capistrano, wrote to Fr. Presidente José Joaquin Jimeno at Santa Barbara: "In the month of February of the past year, and by order of the deceased Fr. Vicente, I went to Mission San Luis (Rey) in order to recover a chalice which had been thrown into the arroyo. At the same time he commissioned me to bring the books which I might find and whatever else might have remained of the church goods; for the linen goods and the vestments had already been brought away by order of the Governor (R. B. Mason). The books I placed in two boxes with some account books and unbound documents. The parish books (Mission Registers) I found torn and without covers; that is to say, the Marriage Register, the Confirmation Register, and the *Libro de Patentes.* So far it has not been possible to find the others. I deposited them, together with some sculptured and painted images, at Santa Margarita, the ranch of the Señores Pico."[1] Hence it is clear that Miss Lorenzana placed the above mentioned two Registers and the *Libro de Patentes* in the keeping of Pio Pico and his brother.

What then, we ask, has become of the Baptismal and the Burial Registers? They could not have been given away or sold by those in charge of the Mission. They were Church property in the strict sense of the word. Hence, if they are in possession of any one outside of Church circles, they are simply stolen goods. As they are clearly labeled, no one can claim that the owner is not known and that consequently he may retain possession of them.

The *Libro de Patentes,* which Miss Lorenzana reported she had found together with the Marriage and the Confirmation Register, lies before the writer. It is a folio which originally had over four hundred pages. The last page now bears number 400, after which some pages have evidently been torn out. On the first page of the front flyleaf are the *Autos-de-Visita* which Fr. Comisario Prefecto Vicente Francisco de Sarría made at Mission San Luis Rey, in 1813, 1816, and 1818, as the accompanying facsimiles show.

The next leaf bears the title page in heavy letters as follows:

LIBRO DE PATENTES, Y DE YNVENTARIO
perteneciente a la Mission de San Luis Rey de
Francia en la Nueva California.—Año de 1808.

The book was therefore begun in 1806. Beneath this heading, comes in another hand the following notice:

---

1 Apolinaria Lorenzana to Fr. J. J. Jimeno. *Sta. Barb. Arch.*

"El Ynventario de Iglesia y Sacristia da principio al folio 321; y Las Ordenes que vienen por conducto de la Mitra de Sonora se pondrán desde el folio 370—para adelante.—The Inventory of the church and sacristy begins on page 321; and the Ordinances which come from the Ordinary of Sonora will be placed beginning with folio 370."

The Circulars of the Franciscan Superiors cover pages 1 to 99. Page 100 is blank. All the folios between pages 100 and 321 appear to have been blank; they have been cut out with a scissors or a sharp knife. The first part of the book closes, on page 99, with a highly interesting note not discovered in the books extant of the missions south of Soledad: "Certifico que el dia primero de Setiembre de 1833 se recibió una Circular del R. P. Prefecto, Fr. Francisco García Diego, de las Misiones pertenecientes al Colegio de Zacatecas, que contenia el Concordato celebrado entre dicho Padre y Nuestro P. Presidente y Vice-Prefecto, Fr. Narciso Duran de que cada Religioso diga 20 Misas por los que murieren de ambos Colegios. Todos nos conformamos, y convenis en una Hermandad tan Religiosa. Y para que conste en lo sucesivo, mandó Nuestro Prelado la presente Nota.—Mision de San Luis Rey Setiembre 2 de 1833. Fr. Vicente Pasqual Oliva."[2]

Pages 321 and 322 of the book are covered with the Inventory of January 1, 1808, as per copy. Pages 323 to 330 have the Inventory of July 1, 1844, not copied. Pages 331 to 368 apparently remained blank; they are no longer in the book, having evidently been cut out. Page 369 is blank; but pages 370 to 400 contain the Ordinances or Regulations of the Bishops or Administrators of the Diocese of Sonora, to which California belonged down to the year 1841.

The discovery of this particular manuscript folio throws some light on the disappearance of the other volumes and may eventually lead to the discovery of the missing Regis-

---

[2] Compare *Missions and Missionaries*, vol. iii, p. 453.

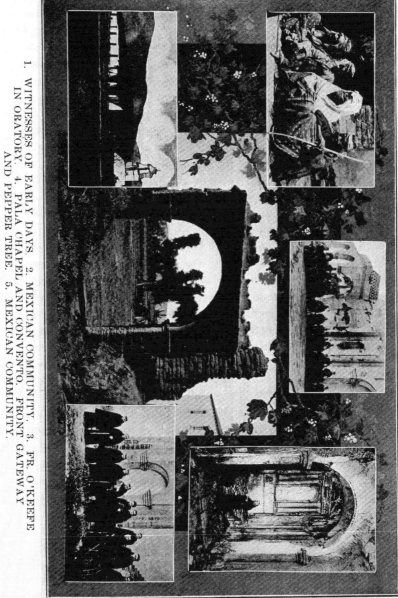

1. WITNESSES OF EARLY DAYS. 2. MEXICAN COMMUNITY. 3. FR. O'KEEFE IN ORATORY. 4. PALA CHAPEL AND CONVENTO. FRONT GATEWAY AND PEPPER TREE. 5. MEXICAN COMMUNITY.

ters. About fifteen years ago, the Rev. José Montañer, rector of St. John's Church at Milpitas, near San José, California, paid a visit to his native country, Spain. At Barcelona, the proprietor of a bookshop told him that in his collection he possessed a manuscript volume pertaining to California. Much astonished, the Rev. Father examined the folio and saw that it was a collection of papers concerning Mission San Luis Rey. The bookseller could give him no other information than that many years before a stranger had come to the shop and had sold it to the dealer for the five cents he had offered for it. Father Montañer purchased it for fifteen cents and brought the unknown treasure with him to Milpitas. The delight may be appreciated only by an old bookworm like the present writer, who at first sight fully comprehended the value of the book. The folio proved to be the *Libro de Patentes y Ordenes* of Mission San Luis Rey de Francia, and most of the documents in it had been written by Fr. Antonio Peyri himself, the founder and manager of the Mission for thirty-four years. These papers were not so valuable, however, as other portions of the folio, because they may be seen in all the mission books of the same class at the other missions. What pleased the writer more were the two inventories dated respectively 1808 and 1844. In them we have some tangible data found nowhere else. The Inventory of 1844 is especially instructive and supremely important. It shows that the church and sacristy of Mission San Luis Rey were well provided with everything pertaining to divine worship.

Still, even these Inventories are surpassed in value and importance by the two leaves or four pages from the missing Baptismal Register. They were lying loose in the book. It is, indeed, remarkable that they were not lost. The first of these two folios contains the entries 4,774-4,780, made in July and August, 1827; the other has the entries 4,867-4,882, made in March, 1828. Those baptized in March, 1828 (ten on March 13), were Indian girls and women ranging from fifteen to forty years of age. The others, baptized on the same day or the day before (the date was on another page not shown in this remnant), were male Indians ranging from fourteen to thirty years of age.

Among those baptized in July and August, 1827, were three children of Spanish-speaking parents. One was Juana, born on July 12, 1827, and baptized in the church on the same day, daughter of Francisco Silvas, native of the presidio of San Diego, and of his wife, Madalena Alvarado, native of the same presidio. The sponsors were José Ant. Silvas, mayordomo of Mission San Luis Rey, and his wife, Clara Cañedo, both natives of the same presidio. The entry is under number 4,776.

On August 1, 1827, was baptized in the church by Fr Peyri, Maria de los Angeles, daughter of José Ant. Silvas, mayordomo of the Mission, and of his wife, Maria Clara Cañedo. The child was born on the previous day, July 31. The sponsors were Antonio Maria Silvas and his wife, Maria Candelaria.

On August 8, 1827, Fr. Peyri baptized in the church a child born on the same day, daughter of José Ant. Valenzuelo, mayordomo of the Mission, native of Mission Purisima, and his wife, Maria Josefa Dominga Albitre, native of Mission San Gabriel. The names of the child and the sponsors are not on the part of the entry.

It is worthy of note that, according to this scrap from the lost Register, the number of adult converts at Mission San Luis Rey was very large, and that after less than thirty years from its founding, the Mission had entered as many as 4,882 Baptisms, very few of which were other than Indian. Where is the Register of which these four pages once formed a part?

From Judge Egan, an old settler of San Juan Capistrano, the writer obtained in 1904 the following additional information: "In 1863, Mrs. John Forster took all the books, etc., which she could find at San Luis Rey, after the soldiers had gone away, to her home, and put them into boxes, which she placed in the attic of her house at Santa Margarita.

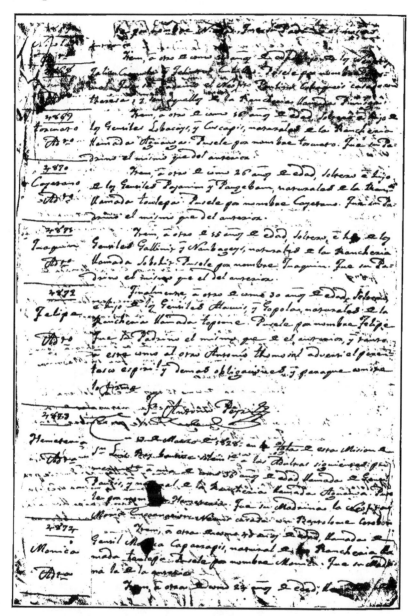

FACSIMILE PAGE FROM MISSING BAPTISMAL REGISTER
OF SAN LUIS REY

There they remained till 1883. When the Forsters left the house, I took two large drygoods boxes of books, printed matter and manuscripts, away and brought them to the Rev. Father Mut at San Juan Capistrano Mission. He searched especially for the Mission Records, but they were not found. The Rev. Father Mut put all the books upstairs. Employes would use the papers to make cigarettes. Tourists took others."

Two manuscript volumes, like the Registers, were in recent years discovered at Mission San Juan Capistrano. This lends some basis for the surmise that the Marriage and Confirmation Registers, of which Miss Lorenzana speaks, eventually found their way to this Mission and that they may be secreted in some private house. It will be remembered that, according to Miss Lorenzana's report, the leather covers had been torn from the two Registers as early as February, 1847. The other folio proved to be the *Padrons* or lists of the Indians belonging to San Luis Rey. The first begins with the year 1798 and includes the names of the converts down to about the year 1910. It is arranged, after the manner of a parish register, by families and in alphabetical order. In the first column are given the names of the father, mother and children in order. The next column has the name of the ranchería where each was born. The third column shows the date of Baptism, while the fourth designates the age of the individual. The last column mentions the number which the respective neophyte held in the Baptismal Register. Widowers, widows, youths and maidens standing alone are recorded in separate lists similarly classified.

A part of the volume is set aside and similarly arranged for the families, widowers, widows, unmarried men and maidens living on their rancherías.

The second *Padron*, a much larger volume but similarly arranged, begins about the year 1808. The last entry in the Baptismal Register, as far as can be ascertained from this *Padron,* was made on October 1, 1843, and bore number

7,061. By that date, therefore, forty-six years after the founding of San Luis Rey, as many as 7,061 persons had been baptized there, very few of whom were whites. It is worthy of note that about two-fifths of the volume was entirely set apart and arranged for neophytes belonging to the *asistencia* or sub-mission of San Antonio de Pala. Hence we find here, too, headings as follows:

Neofitos que viven en San Antonio de Pala: (1) Matrimonios e Hijos; (2) Solteros y Muchachos, Huérfanos; (3) Solteras, Muchachas, Huérfanas; (4) Viudos; (5)Viudas; (6) Viejos, i. e. Old People, Men and Women.

CHAPTER XVI.

Mission Lands Restored to Catholic Church.—Patent Signed by President Abraham Lincoln.

AS STATED in the fourth volume of our larger work—*The Missions and Missionaries of California*—the United States Land Commission and the United States Court declared the sale of the mission lands illegal. Accordingly, all the lands, which the Spanish Laws regarded as Church Property, were restored to the Church. In these legal proceedings the last formality was observed when President Abraham Lincoln, on March 18, 1865, less than a month before his assassination, affixed his name to the title deeds and thereby returned the property of Mission San Luis Rey to the Catholic Church. That document reads as follows:

THE UNITED STATES OF AMERICA.

To All to Whom These Presents Shall Come, Greeting: Whereas it appears from a duly authenticated transcript, filed in the General Land Office of the United States, that pursuant to the provisions of the Act of Congress approved the third day of March, one thousand eight hundred and fifty-one, entitled "An Act to ascertain and settle the Private Land Claims in the State of California," Joseph Sadoc Alemany, Roman Catholic Bishop of the Diocese of Monterey, in the State of California, as claimant, filed his petition on the nineteenth day of February, 1853, with the Commissioners to ascertain and settle the Private Land Claims in the State of California, sitting as a Board in the City of San Francisco, in which petition he claimed the confirmation to him and his successors of the title to certain church property in California, "to be held by him and them in trust for the religious purposes and uses to which the same have been respectively appropriated," said property consisting of "church edifices, houses for the use of the clergy and those employed in the service of the church, church yards, burial grounds, gardens, orchards, and vineyards with the necessary buildings thereon and appurtenances," the same having been recognized as the property of said Church by the laws of Mexico in force at the time of the cession of California to the United States, and whereas the Board of Land Commissioners aforesaid on the eighteenth day of December, 1855, rendered a decree of confirmation in favor of the petitioner for certain lands described therein to be held "in the capacity and for uses set forth in his petition," the lands of the Mission of San Luis Rey, being described in said decree as follows: The Church and the buildings adjoining thereto, built in a quadrangle form, and constituting the buildings known as the Church and Mission buildings of the Mission San Luis Rey, situated in San Diego County, together with the lands on which the same are erected and the curtilage and appurtenances thereto belonging, and the Cemetery adjoining the same, enclosed with a stone wall and the wall of the Church. Also two enclosed gardens, one of which is situated nearly South from said quadrangle and is enclosed by an adobe wall, with the exception of a small portion on the Western side, where the enclosure is of branches or sticks; the other is situated in a direction about North-West from said quadrangle and is enclosed by an adobe wall; said Gardens being the same which were formerly used by the priests having charge of said Mission. The property above described is the same delineated on Map numbered 2 in the Atlas above referred to.

And whereas it further appears from a certified transcript filed in the General Land Office, that an appeal from said decree or decision of the Commissioners having been taken on behalf of the United States to the District Court of the United States for the Southern District of California, and it being shown to the Court that it was not the intention of the United States to prosecute further said appeal, the said District Court on the fifteenth of March, 1858, at the regu-

lar term "ordered that said appeal be dismissed and said
appellee have leave to proceed under the decree of the said
Land Commissioners in his favor as a final decree."

And whereas, under the thirteenth section of the said Act
of third of March, 1851, there have been presented to the
Commissioner of the General Land Office a plat and certificate of the survey of the tract of land confirmed as aforesaid, authenticated respectively on the twentieth and thirtieth
days of April, 1862, by the signature of the Surveyor General of the public lands in California, which plat and certificate are in the words and figures following, to wit:

"U. S. Surveyor General's Office.

"San Francisco, California.

" Under and by virtue of the provisions of the 13th section
" of the Act of Congress of the 3rd of March, 1851, entitled
" 'An Act to ascertain and settle Private Land Claims in the
" State of California,' and of the 12th section of the Act of
" Congress approved on the 31st of August, 1852, entitled
" 'An Act making appropriation for the Civil and Diplomatic
" expenses of the Government for the year ending the thir-
" tieth of June, eighteen hundred and fifty-three, and for other
" purposes,' and in consequence of the annexed copy of a
" certificate of the United States District Court for the
" Southern District of California having been filed in this
" office, whereby it appears that the Attorney General of the
" United States having given notice that it was not the in-
" tention of the United States to prosecute the appeal from
" the decision of the United States Board of Land Commis-
" sioners, said decision having confirmed the title and claim
" of Joseph S. Alemany, Bishop, etc., to four tracts of land
" at the Ex-Mission San Luis Rey, the said appeal has been
" vacated and thereby the said decision in favor of the said
" Joseph S. Alemany, Bishop, etc., has become final.

"   The said tracts have been surveyed in conformity with
" the grant thereof and the said decision, and I do hereby
" certify the annexed map to be a true and accurate plat of
" the said tracts of land as appears by the field notes of the

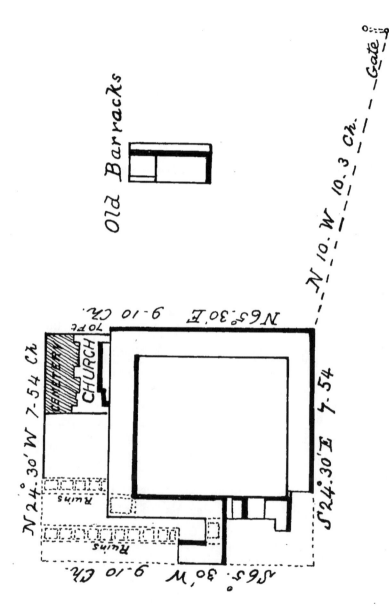

GROUND PLAN OF SAN LUIS REY MISSION ACCORDING TO UNITED STATES SURVEY

" survey thereof made by Henry Hancock, Deputy Surveyor,
" in the month of July, 1860, under the directions of this
" office, which having been examined and approved are now
" on file therein.

" And I do further certify that in accordance with the
" provisions of the Act of Congress approved on the 14th
" day of June, 1860, entitled 'An Act to amend an Act en-
" titled "An Act to define and regulate the jurisdiction of
" the District Court of the United States in California in
" regard to the survey and location of confirmed private
" land claims." ' I have caused to be published once a week
" for four weeks successively in two newspapers, to wit: The
" Visalia Delta, published in the county of Tulare, being the
" newspaper published nearest to where the said land claim
" is located; the first publication being on the 8th day of
" May, 1862, and the last on the 29th day of May, 1862;
" also in the Los Angeles News, a newspaper published in
" the city and county of Los Angeles, the first publication
" being on the 7th day of May, 1862, and the last on the
" 29th day of May, 1862, a notice that the said claim had
" been surveyed and a plat made thereof and approved by
" me. And I do further certify that the said approved plat
" of survey was retained in this office during all of said
" four weeks and until the expiration thereof, subject to
" inspection. And I do further certify that no order for
" the return thereof to the United States District Court has
" been served upon me.

" And I do further certify that under and by virtue of the
" said confirmation, survey, decree and publications, the said
" Joseph S. Alemany, Bishop, etc. is entitled to a patent from
" the United States upon the presentation hereof to the
" General Land Office for the said tract of land, the same
" being bounded and described as follows, to wit:"

(Then follows a minute description of the various tracts
of land, which it would be too tedious to reproduce. We
refer the reader to the engraving for the Mission site.
After the description, the document continues:)

"In witness whereof, I have hereunto signed my
" name officially and caused the seal of my office to
" be attached at the City of San Francisco, this thir-
" tieth day of April, A. D. one thousand eight hun-
" dred and sixty-two.

"E. F. BEALE, United States Surveyor General.
" And whereas there has been deposited in the General Land
Office of the United States a certificate dated June 27th, 1863,
from the Clerk of the United States District Court for the
Southern District of California showing that, in the cause
titled 'J. S. Alemany et al. Appellees vs. The United
States Appellants,' due notice by publication in manner and
form as required by law has been made by the Surveyor
General of the United States for California in the matter
of the approved survey of the Mission 'San Luis Rey' confirmed to the claimant and appellee in the above titled
cause of J. S. Alemany vs The United States, and that the
full period of six months from and after the completion of
said publication has elapsed and no objection thereto having
been made or filed the said approved survey has become
final and the claimant and appellee entitled to a Patent for
the said Mission."

Now KNOW YE,

That the United States of America, in consideration of
the premises, and pursuant to the provision of the Act of
Congress aforesaid of 3rd March, 1851, HAVE GIVEN AND
GRANTED, and by these presents DO GIVE AND GRANT unto said
Joseph S. Alemany Bishop of Monterey and to his Successors, in trust for the religious purposes and uses to
which the same have been respectively appropriated, the
tracts of land embraced and described in the foregoing
survey; but with the stipulation that in virtue of the 15th
section of the said Act the confirmation of this said claim
and this patent, "shall not affect the interests of third
persons,"

To Have and To Hold the said tracts of land with the
appurtenances and with the stipulation aforesaid, unto the

said Joseph S. Alemany, Bishop of Monterey, and to his Successors, in trust for the religious purposes and uses as aforesaid.

In testimony whereof I, Abraham Lincoln, President of the United States, have caused these Letters to be made Patent and the Seal of the General Land Office to be hereunto affixed.

Given under my hand at the City of Washington this eighteenth day of March in the year of our Lord one thousand eight hundred and sixty five and of the Independence of the United States the eighty ninth.

By the President, ABRAHAM LINCOLN.

I. N. Granger, Recorder of the General Land Office.

Recorded Vol. 4, pages 336 to 345 inclusive.

CHAPTER XVII.

CONFISCATION sealed the doom of the Missions in California. The havoc it played with Mission San Luis Rey was heartrending. What was left of the temporalities became the booty of indifferent and selfish individuals. With the passing of the last missionary friar, the trustful Indian neophytes were left helpless, defenseless, and homeless. By degrees many of their number fell victims to the white man's cupidity and became slaves to his whisky and to his vices while others withdrew disconsolate to the sierras. These latter fared badly enough, as we have seen; but to their honor and to the glory of their late zealous missionary protectors, let it be said that they preserved the priceless pearl of their holy Faith and that in consequence Heaven has now provided for them, spiritually and corporally. Their ancient fields and numerous live stock have passed into strange hands. Only a few acres of land around the beloved church edifice still remain, because it was held inviolate by the Government of the United States. The massive and extensive buildings, that once were the wonder of every visitor, have fallen into ruin. To restore them would cost not less than $2,000,000. Such was the estimate which an officer at the request of the Indian Department made to the Government more than fifty years since. Most of the destruction was the work not of time and weather, but of vandals and thieves. Private parties coveted the tiles and timbers which, with other material, they used to construct houses and barns for themselves. Everything useful, and there was much of it, disappeared with the years. The guilty ones are dead, as are also those who confiscated the

SANCTUARY OF SAN LUIS REY CHURCH BEFORE RESTORA-
TION. ACTUAL SCENE AS OBSERVED BY ARTIST A.
HARMER. HE FOUND THE TWO WOMEN CON-
TEMPLATING THE DESTRUCTION AS
HE ENTERED THE CHURCH.

mission lands and evicted the rightful owners. They all
by this time have met their Judge and received their due.
It would be idle to point out the malefactors. Some were
doubtless in good faith, and no one appeared to object to
their proceedings after the Mission seemed to have no
owner. Besides, all the stolen property could not be
recovered anyway.

Only the church edifice escaped complete destruction,
although its interior was brutally dealt with. The accompanying illustration presents the scene as it appeared for
many years after the storm of confiscation and secularization, contemplated with heavy heart and bewildered mind by
the two aged Indian women. Not even the altars were
spared by sacrilegious hands. In this abomination of desolation, however, we state with satisfaction on the authority
of old Silvester Marron, the American soldiers who occupied
the Mission had no share. Emphatically he declared that
the soldiers ruined nothing.

In time, the beautiful dome began to sink and soon the
roof was on the verge of caving in. Thus all was gloom till
1892. In that year, two Mexican Franciscans visited the
ruins of San Luis Rey. They were searching for a site
suitable for a monastery and seminary where they might
educate young men for the Seraphic Order, since this was
no longer possible under the infidel government in Mexico.
Moved, doubtless from on high, the two Fathers resolved to
restore the old Mission church and to erect the novitiate
near by. Rt. Rev. Francis Mora, then Bishop of the diocese, gladly approved the plan. Thus the dawn of a brighter
future broke on the desolate and dethroned Chief of the
California Missions.

The two Franciscan friars were the Very Rev. J. G. Alva,
Commissary-General of the Franciscans in Mexico, and the
Rev. D. Rangel, a member of the former Missionary Col-
lege of Our Lady of Guadalupe, Zacatecas, the same College
that had furnished the first Bishop of California, the Rt.
Rev. Francisco García Diego. Bishop Mora intended to give

the new community spiritual charge of the Indians about Pala, as also of the Spanish-speaking people in the vicinity of the Mission. The priests of that part of the country had more than enough to occupy them and therefore found it impossible to visit San Luis Rey more than once or twice a year. Hence they hailed the advent of the Mexican Fathers as a special blessing to their flocks.

Through the intervention of the good Bishop, permission was obtained from Rome to establish the novitiate. A two-story frame building was erected across from the church, since in the immense mission block not a habitable room could be found. The church was repaired sufficiently to allow the celebration of the holy Sacrifice within its walls. At last, on May 12, 1893, the ceremonies of re-dedication took place. By 10 o'clock that morning, fully three hundred interested spectators had gathered in the church. Four wrinkled old Indian women crouched at the doorway and wonderingly looked on the scene that must have brought fond memories of their girlhood days, when the Mission was still in the heyday of peace and prosperity.

When the Rt. Rev. Bishop, accompanied by Very Rev. Joaquin Adam, Vicar-General, Very Rev. Louis J. Meier, Superior of the Vincentian Fathers in Los Angeles, and Rev. W. L. Dye, Secretary to the Bishop, approached the wide front doorway of the ancient church edifice, he was ceremoniously received by the community of Franciscans in their somber grey habit. They all had come from Guadalupe, Zacatecas. At their head stood Very Rev. J. G. Alva, Commissary-General, who later became Bishop of Zacatecas, where the writer paid his respects to him in 1905. The procession entered the sacred edifice, the cross-bearer and acolytes being followed by three Mexican students, Jesus de la Ros, Manuel Rizo, and Andrés Guerrero, who had come from Mexico to commence their novitiate here; then followed Rev. Fr. Martinez; Rev. Fr. Tizcareño, Secretary to the Commissary-General; Rev. Fr. Ambrosio Malabehar, who

CHURCH AND MISSIONARY COLLEGE OF GUADALUPE, ZACATECAS, BEFORE CONFISCATION.

was to remain as superior of the new community; and finally the clergy named before.

Solemn High Mass was celebrated by Very Rev. J. Adam, assisted by Fathers Alva and Dye as deacon and sub-deacon, respectively. Fr. Meier acted as master of cere-monies. After the holy Mass followed the reading of the *Patente* from Rome authorizing the new establishment. Then the patron saints were announced—San Luis Rey as patron of the mission church, and Nuestra Señora de Guadalupe as patroness of the novitiate. The *Veni Creator* was then chanted, whereupon the three young men knelt before the altar and received the habit of the Franciscan Order from the Commissary-General. The ceremonies closed with the *Te Deum*. Rev. Fr. Joseph O'Keefe of Santa Barbara was appointed by the Superior-General of the Franciscan Order to direct the temporal affairs of the Mexican community *at interim,* to acquaint them with the language and manners of the country, and to supervise the restoration of the Mission buildings as far as was necessary.

At the beginning of 1897, the community comprised Fr. J. J. O'Keefe, Fr. Rafael Fernández, master of novices: Fr. Francisco Álvarez, Fr. José Caballero, Fr. Pedro Ocegeda, Fr. Luis Palácios, Fr. B. Alemán, six choristas or frates clerici, and four lay brothers. Fr. Álvarez, who had been at Santa Barbara years before, was now eighty-two years of age. He died at San Luis Rey and the body was interred in the cemetery next to the church wall.

After serving the Mexican Franciscan community in the capacity of superior and general manager for nineteen years, during which he built the quadrangle adjoining the church, the aged Fr. Joseph Jeremiah O'Keefe desired to be relieved of his burden in order to pass the last days with his brethren at Old Mission Santa Barbara. Fr. Peter Wallischeck, till then Rector of St. Anthony's College, Santa Barbara, was accordingly transferred to San Luis Rey, and he arrived there in August, 1912. As a teacher he had been so long accustomed to the happy, albeit noisy, voices of the young

ABOVE.—INDIAN CHAPEL AT PAUMA.
BELOW.—MARCHING TO DEDICATION OF SCHOOL.

that he missed them near the lonesome ruin of the once
populous Mission. Hundreds of Indian children had in the
past romped about the spacious *patio* and through the mission rancheria, and their voices had mingled with those of
their elders in singing both the Spanish hymns and Latin
chants within the great temple, or in the open air during
the devout processions on the various feasts of the year.
The elders now were provided for, but the children still
lacked the attention accorded them of old in the special
instruction received twice a day from good Fr. Antonio
Peyri and other Fathers.

Fr. Peter then conceived the daring plan of establishing a
day school for the young of the vicinity, and a boarding
school for the daughters of the farmers scattered throughout
the ancient mission district. When he proposed the matter
to the Rt. Rev. Thomas J. Conaty, D. D., the Ordinary of
Los Angeles Diocese, the Bishop at first declared the project
impossible for want of pupils. Nevertheless the good Bishop
cordially gave his approbation if Sisters could be induced
to take charge of a school in so poor and remote a district.
The happy Fr. Peter at once applied to the Motherhouse of
the Sisters of the Precious Blood at Maria Stein, Ohio.
On inspection, San Luis Rey was pronounced to be indeed
the most unlikely settlement for successful activity. Notwithstanding, Rev. Mother Emma, the Superioress General
of the Sisters of the Precious Blood, who had personally
come to view the situation, resolved with the consent of
her Councillors to accept the offer for the sake of the old
memories that cluster around the hallowed spot.

The quarters were thereupon prepared, and in July, 1913,
the Old Mission welcomed the first Sisters, who had come
to open the school in September. That was the dawn of
brighter days for San Luis Rey, which, it is fondly hoped,
may never be darkened. From the beginning the little
institution thrived remarkably. Instead of a lack of pupils,
there was a dearth of room to accommodate all those who
applied. This emboldened the Sisters to add the high school

courses. The plan was rendered possible through the gen-
erosity of a far-seeing benefactor, Mr. Jerome O'Neil of
the Santa Margarita Ranch. The necessary structures were
erected which enabled the Sisters to admit an ever-growing
number of girls who, but for this opportunity, would have
had to forego the higher education which they desired.

A thorough education it surely is that may be secured
from the efficient teachers in religious garb at San Luis
Rey, even if only the secular part of education should be
regarded as paramount. As evidence, but one instance shall
be cited. Early in 1920, the War Department of the United
States Government announced a prize contest for an essay
of four hundred words on the subject, *The Benefits of
Enlistment in the United States.* The competition was open
to the pupils of all elementary and high schools. The schools
·of the Southwestern Military District, which embraced New
Mexico, Arizona, and Southern California from Santa Barbara inclusive, to San Diego inclusive, hence Los Angeles
also, submitted fifty thousand papers by as many pupils.
Not much noise was made over the result for obvious reasons; for it so happened that a young miss of sixteen, who
had been a pupil of San Luis Rey school for four years.
wrote the paper that won the coveted prize. The judges
were Major-General Kuhn, Commander of the Military
District; Colonel Allen Smith, and Captain Warren Carberry.
The presentation of the prize took place at a public celebration held in the school of San Luis Rey on Sunday,
April 11, 1920. Major Fay, U. S. A., made the presentation address.

APPENDIX

—— ——

A.

Saint Louis, the ninth of that name, King of France, was born at Poissy on April 25, 1215, as the son of King Louis VIII and St. Blanche, daughter of Alfonso IX, King of Castile. He was eleven years old when the death of his father called him to the throne. During his minority, the queen mother, St. Blanche, governed France with admirable ability. It is recorded that till his twelfth year, the prince had no other instructor than his saintly mother. Nevertheless, he proved a most masculine ruler and soldier. On May 17, 1234, at the age of nineteen, he married Margaret, the eldest daughter of Raymond, Count of Provence. The marriage was blessed with eleven children. In April, 1236, having completed his twenty-first year, Louis took the reins of government into his own hands but did not cease to seek the wise counsels of his saintly mother.

"During the minority," says Alban Butler, "the kingdom was entangled in many domestic broils, and distracted with seditions and wars in every part, insomuch that it seems a miracle of providence that the Queen, with all her prudence and diligence, should have been able to preserve the state entire, or that the King should be able afterward to compose and settle it in the manner he did, reigning for some years with his sword always in his hand, yet almost without bloodshed. Frederick II, the impious and faithless Emperor of Germany, though he often broke his engagements with St. Louis, as well as with other powers, could never provoke him to war, so dexterous was the saint in maintaining both his honor and his interests without it. Indeed, being exempt from those passions which usually blow the coals, he had uncommon advantage in the pursuit of justice and necessary defence; and, while his magnanimity and foresight kept him always in readiness, his love of peace inclined him rather to sacrifice petty considerations than to see one drop of Christian blood spilt, if possible."

In 1239, Baldwin, Emperor of Constantinople, made Louis a present of the holy Crown of Thorns worn by our Savior. The King sent two Dominican friars, with a suitable retinue, to bring the sacred treasure to France. Five leagues beyond, he himself, attended by his whole court and numerous clergy, met the bearers. Then, walking barefoot, he carried the precious relic into the city. In the same manner he carried it into Paris and deposited it in the chapel of St. Nicholas. He subsequently had a more pretentious shrine erected, where the holy Crown of Thorns was ever after preserved and venerated.

In 1244, St. Louis was stricken with a grave malady which brought him to the brink of the grave. It was on this occasion that he vowed to lead a crusade into Palestine for the relief of the Christians who were being oppressed by the Mahomedans far more cruelly than the Armenians of today, whose sufferings have aroused the sympathy of the whole world. Having regained his health, the King equipped an army and a fleet. Then declaring the queen mother Regent of France during his absence, he set sail from Aiguesmortes, on August 27, 1248, for the Isle of Cyprus, where he had large stores laid up. Here he passed the winter and in the following spring sent a declaration of war to the Sultan of Egypt, who threatened to swallow up the whole of Palestine. On Trinity Sunday, 1249, the fleet put to sea and, after four days, arrived before Damiette, the strong Mahomedan fortress at the mouth of the Nile. Though at first victorious, Louis and part of his army were taken captive. Later, after paying a heavy ransom and agreeing to a truce of ten years, the French King and his army were released. Louis now visited the Holy Places in Palestine with such extraordinary devotion that even the Saracens marveled. In September, 1254, he was welcomed back to France.

Sixteen years later, the saintly King once more set out on a crusade to wrest the Holy Land from the dominion of the inhuman Mahomedans. On July 1, 1270, he embarked with his army at Aiguesmortes for Tunis. At his approach the enemy fled in terror; but a pestilence broke out in the Christian army, and on August 25, 1270, it carried off the heroic King himself, at the age of fifty-five years and four months. His last words were, *"Into Thy hands, O Lord, I commend my spirit."* He had reigned forty-three years, nine months and eighteen days. His remains were taken to France by his son Philip and deposited in the Church of St. Denis. He was canonized in 1297 by Pope Boniface VIII.

Neither executive ability nor military achievements could entitle this King to the halo of the saint. This distinction he merited solely by the practice of every virtue in an heroic degree. For that there is abundant proof in the writings of historians and others who were not in sympathy with the principles that guided the saintly King. They cannot deny that he always led an exemplary life. He took to heart the words that his mother often repeated to him when he was still a boy: "My son, I should rather see thee dead at my feet than know thee guilty of a mortal sin." His biographers accordingly have much to relate of the long hours he spent in prayer, how severely he fasted and performed other penances. By these means and with the grace of God he tried to keep and did keep himself "unsullied from this world."

"The salient points of his character," writes Dr. Walsh in his excellent *The Thirteenth, the Greatest of Centuries* (p. 290), "are his devotion to the three great deeds of humanity as they presented themselves in his time. He made it the aim of his life that men should have *justice* and *education,* and, when for any misfortune they needed it, *charity;* and every portion of his career is taken up with successful achievement in these great departments of social action.''

''The instructions which he left to his son Philip and to his daughter Isabel,'' says Georges Goyau in *The Catholic Encyclopedia,* ''the discourses preserved by the witnesses at judicial investigations preparatory to his canonization, and Joinville's anecdotes, show St. Louis to have been a man of sound common sense, possessing indefatigable energy, graciously kind and of playful humor, and constantly guarding against the temptation to be imperious.''

Between St. Louis and the Franciscans there exists a close bond of relationship. Even before he had assumed the reins of government, he had himself enrolled in the Order of Penance, as the Third Order of St. Francis is called; and this virtue of penance he practiced all the rest of his life in keeping with the spirit of St. Francis. He always wore the scapular and cord of the Third Order, and on special occasions he would appear clothed in the full Tertiary habit. Hence it is that St. Louis is numbered among the Franciscan Saints and is venerated by Tertiaries of St. Francis as their Patron. In the Franciscan Order the day of his death, August 25, is annually commemorated as a feast of the higher class.

B.

Eugene Mofras, the French traveler, in his *Exploration,* vol. ii, reproduced the *Lord's Prayer* recited at various missions. His version of the *Pater Noster* in the Dieguiño was reprinted in our volume— *San Diego Mission*—but doubt was expressed as to its authenticity. It has been found since that no surviving Indians anywhere in San Diego County could understand Mofras' version for either San Diego or San Luis Rey.

Rev. E. Lapointe of El Cajon took pains to secure the *Pater Noster* in Indian from the descendants of the neophytes. With the help of the natives near the Mexican border, the Rev. Father succeeded in obtaining the Prayer in the idiom of the Dieguiños. He tested it among Indians in the northern part of the county, and discovered that they understood it well. Hence we may conclude that this Indian *Our Father* was the same that Fr. Antonio Peyri recited with his neophyté flock at Mission San Luis Rey and at San Antonio de Pala, because the language of the Dieguiños and Luiseños was about the same. The Prayer is herewith reproduced just as the Rev. Father Lapointe reported it:

The OUR FATHER in Indian.

Niawup tat mai apsu mabo etchmak misihche niama atchipoi koi pai ichihua nia pahicha mulpihi mai.

Mihattle nia koshur sauo niniuk ni apsiou pakiennak epohu nieumok meumakle manatle omaho atlich kaumok. Piapehe.

C.

LAND RESERVATIONS FOR THE MISSION INDIANS.

By the year 1917, twenty-eight reservations had been set apart for the Indians in the southern part of California. The majority of these Indians are descendants of the converts who once belonged to Missions San Diego, San Luis Rey, and San Gabriel. Possibly some few can look to San Juan Capistrano as the home of their forebears, but there is nothing on record to show it. Mr. Charles Lummis, in the June, 1902, edition of *Out West*, brings an interesting table, in which he records the acreage of each reservation and describes the condition of the respective lands. From time to time the Government made changes as to the extent of the lands allotted. As finally patented to the respective Indian tribes and adduced in the Report of the Indian Commission for the year 1919, the acreage is placed in parentheses. In alphabetical order, the location, acreage, and description of each reservation read as follows:

Name of Reservation	Acres acc. to Lummis	Acres acc. to Report of 1919	Description by Lummis
Agua Caliente	3,844	(7,205)	Desert, very little water.
Augustine	615	(616)	Desert, no water.
Cahuila	18,240	(18,880)	Mountain valley, stock land, little water.
Capitan Grande	10.253	(15,080)	Portion good, very little water.
Cuyapipi	880	(4,080)	Poor land, no water.
Cabezon	640	(1,280)	Desert, produces nothing, no water.
Campo	....	(1,640)	
Inaja	280	(760)	Small amount, poor land.
Laguna	160	(320)	Small quantity farm land; springs.
La Posta	238	(3,679)	Practically worthless, no water.
Los Coyotes	22,640	(21,520)	Mountainous, very little farm land.
Manzanita	640	(19,680)	Practically worthless, no water.
Martínez	....	(1,280)	Practically worthless, poor land, no water.
Mesa Grande	120	(4,400)	Small amount of farming land, but little water; portion good stock land.
Mission Creek	....	(1,920)	
Morongo	38,600	(11,069)	Fair land with water.

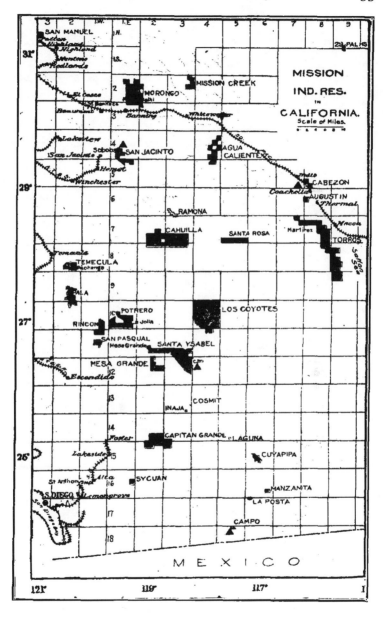

Name of Reservation	Acres acc. to Lummis	Acres acc. to Report of 1919	Description by Lummis
Pala	160	(4,480)	Good land, water.
Pechanga (Temécula)	3,360	(5,195)	Almost worthless for lack of water.
Potrero or La Jolla.	8,329	(8,329)	Portion good, water on part.
Ramona	....	(560)	
Rincon	2,552	(2,554)	Sandy, portion watered.
San Manuel........	640	(653)	Worthless dry hills.
San Pasqual........	....	(2,200)	
Santa Rosa.........	....	(2,560)	Mountainous; timber, but little farming land.
Santa Ynéz........	....	(120)	Good land, plenty of water.
Santa Ysabél (San Jacinto)	29,845	(15,042)	Mountainous, stock land, no water.
Soboba	2,960	(5,461)	Mostly poor land, very little water.
Sycuan	640	(640)	Small quantity of agricultural land.
Torres	19,200	(20,800)	Desert; artesian water recently obtained.
Twenty-nine Palms...	160	(480)	Desert.

D.

The following rancherías are mentioned in the Pedron as the native homesteads of the Indians who belonged to Mission San Luis Rey:

Agua Caliente (Cupa)
Aguanga (Aguangua)
Alape
Atique

Batequitos

Caba
Caguenga (Cahuenga)
Cahuabal
Callua
Casical
Chacap
Chacham
Chajap
Changa (Chunga)
Chelchajon
Cohanga
Corena
Coxenga (Cojenga)
Cucheyac
Cucuas
Cugar
Cupa (San Jose de Valle)
Cuqui
Cusuasna

Gellehua
Gelpa
Guachenga
Guaniba
Guariba (Gariba)
Guegabot

Hebeca
Hopma

Jaba
Jachiquel
Jahuara
Jallagua

Jalpay
Jolpac
Juechinja (Guechinga)
Jugigna
Jugniena
Jujuya

Las Flores
Las Pulgas

Matjay
Melju
Mura

Nesganel

Ojauminga

Pagui
Paixha
Pala (sub-mission)
Palanguaj
Palpisa
Pamga
Pami
Pamusi
Panase
Paumega
Panataguasis
Pasahue
Pasqua
Pimip
Pimisga (Pimixga)
Pimix (Pimihi)
Polabe
Pomame
Potaba
Potumba
Potumeba
Pumusi
Punixhic
Pusulo

Puyalamo

Quejhoha
Quengbana
Quetchinga

Saboba (Seboban)
Sagiya (Siguia)
San Alexo
San Jacinto
Santa Margarita
Sapa
Sebo
Senga
Siljam (Siljuam)
Simoyat
Sobohit
Sogoho

Tahni (Tajni, Tagni)
Talchop
Tasbole
Taubaja
Temécula
Tobaca
Tobacamay
Tobana
Tobe
Tobocac
Tocamonga
Tocanga
Tocanonga (Tecanango)
Topome
Tubac
Tuhuba
Toulepa (Toylepa)
Toysbabal

Yugiena
Yugigna
Yuyiyac

E.

Much uncertainty prevails with regard to the exact course of the *Camino Reál*, as the public highway was called during the Mission Period. We are in a position to determine the route from San Diego to San Gabriel and to Los Angeles very closely. In their Annual Tabular Reports the Fathers Presidentes of the Missions always noted the day of the founding, the latitude, and the distance to the next Mission. The figures were always the same. For instance, the Tabular Report for the year 1802 concerning San Luis Rey reads: "San Luis Rey de Francia, 13 de Junio, 1798;—33 gr. 3 min.;—dista de la antecedente (S. Diego) 13 y medias leguas." The Report for the year 1831 reads the same way.

Similarly the distance between San Luis Rey and San Juan Capistrano is always given as 12½ leagues. This would prove, in the absence of any other authority, that in the early days the Camino Reál from San Diego to the north ran directly to Mission San Luis Rey by way of Buena Vista, not by way of Oceanside, as now.

Through the courtesy of Mr. Cave J. Couts, of Vista, San Diego County, we reproduce in facsimile a drawing which his father made in 1850, when lieutenant of the 1st Dragoons, U. S. Army. It is one of a number of drawings which picture the route from Coahuila, Mexico, to Los Angeles. This particular sketch traces the march from the Colorado River to Mission San Gabriel, and corroborates the statement in our vol. ii, 666-667, that the early Spanish expeditions did not cross the sierras by way of Banning, but farther south. It likewise shows that the road traveled north of San Diego passed by Mission San Luis Rey. This was the case from the beginning, and before Mission San Luis Rey existed. In the Annual Reports the distance between Mission San Diego and Mission San Juan Capistrano was always noted as 26 leagues, exactly the same reported after the founding of Mission San Luis Rey.

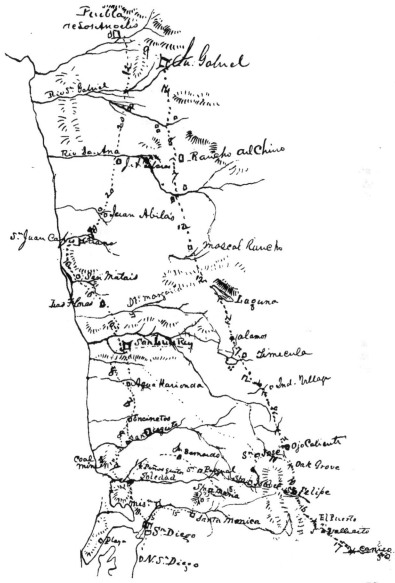

DRAWN IN 1850 BY LIEUTENANT CAVE JOHNSON COUTS

INDEX

LAUS DEO

(Distance to Mission San Diego 13½ leagues)
(Distance to Mission San Juan Capistrano 12½ leagues)

Another Work by the Author of
THE MISSIONS AND MISSIONARIES OF CALIFORNIA
No Fiction. Genuine History.

SAN DIEGO MISSION

OR

The Beginnings of California

BY

Fr. ZEPHYRIN ENGELHARDT, O. F. M.

THREE HUNDRED AND SEVENTY pages on fine paper, bound in Franciscan brown cloth, numerous full-page original illustrations, among which is a true likeness of Fr. Serra, his facsimile entry in Baptismal Register, facsimile of title pages of Baptismal and Marriage Register in hand of Fr. Serra, ground plan of Mission, U. S. Patent, signed by President Lincoln in facsimile, restoring Mission property; Tabular Reports of sixty-two years on agricultural and stock-raising activities, Tabular Report of spiritual results, list and dates of resident and visiting missionaries down to revered Father Antonio Ubach, complete index, etc. Price, cloth, $2.75; by mail, $3.00; in paper covers, $2.00; by mail, $2.25.

"An extremely interesting history of San Diego Mission, the oldest of all the Missions of California, is that of Father Zephyrin Engelhardt, O. F. M. Better than any other account we have seen, this pictures the difficulties under which the Franciscan Padres worked, the immense labor they put into the task, and the hindrance they suffered at the hands of civil and military authorities, hindrance that finally culminated in the secularization of the Mission properties so that the land might be given to hungry civilians. The narrative is full and draws upon all the available documents. It clears up many misapprehensions concerning the Missions and . their conduct by the Padres, etc."—**San Francisco (Daily) Chronicle.**

"It is needless to say that in this new book Father Zephyrin has fully sustained his reputation as a careful, painstaking historian. . . . He speaks always with the certainty of the man who is a thorough master of his subject, etc."—**Los Angeles Tidings.**

Made in the USA
Lexington, KY
02 March 2011